The World We Left Behind

The World We Left Behind

A JOURNEY FROM GEORGIA TO MAINE

Book One

John R Morris, a.k.a. Morris the Cat

ISBN: 0692400370
ISBN 13: 9780692400371

Updated Edition 6/15/16
Edited by: Heather McAdams

In the Press

"The message in The World We Left Behind is one that seems to resonate with a huge portion of the population, no matter their gender, their job, or their financial position, and Morris' struggle to achieve enlightenment while being challenged continually by forces over which he has no control, is a situation that speaks to the internal battle that rages in many of us."

San Francisco Book Review

"There are some parallels between Morris' book, The World We Left Behind and Cheryl Strayed's bestseller, Wild." "Morris presents a realistic view of the people he encounters during this trip." "His best work comes near the end of the book where he describes a one-day solo hike."

Portland Book Review

"THE WORLD WE LEFT BEHIND is part gripping travel diary and part emotional exploration, a young man finding himself amidst the natural beauties and dangers of the wilderness" "The emotional force of the story is amplified by Morris's starkly honest and compellingly vivid writing style." "Morris has a wry, humorous, engaging tone and an innate descriptive ability that makes his journey come to life" - ★ ★ ★ ★½

IndieReader

"Such a good read! Insightful, funny, exciting and revealing. A realistic account of an Appalachian trail thru hike complete with the quirky misadventures that such a quest brings to the unprepared. I can't wait for volume 2 and 3."

AT Library

"The World We Left Behind is instantly engaging. Morris displays a keen eye for detail in every descriptive passage and brings raw nature to life. Dialogue is sharp and involving, and the characters he meets leap off the page. The reader will feel drawn in to the whole experience due to the atmospheric and colorful picture Morris paints. It is a page-turner to the end of the volume." - ★ ★ ★ ★½

Self-Publishing Review

"The World We Left Behind by John R. Morris is an excellent snapshot into one troubled man's journey to discover his life's meaning." - ★★★★☆ *4 out of 5 Stars!*

David K. McDonnell for ReaderViews.com

To my mother and father

I went out on a mission to bring you both back a rock from the summit of Katahdin—if only to give you something so that you would be proud of me.
When I returned home, as you held me in your arms, you both exclaimed with tears in your eyes, "You never had to leave to make us proud."

Table of Contents

Preface

Warning to readers about the following book:
THIS IS NOT A GUIDE that will explain to you how a person hikes from Georgia to Maine. This is also not inside or detailed information regarding the type of equipment or supplies that you should buy or a book about thru-hiking every single inch of the Appalachian Trail.

That's because my journey was very and quite purposefully eclectic and diverse.

What you are about to read is the true story of a man who, in March 2013, decided to quit his job, sell everything he owned, and leave friends and family behind to seek the life of a wanderer for eight and a half months. This was done with the Appalachian Trail as a constant landmark and an arrow always leading north. John Morris (Morris the Cat) would hike through towns, cities, forests, logging wastelands, and quite often even go off-trail altogether through the thick wilderness, deep bogs, and swamps, guided by nothing but the sun or the stars.

He met and lost many friends along the trail who were either stricken with hazards or sickness or simply found they no longer had the desire to go on. Yet still he continued home, with a rock taken from the summit of Katahdin resting within the palm of his hand. It had become his obsession—a mission to see that this rock found its way back to his parents.

This book is meant to awaken those who can no longer find the strength within themselves to rise on their own. Its purpose is to inspire change, simply through words, despite how scary we may sometimes find change to actually be.

There is a world that exists outside our windows. There is meaning in life that far outweighs living from paycheck to paycheck. Do what I did: find your meaning.

Acknowledgments

TO MY FAMILY AND FRIENDS, who gave me the courage and ambition each day to drive my tired, aching feet forward when all I wanted to do was quit.

To my father, for bonding with me more closely at a distance than we ever had in person. My goal was to make you proud of me, as I had felt I had done nothing in my life to have given you a reason to be.

To my mother, who worried about me every day, certain I was hiding in the woods like a maniac and doing drugs or attempting suicide. It is quite hard at times to keep from laughing in disbelief as your mother cries angrily into the phone, "You're just doing this to torture me, Richard!"

To Keven Kirsch: Keven and I hated each other at work. We were mortal enemies and constantly got on each other's nerves. But as he read my online journals and got caught up in my story and my search for ultimate freedom, he found a piece of himself in the words I had typed. He related with my loneliness and depression, and through that mutual understanding, found a friend in me. Keven, you drove nine hours just to hang out with me for a *day* and hike a portion of the Appalachian Trail, if for no other reason than to give me the courage to keep going. You sent food and fell in love with the hiking culture as you met fellow hikers and gave out "trail magic." The world of an AT thru-hiker opened up before your eyes, and you became enamored with the prospect of "leaving it all behind." And at the end of my journey, after nearly a year had passed, you offered me a place to stay as we planned and prepared to meet my parents. Thank you most of all.

To Delta Platoon: The only reason I never left the graveyard shift for those six-plus years was because of the camaraderie of our group. The friends I made in the years I worked out there are my still friends to this very day. Many of you sent me food or helped monetarily. Others helped by way of a forgotten phone charger (John Bison's mother-in-law!) and, of course, in many other ways, like keeping in contact with me, commenting on my journal entries, and making me laugh over the pictures or videos I posted to my Facebook page for the eight and a half months I was gone. It was an honor to work nuclear security with you all and meet your families.

To Lisa Croft and Nancy Jolly: You both saved my life in countless ways while I was walking that lonely stretch of pavement in Connecticut. I hadn't showered in weeks, I was filthy, and I was a complete stranger. Yet you two saw me walking along the side of the road and took me into your home—not knowing who I was or if I posed a threat of any kind. You fed me, kept me warm, and let me clean my clothes, my body, and my gear. You both purified my soul as you offered me a place to sleep, not just for a night but for an entire seven days. I struggled with mental anguish and loneliness in those cold months that preceded our meeting. You were sunshine on the cloudiest of days. I will never forget your kindness.

To Pam and Krystal Bailey: You were both breaths of fresh air that whooshed into the lives of Torry and I, and made us realize that the world we lived in wasn't always so dull and dreary. How is it we could have such a great time doing nothing more than sitting for hours on end with a beer in one hand, a cigarette in the other while listening to music on a cheap motel balcony?

To Dayna Sperling: You read my online journals, and then you and your husband just happened to come across me while I was in Harpers Ferry with my hiker friends, Woodstock and Wales. You proceeded to offer me money, and when I refused, you insisted anyway. Your donation bought the three of us lunch and further inspired me when I came to realize that my hike wasn't all too lonely or isolated after all.

To my journal followers, Al Woolum, Nightingale David, Brian Williams, Jeff Trogdon, Charlie Christianson, Ja Reisbig, Mynetta Januska, Terry Crouch, James Jones, Greg Biggerman (G-man), Frank Balsamo, Jill Brooks Pellerin, Terry Gallagher, Michael Wing, Lenore Borowski, Alan Cook (CookIN), Bramborovy Salat, Betsy Nierderer, Sean Tippens, and everyone else that followed and believed in me: thank you all as well for keeping me motivated and in your thoughts and prayers.

To Devin Payne: With nothing left in me, I had completed my hike and was finally on my way home via walking, hitchhiking, or catching buses and rides from deputy sheriffs, on my way back to my parents' house. We met in Hillsborough, North Carolina. You found me ragged and alone at a McDonald's and bought me an eggnog milkshake. My God, how I must've looked to you. We talked about my life out on the trail, and you tried to explain my exploits to both of your children as they looked upon this complete stranger sitting before them with questions in their eyes. It was great to see a familiar face. It was great to see a friend.

Wendy Wise: You've always believed I would write something someday. Because of your encouragement, I did. Thank you.

To Xinwei Wang, my partial book editor and personal one-person fan base and my wife—thank you for all that you are.

Prologue: The Reason

"Have you ever woken up one day with the certainty that you know how the rest of your life is going to play out? Almost as if you could predict the beginning and ending of each day—before it ever even happened?" I asked him, tossing a small stone into the open blue sky splayed out before us.

Torry looked over at me from the edge of the cliff on which he sat, a Pall Mall menthol hanging limply from the corner of his mouth. Several thousands of feet below his dangling legs, an incredible valley, brightly lit by the sun, opened up. The wind was sharp, cutting wildly into our bones and giving a hint of the early onset of fall on that late-August day.

"You know, some people would call that a blessing," he replied, taking a small puff from his cigarette and exhaling the bluish-gray smoke out his nostrils.

I nodded slowly as I turned away from the scenery.

All at once, the rest of my life played out before my very eyes: the same monotonous schedule of work, sleep, alcohol, television—washed, rinsed, and repeated—for the rest of my life. I felt the onset of vertigo and a thick, nauseating dizziness setting in rather rapidly.

"Yeah, some would call it a blessing, I guess," I said, slipping my hands back into my pants pockets. "And some would call it something else."

Torry removed the cigarette from his mouth, clipping the end of the filter to release the ash hanging from the end. It scattered instantly, disintegrating out into the open valley on the wind.

"So when were you thinking of leaving?" he asked, with a sly grin encroaching on the corners of his mouth. His fine gray stubble glinted like microscopic diamonds around his chin and beneath his nose. It was as if he was aware of some secret that I knew nothing about.

"That obvious?" I asked, unaware that I didn't even have to *try* to spell my life out to him. He could see on his own how badly I needed a change.

"When I had that look you have in your eyes and the feelings you just described, I joined the military," he replied, looking back out into a world that ultimately made us both feel so small from where we stood.

"But I don't *want* to join the military," I said.

"No, but you want *change*. You don't like your job. Your love life is a wreck, and you're unhappy. All you want to do is reset yourself, but the problem is, you don't know how."

"I wanna go. How about that? I just wanna get up one day and walk the hell out of here. Out of *this place,*" I countered angrily, just thinking about it.

He only chuckled, as if my young, immature mind couldn't yet comprehend the complexities of the world.

And maybe to an extent he was right. I had been very sheltered up to that point in my existence, much to my own dissatisfaction.

"Just walk, huh? And where would you *just walk* to?" he asked in a playful tone. His flippancy made me even angrier.

"I don't know. Maybe I just want to disappear from society for a few months. I'm almost thirty years old, and I've only been to five different states. Think about that! I've never even been in an airplane, for Christ's sake. I just want to walk across America and see something different. I want to *do* something other than just live to work every day and work to live!" I'd felt my face flush. I didn't know why this was frustrating me as much as it had been.

Looking back on it now, I suppose a lot of it had been pent-up feelings that I had never vented to anybody before—an unfathomable anger that had been stabbing, cutting, and slicing at my insides for so long that the torture had finally provoked a necessary emotional response of some kind.

It had been a throbbing, infected wound eating away at me.

And in that moment, it was the words and expression and passion in what I was saying that seemed to ease and heal the pain.

"Kinda sounds like you're speaking of a walkabout," he replied.

Well, I had no idea what a walkabout was at the time, but as Torry gave me the details, I listened intently. He spoke of Australian Aboriginals who, in their adolescent years, went out on journeys into the wilderness, sometimes for as long as four or six months. They slept in the bush, learned to hunt and how to survive in nature, and came back with tales of heroic deeds and stories of what they had learned on their spiritual journeys.

As Torry talked, I began to imagine my life away from civilization. I wondered how long it would take for me to run screaming back into society with my tail tucked between my legs. If I actually decided to go through with this crazy idea, I wondered if I could actually find the strength to make such a bold decision feasible.

Yet still a deeper, more primal urge within me awakened. Torry's words became like a mantra in my mind. As he talked I thought of ways that I could make this walkabout he spoke of happen in my own life.

Morris the Cat standing at the summit of
Katahdin and overlooking Knife Edge.

CHAPTER 1

The Seeds of Change

"THE PACK'S A BIT EXPENSIVE," I told my father as he placed fallen branches into an already burning pile.

He had only just recently picked them up from around his yard after the storm we'd had just a few days before.

"They usually are," he replied, more toward the earth than to me.

It was *all* he said.

"I've also been looking at water purifiers but haven't decided on one just yet," I added, almost making it blatantly obvious to him that I was looking for insight of any kind. Instead all I received was a grunt of acknowledgment.

I sighed angrily and tossed the twig I had been mangling into the fire.

I suppose my father still found it hard to believe that I was going to go through with it. Maybe he'd thought I was all talk? Truth was, I had told quite a few people of my plans and been looked at as if I was certifiably insane. It wasn't without reason I suppose, but I had still found it insulting. And while my father hadn't outright said to me, "You're full of shit," part of me believed that was exactly what he was thinking.

I dropped the subject, thinking it was one he hadn't felt like talking about.

And maybe it wasn't something for me to converse or ponder over, with the recent breakup with my ex-fiancée still fresh in my parents' minds. Maybe it seemed that I was trying to run away from what had happened.

I was aware that self-diagnosis could be dangerous and critical analysis could just as easily be crippling as well. I knew I would have more than enough time to contemplate my own depression that evening in my apartment alone, with a bottle of alcohol.

For the moment, I slipped on my disguise. I wore the facade of a man who had everything that he wanted in life. I smiled at jokes while I was really a hundred thousand miles away in the confines of my own mind.

My sisters were over for the weekend, and as was typical of our family get-togethers in our adult years, we were planning a big feast. My father had gotten out his cast-iron kettle and was in the process of firing down coals to cook the huge pot of beef stew he would soon be brewing within the pit.

My nephew and I had already started to devour the cornbread he had baked over the flames. We picked at it like hungry vultures.

It was October 2011, and late afternoon sunlight burned the sky like a wildfire. I enjoyed the cool air and the smell of burning wood as distant trucks ground their transmissions loudly, changing gears on the nearby by-pass. Most important, I imagined I was anywhere but home.

It was later that evening that I looked into the lonely walk-in closet, which was barren save for the two REI bags pushed far into the left corner. It was as if the things inside had left me ashamed of the very purchases I had recently made. Truly, I was well aware that I had spent far too much money on the contents of those satchels. My convictions had been true, and my heart had stood ready. But as every day passed by, I began to think of different reasons or excuses as to why I shouldn't do it.

Why I shouldn't go.

The hell is wrong with me? I should be saving for my future. I should be trying to further my education or career or move up within the company.

In truth, I didn't have some grand plan for my future or a pension. There was no retirement fund headed my way down the road of life. I was a loser, scratching to get by in the world with a GED and no college education, whose best paying job had been as a security guard.

Now here I was, contemplating taking on a monumental hiking challenge up the East Coast. I didn't even know that much about it, other than what I had read in books and online journals.

My father had taught me to be successful, yet at twenty-eight years of age, my savings (if you could call it that) existed as a mere joke.

A couple thousand bucks. That was it.

I had always been pushed and driven to pay attention to building my credit: imaginary numbers which only existed to keep your average American in constant debt. It was a state of being where you *always* owed some financial institution *something* and somebody *always* had a foot on your neck.

Now here I was, thinking of throwing that world away.

I had examined my thoughts about being irresponsible, and it was like a shot of adrenaline every time that I did—to rebel against something and feel *right* for doing it. But these brief escapes of rebellion lived and died within the boundaries of my own mind.

Quite often, I felt this was because in one way or another, we were all reflected in our actions. We are made transparent by our decisions. We aren't what the world makes us so much as we are made by what we *allow* the world to change us into.

In November 2011, I was still making my choices and hoping that the world would induce change inside me where I found no strength to make life decisions on my own.

I had always been weak that way.

With a failed relationship in one hand and a job going nowhere in the other, all I saw was questions about my future. A life of living alone, working, and dying (after having been shoved away into some rest home and forgotten about).

As I stared into that closet with my REI bags in it, I wondered what else I had to hold onto anymore.

Sure, I had always loved the outdoors. But did I love it so much I was willing to make it my *life* for the next six months? Quit my job, and leave my friends and family behind to fear for my safety or the chaos of an unpredictable future? I wasn't ignorant or blind to the fact that we live in precarious times, where holding a job was such a precious privilege, one in which you'd *never* think twice about leaving whatever place of employment you could get.

The very idea of just giving it all up and walking away is so incredibly taboo and careless, we keep the thoughts bottled up like secrets within our minds. Divulging only to ourselves in daydreams, as if we're ashamed that an act of such incredible freedom would ultimately prove our insanity—as well as our inevitable downfall.

You see, there was this contrived feeling of life suddenly stopping and the world not moving forward because I chose to walk on a 2,188-mile expanse of trail that absolutely terrified *and* intrigued me. While it was a laughable thought, was I to trade five to six months of my life for sixty years of regret, wondering *if* I could have ever pulled it off?

We are all so scared of change in some way or another that a break from the norm makes us believe that everything will come crashing down around us like a mountain of crystal wine glasses should we choose to do something as incredible or as insane as hiking from Georgia to Maine.

The people's faces alone offer humor. They fumble over their thoughts as they try to form words for something that makes so little sense to them.

"You're trying to tell me that you don't want to bathe for days at a time. You *want* to get blisters and cuts, and you want to be in a state of constant, aching pain. You *want* to risk being killed by bears, eat crappy dehydrated dinners, sleep in the cold, or walk in the rain for two-thousand-plus miles and get nothing for it?"

"Yes," I would reply defiantly every time.

When they proceeded to ask me why, I never had a complete answer for them though. I've never lived a strongly spiritual life, and I've always been a skeptic when it came to such magical things as *religion*. Because in moments of weakness, we look to something greater than ourselves to pull us through whatever hardship we're dealing with. What makes that any truer is the fact that we don't have to justify that truth through any physical or scientific evidence.

We simply say, "I have faith," and then we move on into thinking everything will be OK. I'd like to give these people an answer as simple as "God told me to do it" or "Maybe I'll learn something about myself. Hell, maybe I'll even get one of them there things called an *eeee-piff-a-nee*."

But ultimately it came down to a feeling inside me that something was pulling my heart, my *soul* perhaps, to seek the distant forests of Georgia—whether that force be the unaccounted beauty of mountain summits I had never seen or the challenge to push myself harder than I ever had before in my life.

We all want to escape from things. Eric Hoffer, an American writer and social philosopher, said it best, "We feel free when we escape—even if it be from the frying pan into the fire."

Maybe I would gain something, or maybe I would lose *everything*. For all I knew, day one on the trail I might break my back somehow and thus never be able to work again. I might lose the tiny threads of any or every relationship I still held on to—and both financially and physically cripple myself. But the fear of not pushing myself to *try* was what haunted me the most.

Those nights sitting alone in bed and staring at the ceiling hurt most.

Distant gazes at an intersection stoplight enraged impatient drivers behind me, and daydreams pulled me from social gatherings as I stared off, wondering, "What if I left this all behind…?"

Well, I didn't want to die wondering, "What if I could have done this?"

I wanted to die being able to say, "*I remember when I did…*"

Wendy had moved all of her things out a month prior, which was why the closet was mostly empty. In her doing so, I realized both how little I actually owned and how lonely it made my apartment feel. Not only because the closet was now a bare, white-walled holding cell, but because pictures of her and her family that had been scattered around the walls of our dwelling were now gone. The only proof they had ever even been there were the holes or nails where they had once hung. In truth, the finality of her leaving simply felt too real to deal with, even on my most energetic days.

Furniture we had spent hours mulling over in busy bargain-basement department stores had been decided upon and separated between us like selfish parents trying to decide who wanted which child more. We adopted the things the other person didn't want or paid each other off for them, no longer as a couple but as complete strangers bidding at an auction.

I turned to take a look around the empty guest bedroom Wendy had spent her final months in, separated from me by thin walls. Random bills or receipts of no importance were scattered about here and there, along with trivial items she hadn't wanted and had forgotten to throw away when she had cleaned her stuff out.

Among the forgotten remains was a black-marker caricature of her and me that we had gotten at a local flea market years before. I knelt down slowly and ran my hand across the ripped edge that had been torn between our images.

When I had finally given in and allowed her to remove her name off of the apartment lease, it hadn't been without a fight.

When the nights and the cold between us grew incessantly, I could hear her in the other room crying over the bad situation that had become our everyday lives, and it had made my stomach roll with anguish. I didn't want to hear it. I ran away from it by turning on the fan or listening to music and trying to drown out her sobs.

But I couldn't.

In the end, the move-out had gone smoothly though. That was the funny part. All of the arguing and turmoil ended once it was finally agreed that she was leaving. Still, we had been good about hiding the crumbling structure that was our relationship from friends and family. But that's the front we always put up, isn't it? An act is so easy to carry on when the people around you love you both so much that they don't want to see the seams stretching or the rips curling up under the edges of a relationship. They can't see it.

They're absolutely blind to it.

And yet still, Wendy had had a light in her eyes on the morning she'd left that I hadn't seen in years.

I had first seen it after our first romantic moment together at a crowded bar on karaoke night as she forced an intoxicated kiss on me in a moment of spontaneity. She had smiled with a naughty-but-I-don't-give-a-damn look that makes me laugh to this very day. It was a light in the darkness that showed the promise of what was to come in a new relationship unaltered or unscarred yet by petty arguments or jealousy. It was a hope that I was everything good that other men hadn't been to her in the past. It was the desire and passion to feel a fairytale *love* in a world where miracles and myths seemed to have died out long ago.

She had looked at me with that gaze not so much at leaving "us" behind but of the adventure of change and the unpredictability of what was to come with the departure of our relationship.

It was her smile that could always cause me to fall in love with her again.

Sometimes within seconds.

Only when she turned away…it was gone.

It was as fleeting as a shape in the clouds you wanted to point out for a friend or a sibling that just couldn't see where you were directing your finger up in the sky, all before the wind broke apart the image forever—and just as frustrating.

I visited REI quite a few times over the next couple of months as my interest in hiking began to peak. I had been doing ten-mile walks four days a week on my days off, but that had only been to keep my mind busy. To keep from sinking deeper into depression, which would rather I drank all night and fall asleep half hanging off the couch intoxicated.

Was I ready to attempt an over-two-thousand-mile trail of mountain ranges and desolate forests in the middle of nowhere simply because I had walked ten miles on a flat sidewalk a few times?

As the month of November rounded out, I bought a Gregory Baltoro internal-frame backpack for $283. I purchased a ninety-two-dollar water purifier and a ninety-dollar ThermaRest self-inflating air pad to trap a bit of body heat beneath me when I slept on the earth at night.

Then I started to get carried away.

Suddenly I felt as if I might need parachute cord, miniature towelettes, wet naps, and a whole new first-aid kit. I bought a folding saw and pined over a hand ax as well before I thought better of it because of its weight. I started stocking up on dehydrated food and MREs next.

I didn't have a set time when I was supposed to begin my hike because I still needed enough mental strength to realize that life *wasn't* just about working until you died. It was about enjoying the time you had while you were still here on this planet.

Only I wasn't ready to hear that yet or take it into serious account.

I began looking on websites and reading books and Internet blogs about people who had quit their jobs and went out in search of finding some purpose in their lives. Some came back happy, with a renewed appreciation of family and loved ones, while others gained nothing but a wealth of experience and the self-satisfaction of completing such an epic feat.

A few others had called it "a complete waste of time."

That was usually more typical of people who had quit hiking after a couple hundred miles or less.

My excitement grew all the same, along with my purchases.

I bought hiking socks for fifteen dollars and trek poles for thirty. I got Storm Proof Matches (five bucks for a pack of fifty) and wetsuit socks for thirty-seven, to keep my feet dry when walking through streams. Money for each trail item was pouring out of me before I had a chance to fully inspect or learn a thing about the piece of equipment I was buying.

When I finally had the items I needed to take on a small hiking excursion, I looked up a map around Troy, North Carolina and the Uwharrie Trail head off Highway 24/27. This place was an hour and a half from where I lived, and I couldn't think of a better place to get a taste of cold-weather camping and try out my new equipment.

The sun broke through the skeletal branches above me in a thousand beautiful spotlights, which lit up the ground like a disco ball.

It was going to be quite the beautiful day.

I attempted to pick up my pack but was shocked at the weight. When I tried again, straining, I decidedly let it fall to the gravel parking lot. I then attempted to sling it over my shoulder and was shocked at how extremely hard that actually was to do.

"Geez, what'd I pack in here? Bricks?" I asked myself out loud. Maybe I had gotten a little carried away at REI. Or maybe the employees had gotten a little carried away at *telling me* what it was I was supposed have been buying. Regardless of whose fault it was, I struggled momentarily again before I lost balance and fell backward onto my butt. My backpack fell over as I shook my head slowly with disdain.

At that very moment, a hunter walked into the gravel parking lot with his two sons, both of whom were decked out in orange-and-green full-body camouflage overalls. As I braced myself against the trunk of my car, my spine had already started screaming out in pain as I stood. I offered a humble smile despite my embarrassment.

Here I hadn't even left the parking lot yet and I'd already pulled a muscle in my lower back.

"Here, let me show you a trick," the hunter said, setting his rifle against the side of my car. I eyed it warily before looking back at him. He squatted down into a lower position without fully bending over and then proceeded to pull the backpack up onto his knee. He then swung both arms beneath each strap like a breeze and stood.

"If you don't want to strain your back, always try to get the weight halfway up to your shoulders. Man alive... whatta ya have in here?" he asked in surprise, tugging at the straps. He slowly slipped the backpack off again and set it upright in the trunk of my car—pivoting it against the inner quarter panel.

"Well, enough stuff to go from Georgia to Maine," I said proudly. I expected (and sort of wanted) him to nod his head in approval of my response.

Instead he only laughed.

"Ya know, it's gonna get cold out here tonight," he said, not really interested in my desire to walk the AT someday. "You hiking the whole twenty-mile Uwharrie Loop without stopping?" he asked, with a tone too sarcastic to really even care to hear my answer.

As it was the end of November and with the light fading at around five, I hardly found it logical that with a sixty-pound pack on I'd be jogging up and down these mountains in time to make it back to the parking lot that same day. Besides, darkness was only four hours away.

All the same, I kept the thought to myself. Especially since the guy was holding his rifle in his right hand again.

"Well, that's the plan, hopefully," I lied, slowly trying to put the pack back on. When I did, I tried to control and hide the look of anguish on my face from the heft of my load, if for no other reason than pride. I adjusted the straps atop my hips and pulled the shoulder harness tight, wincing at the strain in my back.

"Son, that's some heavy mileage. You aren't gonna have enough time for that. Hate to say it, but ya shoulda planned better. Good luck though," he said, laughing and shaking his head as he walked off with his two children. Suddenly, I thought about why I had come out here.

It was to get away from people like *him*. People who said on a daily basis that I wasn't capable of doing something, or *anything* for that matter. I prayed I wouldn't see him further on down the trail, with his overconfident and cocky attitude.

I headed out northwest down the Uwharrie Trail.

While the weight in my rucksack was already straining my shoulders, I *was* appreciative of the pack and how well it evenly distributed the weight. The thing I would come to find that I had enjoyed most after my initial trek was how neither my hips nor my shoulders had any real lasting soreness or pain in the days to come. This was despite the fact that this was the first overnight backpacking trip I had ever taken.

Mountain laurel twisted and turned, erecting their crooked trunks out of the ground like cartoon trees from a Dr. Seuss book. The trail ran downhill in the first mile, passing a series of hiker- and camper-made sites with rock rings in the middle of their clearings. These places were usually adjacent to a water source of some sort, such as a small stream or creek. There were many of these close to the parking lot for those enthusiastic backpackers whose steam ran out once they were a mile or so in and discovered there was no beer, television, or hot chicks in bikinis waiting for them around the bend.

But while there were several small clearings for camping already made along the Uwharrie Trail, my sense of adventure made me want to steer clear of such pre-established sites all together. Out there you were allowed to build a fire wherever you wanted, which added to the excitement of being outdoors, and I wanted to experience that little pleasure to its full extent, as simple as it might have sounded to most.

Hell, I'd dropped over a grand on gear so far, and wasn't it my *duty* to see if the stuff I'd purchased actually held up?

As I hiked, I began to imagine grand scenarios in my mind, pretending that I was lost and the world was searching for me. Scenarios in which I had become a fugitive from the law, and my only escape was into the wilderness. Out there I would survive only by catching wild game. Knife fight outlaws and save little mountain towns from danger or bad guys before walking down the road with heroic theme music playing me out.

Instead, in the real world, I was sweating profusely and gagging on bugs buzzing manically around my face and dive bombing my eyeballs, all while I tripped and stumbled over rocks or crashed headfirst into trees without paying attention to where I was walking.

A little over a mile in, I came to a place called Woodrun Creek. It was here I decided to test out my trek poles.

The water was amber-colored from the bed of pine needles resting on the bottom and even appeared a bit stagnate for a moving stream. I hopped from rock to rock, balancing in my horribly cheap hiking boots and then steadying myself with the trekking poles.

"Not bad," I said to myself as I pushed on up the winding hill. I had been on the fence about purchasing the poles. I thought they were an unwarranted expense that I could easily replace with a hiking stick or two found in the woods for free, but I was wrong. The light-weight titanium-aluminum poles were sturdy and more than long enough to be used for either single-handed hiking or the double-ski-pole method, which is the way I had decided to use them.

They were good at keeping me from falling on more than a few occasions along the way, but I couldn't deny how dorky they made me feel.

I say that because, while I was aware they were essential tools, whenever somebody passed by, clad in fresh North Face synthetics and a school-sized backpack on, I began to wonder if I looked cheesier than *they* did. It wasn't like I was hiking across the Alps or over ten-thousand-foot mountains out there.

I took a quick break to admire two male squirrels arguing over a female…and strapped the poles back to the outside of my pack.

As I took to struggling with my pack again, I hefted it to my knee and then slipped my arms through the straps as coolly as the hunter had done it back in the parking lot before I'd even set out. Too bad one of my arms missed, and the weight of the pack falling back on one shoulder pulled me backward to the ground.

I still had some learning to do.

The trail ran along the base of some unnamed mountain for a short time and then slowly began to ascend between two peaks. My heart was pumping and my lungs were heaving as I dropped my sweater immediately and hiked on in short sleeves. Nestled down into the valley was yet another creek that had erased all sense of anything to be called a trail for as much as twenty feet or more due to heavy backwash and runoff from previous storms.

Impenetrable wooded views atop 500-million-year-old volcano tops left you begging for an outcropping somewhere—*anywhere*—so that you could see an un-obstructed view of the landscape below. I never got any of those scenes though. Instead, I had to settle for summits covered by leafless trees and barren brush or briars.

Only a few miles in and already my feet were beginning to hurt as I climbed steep inclines and stamped across broken boulders with jagged edges.

While I had spent gobs of money on all my equipment, I just couldn't justify buying $140 hiking boots. I knew my feet were important when it came to hiking but REI, like *most* outdoor retail stores had grossly overcharged on *several* of the things they had sold me (most of which you could find on Amazon for *half* the price). As a result, I opted for twenty-dollar boots from a nearby Walmart.

Well I was paying for that decision now—and only seven miles in.

As I limped painfully along, I passed a Boy Scout troop in the midst of packing up and heading out from a flat section of land on top of one of the many summits of the Uwharries. One of the Scout Leaders told me they had seen wild dogs chasing down deer about thirty feet from their campsite the day before. One of the dogs, according to the Scout Leader, had bit down on a hunk of flesh along the deer's side and had held on until it had been brushed off into the side of a tree. He told me they had then searched for the deer remains off-trail for a bit by tracking their path through the leaves on the ground.

After a while they had given up.

It was a very interesting story to me because the rest of that day, I periodically thought to myself: *How would I stave off a pack of hungry wild dogs if I had to?*

I never saw the beasts the Boy Scout leader had been talking about though. But I would occasionally hear howls and barking in the distance throughout the night and later into that evening, which always made the hair on the back of my neck stand up and adrenaline shoot through my veins.

The barks were so far away though that it didn't immediately appear as if anything posed any real threat to me.

At least that's what I told myself several times during the night, if only to get a little sleep.

The southern portion of the Uwharrie Recreational Trail weaves and intertwines with the Dutchman's Creek loop in a figure eight. When I reached the intersection in the middle of the national forest, I took a breather and tried to decide where I would be setting up for the night.

It was five o'clock when I chose my place of rest, on the summit adjacent to the trail by half a mile.

Oh man, was I excited.

So much so that I laughed as I eagerly broke out my waterproof matches and gathered nearby rotted tree limbs and stones. I proceeded to clear the leaves carpeting the forest floor, down to the dirt, using a dead branch with a cluster of twigs at the end as a rake. I cleared a five-foot-diameter outer ring around the inner rock circle I had built, to avoid flying embers catching the nearby leaves on fire and burning down the forest.

After warming my hands in the flames of the pit I had created, I set up the decade-old hammock tent my father had loaned me, no more than five feet away to soak in the radiant warmth beating off the flames.

What struck me first about this specific hammock was how incredibly *thin* the material holding it together was.

Was this meant to have been a summer hammock of some kind? Because I not only became insecure about its ability to sustain my warmth but also its ability to even support my weight.

When I eased down into it, the ropes I had tied to two different trees about six feet apart shifted and tightened. As this had been my first time setting it up, I had unknowingly set it down too low. I was practically sitting on the ground. I wondered momentarily how pathetic I looked in that U-shaped position.

"Well, damn," I whispered, and my words vanished into clouds, dissipating before my very eyes.

After several failed attempts to hang my father's hammock the correct way, I finally settled into it long after dark had already come.

My view was absolutely beautiful as all remnants of the sun disappeared from the sky. From where I was camped, there was a 360-degree view of five surrounding mountaintops, poking out from leveled fog that had started creeping into the valleys below. It appeared as if I was in a giant bowl of cereal and the fog streaming in between the basins was the milk.

As I readied myself for dinner, it only took a second for exhaustion to set in rather rapidly.

Boy, I was exhausted. I had done eight miles in roughly four hours and planned on rounding out the remaining twelve the next day.

I couldn't sleep much as I lay there though.

I kept thinking about wild dogs or rabid black bears attacking me in the night and different ways I'd fight the beasts off.

I had awakened three times during the night from the sheer cold alone and had adjusted myself time and time again quite unsuccessfully. I had every piece of clothing I had brought with me for those two days wrapped around my body, including the extra socks that I had fitted over my gloves because my fingers kept becoming numb as the evening progressed.

I hated being such a newbie at this outdoor lifestyle. I should have been better prepared.

My home for the evening was a Hennessy Hammock, which acted as a hybrid of a tent and a hammock. It had a sewn-in bug net with a separate rainfly you staked down over the top of it. You got in by entering from the bottom, as it was suspended in the air, and then sat down with your legs on the sides of the entry gap.

Velcro strips closed the portal to the outside world. The only issue was that I had chosen to sleep atop the summit of this ancient inert volcano. This meant that wind blew beneath my hammock and between the two trees I had tied off to, chilling me even more throughout the night. The flimsy material of the hammock did *nothing* to cut the wind either. The ThermaRest I was using beneath me was absolutely worthless as well and had slid around beneath my constantly shifting body all through the night. I would wake the following morning to find it was *sideways*, encroaching up and around my torso.

I think at some point I had even begun to wrap it around my body like a giant synthetic tongue, hoping for *any* kind of warmth it might actually provide.

When morning came, my throat was raw and my eyes wild from the cold. I said, "The hell with breakfast," and came to the exaggerated assumption that I had to get moving or else I would freeze to death.

But trying to get your numb fingers to work when they're quaking, tugging on frost covered knots can almost become impossible. They had turned a blushing red, and I could feel *nothing* below my knuckles.

When I had finally gotten back on to the trail, I began *pumping* out the mileage, if only to build up body heat. Every climb was welcomed, though self-defeating all the same, as my lungs whisked in the harshly frigid air and made my sore throat throb even more. There always seemed to be a tradeoff of some kind out there in the wild.

After about two miles, I stopped hiking, as my feet were screaming out in anger at me.

"What! What? *What's the issue now*!" I shouted out loud in frustration, to nobody, as I threw my two-ton backpack off quite suddenly and limped toward a boulder.

I had thought it was sweat that had been giving me a squishy feeling between my toes, but when I saw the dark red stain on my sock after removing my cheap boots, it told me a completely different story. As I removed the piece of clothing completely, I found that I had lost my middle toenail, which fell out of the material and onto the ground.

"Gross…" I muttered, oddly curious as I examined the hardened collection of dead cells that made up the nail. Dried and moist blood had collectively encompassed the rest of my toes. Upon further examination of my feet, I found myself looking down upon two huge blisters as well, one on the same mangled appendage that was missing a nail and the other on the underside of my big toe, which had already ruptured and begun to bleed too.

"Stupid boots!" I shouted, slamming them angrily on the ground, as if that would've fixed anything. But in truth I knew it was *my* fault for being so frugal and not shelling out the money for something better at REI.

When I finally made my way back to my car later that afternoon, I was limping.

An elderly couple passed by, eying me carefully, as if I was in dire need of medical attention. The old man turned and gave me a wizened look. He had seen my crippled gait while I had been stumbling into the parking lot and wasn't too shy to state the obvious.

"Bad boots make for a bad hike."

I answered with an "Amen, brother" as I threw my pack into the trunk of my car and slammed it shut.

"Where'd you come from?" he asked. I wiped sweat from my brow despite the fact that it was twenty-three degrees outside. The sweat hadn't been so much from the temperatures at the end as much as it had been from the sheer pain radiating throughout my feet and the utter displeasure I'd had in pushing on.

"Did the Uwharrie Loop. Trying to prepare myself for the Appalachian Trail someday," I exclaimed, leaning against my car and drinking purified water from a stream I had stopped at earlier. I had filtered it with my

Katadyn Backpacker Pro water purifier. While the water was still a dirty amber color, it tasted clear, clean, and incredible all the same.

"Well, now, really? My brother did half of that trail—oh, I'd say maybe twenty years ago or so. He was in his mid-fifties. That's a lot to put on your plate," he said, laughing a little. It seemed as if an old spark had reignited within the old man's eyes.

Meanwhile his wife looked impatiently at their car, clearly not as interested in our conversation as we both were.

"My father did a hundred-mile section from Harper's Ferry down south through Virginia ten years ago. I had hoped to hike it with him on some parts along the way someday. He came back with wild stories of the crazy places he'd stayed and odd people he had met and some of the adventures he'd had while he and his friend were out there. I don't know. It struck a chord in me, and I've always wanted to do it since," I exclaimed. And in truth, the sheer adventure and stories my father had come back with really *had* made me want to give it a try.

As the elderly man's wife started their car, she got out and circled to the passenger side, giving me a look that almost appeared to be a plea to wrap things up. I smiled and nodded my head at her, though I was thoroughly enjoying conversing with somebody that had actually been interested in the possibility of my future exploits.

Hell, everyone else I'd told had either brushed it off or declared that I was crazy to even think about it.

Here this complete stranger looked as if he was about to invite me out to dinner to talk about the outdoors and nature and life off of the grid.

"Well, I better get going. It was nice to meet you," I said, extending my hand.

"My name's Earl, and you are?"

"John." I replied as he clasped my hand and we shook.

"Well, good luck, John, on your hike along the Appalachian Trail. I hope to read about you someday," he said, as if it was some monumental journey that would be printed in every newspaper across America.

Here a complete stranger had shown such incredible interest in something I wasn't even sure I was really ever going to do. I was still far too scared and disorganized to even know where to begin.

But it was a seed my father had planted in my mind seven years before and only now was it beginning to sprout under the circumstances that had become my life.

Cheerfully, excitedly, I got into my car and drove back into civilization.

The Uwharrie Mountain Range in North Carolina was originally not a part of North America. It was in fact a non-native chain of volcanic islands believed to have once existed as a string of ocean floor outcroppings around the late Precambrian to Paleozoic eras (460–630 million years ago). That is why it does not appear to be an extension or a snippet of the Appalachians. It is believed that the Uwharrie's peaks were once as high as twenty thousand feet but in time had eroded down to a maximum height of around eleven hundred.

Climbing these little summits today didn't offer grand or exciting views or much of a challenge. But as they were only less than two hours away from where I lived, they were about as practical as it got for me and my hikes.

I sat on my balcony reminiscing over the short excursion I had taken just a few days before, now from the safety of my home. I was eating alone and watching the heavy wind blow the trees back and forth in front of me, predicting the future for the evening and the storms that were on their way. I was dressed and ready for work and had prepared myself a rather bland ham and cheese sandwich for my dinner. Now I ate it alone, with a large glass of orange juice in hand.

I didn't have much for company, save for a few boxes packed with my belongings, and the band Abba playing their song "SOS" over my neighbor's outside radio. She was jiving and lip-syncing, "When you're gone, how can I…even try…to go on…" as she folded the laundry she had hung up to dry above her railing.

I smiled, wondering how embarrassed she would've been had she known I was there.

But the smile quickly faded after taking another bite from my "dinner."

I looked down at my sandwich and thought about how dry and plain it was. Wendy had always made the perfect sandwiches, even going so far as to cut them in half for me and remove the bread crusts. She also always wrapped the tomatoes separately in cellophane to keep the sandwich from getting soggy.

Shut up! Stop thinking about her!

But I sometimes wondered if my newfound loneliness spurred the want inside me to run away from everything. I slunk in each day to work, drifting in and out of mental consciousness and sitting in remote positions stationed around the Nuclear Plant as part of my job. I felt like a mindless zombie shuffling from one connect-a-dot to another for thirteen hours—under command and constant threat of job loss for so much as forgetting to iron pleats into my uniformed pants legs.

Then I went home.

I jogged three times a week, ate a bowl of cereal every morning for breakfast as I watched the news, showered, and then went to bed alone.

Woke up and made myself a quick dinner, either something microwaveable or something without much prep time.

Went back to work. Proceeded to watch more cameras, walk in more circles, armed to the teeth with weapons, and make idle conversations in passing to coworkers as my eyes glazed over and my mind separated from my body.

This was my life, at twenty-eight, and I had no one to blame for the monotony but myself.

I grew up believing the world had owed me something from the hardships I had faced as a youth. I used it as reasoning with a sense of entitlement to never push myself very hard to achieve something, always subconsciously believing I had earned a place in life just because I had survived it thus far. I had made my world successful and routine because of a father that never haggled, argued, or asked why in his life. He simply followed the rules. And as a result, I followed suit as his son.

The mind is a wonderful thing to run away to. I escaped into daydreams all the time when I was at work. Most people seem to take each situation in life and look for the worst-case scenario before attempting to tackle it. Or at least I always did. That was the only way I justified my jump from the norm to the "abnormal."

John Bison, who was a friend of mine from work, had let me borrow a book entitled *AWOL on the Appalachian Trail*[1], which had been written by someone called David Miller.

---

[1] Miller, David. AWOL on the Appalachian Trail. 2nd ed. Lake Union Publishing, 2010.

By *borrow* I mean he had unknowingly *given* me the book because I never returned it. Having read through it several times, I had become engrossed in its words. And not so much because David Miller was a literary genius of some kind but because of the subject matter *within* those words.

After my trip to the southern portion of the Uwharries and reading David Miller's adventure along the Appalachian Trail, I was so eager to jump back out into the wilderness that it was all I could ever think about anymore. I flowed through the following workweek like an excited rower slogging tirelessly in a sea of wet cement. I wanted to escape from the gray, radioactive tomb I lived in four days a week.

As I sat in watch towers and looked out the windows at the night sky, I longed for the fresh smells of the forest, the secluded nature of the woods, and the peace and beauty that followed suit.

Wendy sat first, and I followed. The sunset beaming through the window behind us painted the skies in hues of purples and deep burnt reds. Strands and strings of clouds stretched out bright with neon orange lines running along the edges of the massive formations—all within in the remaining rays of sunlight. It had made for quite the relaxing atmosphere.

Wendy took to thumbing through the menu with what appeared to be distant thoughts residing in her mind. You could see her thinking at a thousand miles per hour. Silence, not yet uncomfortable, hung in the air only momentarily as I glanced over her. She hadn't changed much in the past six months, yet she had a rather radiant glow about her now that I had never quite noticed before. I couldn't describe it other than to say it was different from her usual presence and easily seen through the silhouette created by the setting star on the horizon behind her.

Our waiter, a teenage boy so nervous he was practically shaking, took our order and then vanished into the kitchen eager to be out of the limelight of an awkward two-person audience. He must've been new. I sort of expected a cartoonish dirt cloud to trail after him in what appeared to be a rather rapid escape on his part.

"So tell me about her. I guess you both have been arguing some, huh?" Wendy asked, taking a sip from the Long Island Iced Tea she had ordered while looking up at me over the edge of the glass.

"Now how would *you* know that?" I asked matter-of-factly. She only smiled as if she had hidden sources she'd die for before ever divulging to me.

I bet it was Paul.

He was a mutual friend of ours.

"She's just…" I began, before reconsidering what I was going to say.

"Ya know, at least I didn't move on and get married like you did," I finally spat out sarcastically.

It was true that Wendy had been dating again. More often than not, it felt awkward whenever we talked about our dating. Only because I wondered dreamily if we were destined to come together again.

There was no denying I still had feelings for her.

But Wendy didn't have many friends aside from Paul and I, so the topic came up quite often in our conversations together whether I wanted to hear about her dating life or not. Quite regularly I got to hear about her failed or creepy dates as well as the ones that had gone well.

"Been writing any more lately? Making your YouTube video skits?" she had asked, changing the subject.

I laughed passively and replied with a shrug. "Here and there, I guess." I said it more to my plate than to her.

Truth was, she had wanted me to meet her new boyfriend, Chris, and it was the topic of almost all of our conversations as of late. And while he seemed to be a nice guy from what she had told me, his cemented existence in Wendy's life wasn't something I was completely OK with yet. And really, could I ever truly be OK with that?

Suddenly her phone buzzed, and she reached into her purse to retrieve it. She laughed out loud and began typing away as if I wasn't even there.

"Chris is great. Did I tell you that he's got tattoos?"

I gave her a cynical look of awe she never witnessed, having been so glued to the four-inch screen of her smartphone.

"My God! Tattoos, you say? In this day and age!" I replied over enthusiastically as I crammed another green bean into my mouth. "Yeah, you did. Are we going to go over all his amazing traits again for another hour?" I asked, looking down at the scant dipping sauce we had left between us.

"What? We're always talking about you and your girl…or girlfriends…or whatever…" Wendy began.

"Right, because I have women practically *beating down the door* to be with me. Besides, the topic comes up because you're always asking. Right now, I'm dating someone, and we're just friends, seeing where things go. Did we have a few early arguments? Yeah, but does that mean it's not going to work? No," I replied, a little exasperated.

"But you don't think it's strange you're arguing this early in the relationship? I mean if you're gonna be boyfriend and girlfriend…" Wendy said, but I closed my eyes and began waving my hands back and forth, cutting her off.

"You're talking about months down the road. Even then, that's *maybe* if anything ever even works out. I've already told her I'm going to date other people and that I expect her to do the same. I'm not out there having sex with random people or making out with strangers. Besides, I don't sleep around, and you know that about me."

"I do," she agreed.

"And that doesn't make me less of a man either," I added, before taking a long swig from the Corona Light I had ordered. I had wanted something light to go with my meal but was now wishing I was pounding down shots.

"Who ever said that?" Wendy asked, confused.

"Some of the guys at work ride me about it. And other things. Just forget it."

Our waiter stood in the doorway to the kitchen, scared and looking out at us as I finished my beer and tried to wave him down. It looked like he had begun shaking nervously again, purposefully averting his gaze from us for a few seconds before disappearing into the kitchen.

"Well don't lump me into your work friends. I'm just saying be careful. I don't want you to get hurt."

"No problem, Mom," I replied, wishing the conversation had ended long before it ever even started.

When our food came, our conversations swiveled around the amazing new apartment she had found in Durham at her new job. After three years the excitement of the living space I had once shared with an ex-fiancée had died off. A 1,350-square-foot apartment for $600 a month was nothing to laugh at though, and I knew when

I eventually needed to move out that I would miss the space, the price, and the location.

But when a bunch of memories sink into the surrounding walls, cleaning house and moving on can also mean finding somewhere else to live without the bad memories trailing along as well.

Starting over completely and evenly.

Because those walls within our old apartment still held the arguments.

The memories.

The shouting matches had sunk in and been absorbed into those thinly painted white surfaces.

And the daily reminders haunting my drunken nights alone had become relentless.

When you're argumentative, and you've got your face...

The lyrics softly sung into the air over the TGI Friday's ceiling speakers as I lifted my head. Wendy was going on about her new boyfriend once again before I finally cut her off.

"Remember this song?" I asked her as a smile slowly crawled across my face.

I began to slightly hum and harmonize with the lyrics as Wendy stopped talking long enough to listen along with me for a moment.

"Oh yeah! You downloaded this for me after one of our fights a long time back didn't you? As an apology. Yeah, I liked it," she said, remembering.

I smiled in slight awe at such an obscure song ran-domly playing right then and there.

"Bet you and Chris don't have a favorite song yet," I said, forking a grilled chicken skewer chunk into my mouth and grinning at her.

"We've been dating like two weeks," she replied, not remotely taking me seriously.

"Let me see his pictures again," I said, grabbing her phone and thumbing through her text messages rudely.

"Oh wow, quite the assortment of naked pictures you've been trading each other," I lied playfully.

"Oh yeah, tons of naked pictures. Give me my phone back, and I'll show you what he looks like." She immedi-ately jerked her cell back into her own possession. "Don't touch my phone," she added childishly, as if she was play-ing the part of a selfish little girl not willing to share her toys.

She proceeded to show me Chris's picture, at which I immediately began to scoff.

"So what's it like dating the lead singer of Limp Bizkit?" I asked as she simply glared back in anger.

"Fred Durst, everybody," I went on, out loud to an imaginary audience with my hands up in the air. I was crassly waving her phone back and forth.

"Oh, shut up," she said, snatching it from me again and putting it back in her purse.

"I'm telling you, I'm hotter than him," I said, if for no other reason than to rib her a little bit.

"No, he's hotter, and he's got a better personality than you as well," Wendy finished coldly as our song ended over the speakers.

"Ouch," I mouthed quietly.

When we finished dinner, I yearned for a cigarette but only because Wendy had one, flaunting it right in front of my face outside in the parking lot.

We stood where purple traces of daylight were all that remained, and the orange parking lot lights had already triggered. We talked about our parents and how our families were doing just to pass idle conversation. In the darkness, her face was illuminated by the bright light of her smartphone as she exhaled a thin stream of smoke into the air.

She was texting Chris again and laughing.

I looked away for a second as she began talking about her eccentric interest in this new guy of hers once more. When I was about to tell her to shut up and make an excuse that I had to go, I got caught up by something in her eyes that I hadn't seen in a long while.

It was happiness.

Something hit me hard within my heart at that very moment as I saw the curves of a smile pull at either ends of her lips.

And then it came to me all at once, what it was I was feeling.

It was in fact jealousy.

It wasn't jealousy solely because she had moved on or because she was no longer in a relationship with me. Oddly enough, it was because she was happy, whereas my nights had usually ended in drunken depression.

The jealousy in my heart turned to reflection as she took a final drag and dropped the butt of her cigarette to the asphalt. "I want to tell you something," I said softly as she looked up at me.

"I know, stop talking about Chris…"

"No, not that at all. I'm gonna try and say this without looking or sounding stupid."

A slight look of bewilderment crossed her face, uncertain of where I was going with the conversation or what I was about to say.

"It's just good, that's all," I said, my voice wavering momentarily. I grasped listlessly at resolve and composure but found nothing.

"What's good?" she asked, putting her cigarettes and lighter back into her purse and looking up at me. I had always been taller than her by a good thirteen or fourteen inches, but I was also standing on the curb and she wasn't. When she looked up at me, the orange aura of street lamps brightened her face. And once again she was glowing.

"It's good to see you smiling…it really is," I said, looking down at the ground in shame as my voice wavered.

I didn't want to say it. Something inside me, possibly pride, stood defiantly in the way of the words I was yearning to pour out of me—words and understanding that had been kept inside for far too long out of spite.

I exhaled softly, feeling my breaths shatter only slightly. When I looked into her eyes again, I found myself remembering the first time I had told her I loved her, so many years before. It had been a special moment in time. One that would always be ours.

But still a moment that I was aware we would never go back to.

I continued on, tears brimming on the edge of my eyes. I was an expert at false smiling and managed to cough out a nervous laugh, mostly because I was embarrassed by my own reactions.

When I looked at Wendy, her face changed from concerned to endearing.

"It's been forever since I can remember you being happy," I said, wiping my eyes.

"John…" she began, seriousness taking over her facial expressions completely. I couldn't let her stop me though because they were words she needed to hear.

"And while maybe I wasn't the one to be able to do it…it's good to see you found somebody that *could*."

She looked down for a moment with tears of her own lightly cresting.

"It's about time you were happy, that's all," I concluded.

It was conceding defeat.

It was a collection of words and a statement that would foretell our futures till the end of our days.

And it hurt to accept them. To willingly say good-bye to our past.

Wendy embraced me then and held on before whispering, "Thank you." As she did, a peace came over me in that moment that I couldn't fully understand.

It was hard and painful to watch each other move on, but it didn't seem right until there was an ultimate reason, an ultimate goal: each other's lifelong happiness. It was all either of us had ever wanted for each other, and when it wasn't achieved through a relationship together, it felt right to see it now from a different perspective.

It felt good to see her move on.

When Wendy drove off, I sat in my car for a moment scrolling through my old iPod. I found the song that we had heard inside TGI Friday's and played it. The lyrics talked through the scenes of a quarrelsome relationship that easily fit the mold of our own past.

The song was "Marty Bum" by The Arctic Monkeys.

I listened to it nine times on my way home.

Tiny flowers found along the Virginia Creeper Trail
in Damascus, Virginia, during Trail Days.

CHAPTER 2

Final Preparations

IT WAS 2:00 A.M. SEVERAL weeks later, and I was intoxicated again, lying face down on the floor in someone's bathroom. I awoke dazed in a puddle of my own vomit. I suppose I hadn't been fast enough to reach the toilet.

I watched with cloudy eyes as a black beetle scurried behind the trash can beside the toilet as if terrified of the *beast* waking nearby. My head was bleeding slightly from the counter's edge it had struck on my way down. My brains felt scrambled, and my vision was blurred.

I felt as if my skull was on fire and alcohol had fueled the blaze.

I tried to remember or grasp where I was as I sat up slowly and touched the dried puke on the side of my face. *How had I gotten here? Where was I?* I asked myself.

I looked behind me and found I had stripped my clothes off, almost like a path of breadcrumbs leading from the front door. It was then that I realized I was inside my own apartment.

My entrance door was still wide open from when I had stumbled in.

After crawling on my hands and knees toward it, using what felt like all of my strength and cognitive skills to shut it, I slowly got to my feet and clumsily shuffled into the kitchen. I was eager to get the taste of puke out of my dried-out mouth.

I grabbed a carton of orange juice from my refrigerator, drank thirstily, and then dropped the rest of the contents onto the floor on my way back to the bathroom.

I took a hot shower, thinking about my life and how depression had been racking my mind more and more with each passing day.

Part of me believed that finding a different job would have made me happier. Another part of me thought that moving on would've been healthy. Yet, self-loathing had set in again over the last month as I went through bad date after bad date just trying to do that exact thing.

To move on.

But each failed meeting was another reason to find something wrong about myself that I needed to change.

In time, I began to despise the thought of ever dating again and yearned to just leave everything behind. But my experiences on the Uwharrie Trail had left me feeling weak and pathetic. Not yet ready to confront the wilderness.

So I combated that as well, by drinking.

Only I was doing more than just drinking. I was killing myself.

The four nights I had off work each week became dark days lying on my couch with the curtains drawn as I drank and watched television. I stopped jogging, working out, and biking. I started giving up on everything.

I stopped going to parties or get-togethers with friends, as I no longer had the patience or the willpower to deflect playful comments made by them about my growing weight and the gut I was starting to gain.

Early on in the last evening, before a drink ever even touched my lips, I glanced over my phone's contact list and picked random friends or acquaintances to ask if any one of them wanted to sing karaoke and get drunk with me.

Two responded.

My friend Thomas and my ex-fiancée, Wendy.

She had shown with her new love interest in tow, of course, who she had been badgering me so incessantly to finally meet. She had a cool demeanor about her. No chink in her armor whatsoever.

There was a slight urgency in her eyes though that made it imperative I enjoy Chris's company and that I remain decent and respectable to the new guy in her life.

But my world was an inebriated blur that made me feel more bitter than anything else. Several times I found myself wanting to just blurt out at him in rage, "Can we just be honest here with each other? You realize you've stolen *my* fiancée, right?"

Only I had kept my mouth shut.

When Wendy appeared, I found it funny how much more stunning an ex becomes when you realize that they'll never be yours again. I watched her eyes look lovingly upon Chris as the four of us passed time with darts, cigarettes, alcohol, and idle conversation that never really spanned out any further than a few words or acknowledgments.

And as we all stood there, I watched as she now looked at him like she had once looked upon me.

Was it inconceivable for me to be hurt by that?

When Thomas left, I was alone in my torment among them, during which I kept absolutely silent. It was odd to be the third wheel with a former fiancée.

As I watched them, I was aware that Chris was kissing her whenever I vanished to the bar to collect drinks for the three of us or to use the restroom. I was sure that Wendy knew the blatant display of courtship in front of me would hurt me more than I already hurt inside.

And she was right.

I could almost believe for a second that she had possibly asked him to *tone down the affection* on the drive over, out of respect for me.

But it still hadn't stopped me from knowing. So I walked home, barely able to see the lines of the road or the sidewalk on which I traipsed. It wasn't a long walk, as the bar was less than a mile from where I lived. But it hadn't been a nice walk either. I remembered leaning against a light pole somewhere, fighting back the nausea and one hell of a headache as I emptied the contents of my stomach onto the pavement.

How I got up the stairs to my apartment from there, I don't know. And now here I was. Washing puke and dried blood off of the side of my face and wishing the water could sink in a little deeper and rinse away my loneliness.

After I'd taken my shower, I stepped out and caught sight of my phone on the floor beside the toilet. It was blinking with a notification of some kind.

The red LED light beckoned me to answer Wendy's text message of concern.

I blinked out of the last few minutes of reflection and concentrated harder than I ever had before in my life to respond to her while clumsily tapping a screen too small and blurry to see with inebriated eyes.

She had messaged me to ask if I had gotten home safely.

"John Morris, ever the vigilant drunk," I replied.

I momentarily thought of the Appalachian Trail again as my sozzled world spun in circles. And as I stumbled toward my bedroom, I dreamt of vanishing from civilization as I had a million times before. Most importantly, I thought of everything I'd be leaving behind.

I hated myself. I hated my life up to that point, and I hated the type of person I had become.

Moreover, I came to realize everything I had already lost.

My future, my life…my *everything* was gone.

Wendy had moved on.

As I fell naked and still wet from the shower onto my bed, I used what little strength I had in me to bring my phone up toward my face.

In a swift, deliberate move, I deleted her from my contact list. I never wanted a reason to have to talk to her or bother her again.

If my life was to go on, there had to be no regret in my decision to make it happen.

My smartphone asked for confirmation that I wanted to remove her permanently from my list of contacts.

I looked behind the pop-up window on my four-inch screen at the last text message she had sent me.

"Glad to hear it. Have a good night." she replied.

"You too," I said out loud as I clicked yes to delete and felt my heart break.

It was my first day off work, and I was already on my way back out to the Uwharries. My goal was to attempt the entirety of the forty-mile recreational Uwharrie

Trail Loop, if only to test myself both physically and mentally. I wanted to get a greater understanding and knowledge base for some of the equipment I had blindly purchased under the "protective eyes" of the REI sales associates.

I also wanted to figure out what I could dump from my oversized backpack.

The morning was bright and crisp. As it was winter, the air had a minute sting to it that would nip lightly at your cheeks whenever a sudden breeze whispered through the trees. Red robins lined the skeletal branches above, chirping out loudly as their heads tilted left to right, looking upon me curiously.

Two miles into my hike, I crossed paths with an elderly man walking with his daughter. "Nice trek poles," he said, pointing toward them with his wooden hiking stick. At first I thought he was mocking me, but I responded with a thank-you all the same, quite cheerfully.

"You heading out overnight?" he asked.

I confirmed his inquiry with the nod of my head. I went on to inform the gentleman of my desire to thru-hike the entire AT one day, rather gushing about it, and that I needed to acclimate to hiking longer distances as a result. It hadn't been my intention to blurt out future hypothetical plans, which were far from coming to fruition, to complete strangers. But deep down I wanted an ear to vent my dreams.

"Interesting. I hope to read a journal entry about you one day in one of the shelters."

I wasn't sure what he meant by that exactly, so I asked him to explain.

"Basically, along the Appalachian Trail, you come across these shelters that you can sleep in and—"

I quickly interrupted him. "OK, now, I read something about these sheds or shelters—whatever—in a book about the AT."

"So then you understand the concept. Well, anyhow they aren't really sheds. Then again, now that I think about it, some of them are *run down* enough to look like sheds, or worse," he said, reminiscing with a laugh before continuing on.

"But anyways, these shelters have journals in them usually maintained by local hiking clubs or Boy Scouts within the general area. These logbooks are a *good way* to keep up with the friends you make along the way. Say you were hiking with a nice guy or gal that you generally got along with for a week, but he or she ended up getting ahead of you. A good way to keep up with the person's progress is to follow their entries in the logbooks kept within those shelters along the way," he explained.

I didn't know why, but I was getting more and more interested with all of these little things about the trail I was learning. I had read about "trail magic" and "trail angels" and was starting to become engrossed in the

Appalachian Trail culture, which seemed to in all honesty be a culture in itself.

Three hours into hiking and the sky above had darkened, causing the once proud sunshine to slip beneath the cover of darkly bruised clouds. It made me think that the sun had woken up briefly, said, "Nope!" and then decided to crawl back into bed.

I stopped on a rocky outcrop forty feet off of the trail and sat down with a bottle of water and an apple-cinnamon cereal bar in hand. I pulled my earphones from my ears and listened to the soft rustling of the wind between the dead leaves still clinging to their mothering branches and relished it. I took deep breaths and found comfort in the smells of thick forest vegetation. It could have been pouring rain in that moment and I would have been completely fine with it, I was so at peace.

That is, until I had a passing thought about my change of clothes.

Around me, occasional drops were starting to patter as I quickly began to search through my pack. In doing so, I saw the empty gap where my second pair of clothing should have been. I repacked my things, suddenly remembering I had left my other outfit in my compression sack on my dining room table before heading out.

"Damn," I muttered as I let my pack fall on the ground and rested my head in my hands.

As I stared down at the leaf-covered earth beneath my feet, what I thought had been wind was actually a wall of heavy rain, advancing on me. When I looked up, I actually *saw* the downpour headed my direction.

"Crap," I uttered, jumping to my feet.

Suddenly that "thick forest vegetation" smell that had brought me peace and admiration of the wild minutes before no longer meant a thing to me.

I took off along the side of the trail, quickly throwing my pack onto my shoulders midway into the process. I ignored the loop that I saw the trail cut off to on the left, and instead I jogged straight down the slope in front of me, completely off the path altogether. As I ran, I stopped every couple of minutes to hear the wall of rain still advancing south, in my direction. I actually began to believe that I could simply outrun the cloud far enough ahead to set up a quick shelter before it reached me.

Most important to me was the fear of being unable to start a fire in the rain. I didn't want to get soaked and freeze to death when it dropped down to the mid-twenties later that night. It would have been just another crappy factor I'd have to deal with in my nubile experience within these wilds.

While my jogging abilities were average at best, I had never jogged with fifty pounds of gear bouncing around back and forth on my back before either.

Because of this, I took my first fall that moment when, while running, I tried to pivot myself with one arm over a fallen tree like a B-movie action hero of some sort.

I landed perfectly with both feet on the ground on the opposite side of the tree. The only problem was that I had landed on a downward slope, and the weight of my backpack slung out—pulling me backward down with it.

I rolled down the hill a good twenty feet, and the earbuds I had placed in my ears were ripped out painfully during the process of tumbling. It left me feeling as if my eardrums had been sucked out with them. My descent finally stopped with me landing elbow-deep in a muddy wash at the base of the hill.

Behind me the wall of rain was still advancing, but it was a distant thought as I pulled my arms from the black muck.

Black muck that, I might add, had the distinct smell of sewage runoff.

"Way to go, dummy," I growled bitterly at myself.

As I got up slowly, I was surprised I hadn't really hurt myself that badly, other than my pride.

After getting to my feet and scrubbing off as much mud as possible with handfuls of dead leaves, I readjusted my straps and then made my way across the stagnant mud stream rather carefully.

The trail looped around back in front of me about a good sixty to seventy feet up and then climbed a good ways skyward before vanishing around the upper cusp of the worn-down mountain before me.

The rain wall was closing in from behind, so I ran up the steep slope, trying to get to the more level surface of the path. I knew that if I could somehow manage that, I could take off running again.

Clearly I hadn't learned my lesson.

Each step up was becoming just as pointless as the last. I kept slipping and sliding back down the steep hillside as the loose dirt and leaves gave way beneath my feet, slowing my ascent. Rain drops began pitter-pattering here and there around me, and suddenly I could imagine myself in third person. The image was of me fruitlessly climbing nowhere as the rain wall hit me and ended with a close-up of my face as I stood with a glum expression and mud dripping from my arms.

Streams of cold rainwater ran along my face or dripped down from my forehead in droves as I stood there.

It was in that moment I thought that if I had simply stayed on the trail instead of trying to go all Survivor Man, I wouldn't have even been in that predicament to begin with.

Further down, I found an easier grade to climb up from the muck stream and trudged on through the rain.

After hours of walking in that downpour, I set up my refugee campsite in the rain. I was within a dense section of forest next to what someone had titled Twin Snakes Creek. The name had been engraved onto a thin wooden board and nailed to a tree along the side of the trail.

I cursed the skies for the flood that it had brought down upon me, and as immediately as I had, the rain stopped.

"That's what I thought!" I shouted defiantly, as if I had intimidated Mother Nature herself.

I managed to get a small fire started, mainly from bark I had taken from a dead yet still-standing tree. I had also taken nearby branches and carved the outer wet layer of bark off and shaved out the dry pieces into splinters within the middle for kindling. This was a technique my friend and coworker Torry had taught me on one of our many day hikes taken together, long before the depression of my broken love life had stolen the determination and willpower to do so more regularly. I had a spark starter (and a lighter as back up) and decided on the easiest solution.

I'd test the spark starter some other time, because right then all I cared about was getting dry and warm. I took off my wet shirt and pants and squeezed as much water out of the synthetic-based quick-dry clothing as I could.

My fingers were rosy and numb as I shivered in my wet boxers over the weak, waning fire.

"What am I getting myself into?" I muttered out loud as I thought about the AT. It was depressing to think that something as simple as precipitation of some sort could ruin your entire view of such an epic journey.

I broke out my sleeping bag and an old beef stew MRE from 2004 that I had bought in a case of twelve for sixty bucks. As I hunched over the dwindling fire, I took out a can of spam and cut chunks into the soupy mixture I had created. With the remaining portion of potted meat, I skewered the chunks onto a green twig I had broken off from the tree supporting my tent.

The greasy meat popped and crackled as the flames licked voraciously at it.

I ate the pieces hungrily, feeling calorie-starved.

That night, I slept nude within my sleeping bag and was rather surprised at how warm it kept me. This was of course despite the fact I was still far too cold to sleep at all, and I could no longer even feel my fingers despite packing them beneath my armpits.

As night began to fall, I got up to pee twice, which is never fun when you're completely naked.

I had enjoyed utilizing the streams in the national forest for fresh water just a little too much, I suppose. It had been the realization that I could find any old rotten, stagnant puddle and drink out of it using the purifier I had purchased. The filter claimed it could even strain radioactive isotopes out, but where the hell was I going to find that around here?

I fumbled awkwardly around within my hammock tent, looking for my headlamp. When I rolled over to grasp at it, I ended up falling out through the center entry port of the hammock onto the cold, rocky ground.

"Christ!" I screamed out both in pain and sheer anger as my hand immediately shot to the sharp pang on my back where I had fallen onto a jagged stone.

Around me, the frigid air kissed at my bare flesh as I struggled with my sleeping bag zipper in the dark.

Ice was already starting to form on the dead leaves carpeting the forest floor. A sharp breeze cut through, rustling the bare branches around me. I learned another valuable lesson in that moment. Don't set up camp so close to a stream if your clothes are soaked and it's less than thirty degrees outside.

You'll only stay wet, frozen, and cold as the fog drifts idly over you and your belongings.

As I nakedly shuffled away from my hammock, an aching throb in my lumbar region reminded me that even on such a simple excursion, things could easily go downhill in the blink of an eye.

How could I ever be ready for six months of this, day after day, on the AT?

As I released my bladder, my headlamp went back and forth, cutting through the night like a knife.

Thousands of bright rainbow-like sparkles lit up around me like diamonds pasted to the tips of leaf fall. I knew it had begun to frost outside, because my bare toes were numb from standing on the frozen forest floor. But the diamonds shining brightly from random spots on the earth around me stood out like stars in the sky.

When I was done, I approached one of these glittering orbs, only to see it was the eyes of a rather large wolf spider.

I quickly approached another sparkle nearby, only to see that it was also the eyes of yet another wolf spider. It wasn't until I did a complete 360-degree turn though that I became aware of the thousands of spiders' eyes all looking in my general direction, clearly aware of the giant stomping around in their territory.

It made me glad that I wasn't sleeping on the ground that night.

Morning came, bitter and unrelenting, and wind gusts definitely didn't make things any more bearable. I tried to figure out where I was on my phone but soon realized that once I had trotted off-trail, I had passed and forgotten any noticeable landmarks that would've given me a general area location.

If anyone was within a mile of my campsite that morning, they got an earful as I threw on my cold, wet, frozen clothes, which hadn't seemed to have dried one bit over the embers of a dying fire throughout the night.

I had thought of putting the wet clothes in my sleeping bag during one of the many early-morning shiver fests I'd had during the night, in hopes that my body heat would've helped them dry. This was a trick I had read about in online journals about the Appalachian Trail from those that had hiked it. The only problem was, I felt there wasn't enough heat coming off of my body throughout the night to make it feasible, and I didn't want wet, freezing clothes crowding my feet within my semi-warm and dry sleeping bag.

After packing my things and finding my way back to the trail, I began to hate the woods. I imagined my comfortable couch and my big screen television back at home. I thought of buying a huge bag of pizza-flavored Combos and Snyder's Hot Buffalo pretzels and pigging out under a warm blanket to a movie.

Instead, I was freezing to death in the middle of nowhere, aching, angry, and blistered. I turned on my phone and looked at where I was at on the map according to my GPS.

Staring at the tiny screen of my smartphone, I found the southern trail head was twenty-eight miles further away and knew that if I decided to stay on the path, I'd be out there another night, with my slow progress, in freezing, wet clothes.

"What a joke," I said, more of myself than as a statement of my predicament. Was I bound to be the impulsive type the rest of my life, who got a wild hair up my ass from time to time and made life decisions in the blink of an eye?

It started to feel like that was the case.

Here I had thought of taking six months to hike the entire Appalachian Trail, but after one idiotic mistake after another, I was already heading back home from what was supposed to be a two-to-three-day trip through the Uwharries.

I felt like a failure and no longer thought I was *ever* going to hit the trail.

It was several months later, and I had given up on the online dating website, ironically entitled Plenty of Fish. I had deleted my account with a rather jaded point of view, one which seemed to turn my vision red whenever I thought of wasting any more of my time on another first-and-last date from there. In life though, I always found it odd that you could sometimes stumble upon love, or a relationship, at times when you weren't even looking for it.

It wasn't hard to see that I was lonely.

I attempted to fill whatever I thought the gap was in my life by looking for a companion of some sort.

Yet deeper down, a part of me knew even having one wouldn't satiate my taste for change.

It was September 28, 2012, and I lay in the bed of my father's Chevy Colorado beneath the eclectic ambiance of a crowded beach. Above, the night had started to come in like the tide washing upon the shore. The once-pink skies were being washed away by purple wisps of night like dissolving grains of salt, leaving only the starlit heavens overhead.

I had decided to tag along with a group of my friends and had been peer pressured to camp at the beach for the weekend in a community setting. This was only to break up the monotony of a bland life riddled with alcohol and depression.

I had no idea my way of life had become so transparent to the people I called friends. Still, I found it odd they found comfort in my out-of-control drinking in their presence as opposed to my doing it alone.

The small coastal town of Pleasant Island resembled nothing more than fragmented pieces of North Carolina that had broken away from the mainland in their pursuit to be free entities. Freeman Beach was a small peninsula that (for an outrageous twenty dollars a day) you could drive your vehicle out onto and stay overnight. The bigger your party the better because you usually ended up mingling with every other celebration taking place on that eroding string of sand anyway.

Sometimes huge herds of communities merged as strangers mixed, alcohol flowed, and music blared.

But I was a million miles away from all of that noise and their senseless pursuits as I watched *her* silhouette upon the shoreline.

Her dark hair flickered brisk but briefly in the moonlight as she walked along the beach alone. A somber look on her face stood firm and undeniable. And then she was gone from my sight.

Truth was, I knew why the somber face had been there.

She had come out with some of our mutual friends to enjoy herself and a weekend with the salt and sand and water that felt so primordial and ingrained within us all. The only issue was that the friend she had come with had complicated things by making intoxicated moves on her all night.

After she pushed away quite a few of his inebriated advances and kisses upon her neck, he had become irritable and began bouncing around other people's parties dotted in the darkness by firelight.

The beach was a maze of these sand pits, flames, and collections of people. But nobody had a physical description or definition, as they existed only as blurred shadows and drunken fits of laughter. It was the haze and hum of the crowd that had stolen purpose and reason, replacing it with disguise.

Still, *she* had spotted me lying in the bed of the Chevy truck and staring up at the skies. I had a cigarette dangling idly from the corner of my mouth and a cold beer balancing upon my chest.

I was unaware of her presence as she approached until I smelled the sweet scent of her perfume mixed with suntan lotion and sweat. It was a beautiful smell.

"Why do you do that?" she asked as she leaned over the side of truck, looking down at me.

I started to sit up, rather startled at her sudden presence and managed to catch the beer before it fell.

"I'm sorry. But that's a rather vague inquiry," I replied, attempting to smear my intoxication away from bloodshot eyes.

"Smoke, is what I meant." Her serious expression wildly flashed within her dark-brown eyes. It made me feel as if I had insulted her in some way by asking that she clarify her question.

"Well…because it calms me. Makes me feel good, I guess," I responded, setting my beer down by my side.

"Makes you *'feel good,'* you say? How so? By killing yourself?"

"I'm not killing myself…" I tried to counter, so she reached over and grabbed the pack of cigarettes that had been laying by my side and flipped the pack around to face the warning label toward me.

"Might as well be sucking on your truck's exhaust pipe," she said, tossing them back to me. I caught them against my chest, with a slow grin rising.

"Well *that* would just be uncomfortable and odd," I responded with a smirk. She smiled.

"I hate those things," she explained as she sat beside me on the tailgate of the truck and eyed the cigarette I was smoking. She proceeded to snap her fingers and say, "Let me see that."

After handing her my smoke, she took a drag off it.

I began to comment on her hypocrisy when she placed her finger against my lips.

"Yeah, yeah…" She trailed off as she blew a perfect smoke ring into the humid, ocean night's air.

We talked for a while, her and I. The topic was mainly centered around the drama she was experiencing with her friend. As she explained the knots and tangles of her life up to that point and how it came to be, I wondered what it would've been like to have been loved by her.

Would it have been complicated or overly maintained? Would our world become meticulously scheduled or left airy, open, and free to spontaneity?

It was no question that my loneliness and lack of self-confidence bore my heart to my sleeve. Willingly I offered it out before her as soon as she had smiled at me, and in doing so, I subconsciously asked that she forever *be mine*. While I was aware of how pathetic that made me look, the underlying irrationality it drilled into my brain was almost absent from thought.

But as I watched her mouth move and her lips form words, everything slowed down before me.

I changed my focus to her eyes as they looked between the day's dying light and then to me again. Each time her eyes touched mine, I felt the warmth of her smile spread lightly within the magic of her dimples.

It was a passing expression that held immediate ground within my heart. Just the subtle answer to a loneliness I could no longer bare to feel anymore, awakened once more by nothing more than conversation.

Maybe that defined me as broken? And truly, maybe deep down I still was? But in those moments in her company, I ultimately didn't care. While I knew that I was falling for her rather too easily, I thought it better than looking at love with jaded eyes like a cold virus.

Almost as if it was a sickness that took over when my immune system was too weak to defend against it.

When her cell phone rang, she took the call and vanished into the gypsy night of beachside parties, bonfires, and rows of trucks or Jeeps that darted in and out of the darkness along the shoreline.

And her name was Melody.

Everyone had somebody to hold in their arms that weekend. That is to say, everyone besides her and me.

But that was fine.

I made do by drinking my desolation away and keeping myself within my own personal intoxicated shell. It had worked for the most part, but only so much. Ultimately as I watched people and friends kiss each other or toss words of endearment back and forth around the fire pit, I began to feel like the odd man out.

Cigarettes, chips, and alcohol were all I lived off of those two days. I kept a constant buzz and thought of distant worlds far away. I found myself walking off alone along the shoreline or swimming out to sandbars to daydream if only to escape the reality that the following night I would be back at home, thinking of this place. And dreaming of *her*.

I stared upon the blanket of stars above me, and my only company were the inebriated dreams of the lonely, which brought the lips of some faceless woman to mine.

I'd like to believe the woman of my dreams *had* in fact been Melody. But it was only a wish.

In the early hours of morning, I arose to the ocean's salt on my lips and the sun's cherry-red burn upon my skin.

I was with all of my friends, and simultaneously I was all alone.

Yet with a morning beer in my hand and a bag of chips in my lap, I was God.

And halfheartedly, I was content.

I guess you could say I had everything I wanted.

I was in a brand-new relationship with somebody I had truly come to care about, and I still had a great-paying job that made having a financially successful future actually possible. I was in fairly good shape, and my new girlfriend, Melody, was rather active, so she enjoyed working out together, hiking together, and generally being in my company no matter what we decided on doing.

She lived an hour's drive away, so our visits usually only came about on my days off from work.

But still, here I was with my troubled thoughts.

I was still setting aside money for some reason, like a hoarder—not to save for my future. Instead, I was saving for some life-changing event I still believed might eventually happen.

And there were arguments because of this. Lots of them, which had been about the subject of my wanting to hike the Appalachian Trail. Only, of course, whenever I had the courage to bring it up to her.

When I asked Melody if she'd be OK with me being gone for six months, she would always respond, "We haven't been together long enough to establish a strong relationship. I've only known you for four months, and now you're going away? How is that fair to me?"

Then my argument would always be: "This was a dream of mine long before I ever even met you. I'm not going away and never coming back."

Then she would change the subject rather dramatically, most times before I was even done talking.

She didn't want to talk about it right then and there, she would often tell me, as if in a few hours I'd forget about the whole foolhardy idea like it had never happened and everything would be just fine.

But that wasn't the way I worked.

I sat another night in another dreaded rotation at work, one which would leave me doing security patrols in the cold November rain. The storms breaking off Hurricane Sandy would be hitting later in the early hours of morning, and in my dreary, depressed haze, I didn't think to bring in my work-issued rain jacket.

It was going to make for a long, cold night.

Truly, I barely thought about much anymore when I was at work. I sank deeper and deeper into misery despite not having a reason to be melancholy about life truly at all anymore.

I had everything I needed. Everything that I had been taught by society that was supposed to make me happy.

But I wasn't.

At times, I stood in the doorway to my closet and stared at the thousands of dollars I'd spent on hiking gear and simply shook my head with regret as I turned off the light and closed the door.

When I imagined my future, it scared me. It was frightening only because my lack of education left me wondering what would become of me when I finally got the gumption to say good-bye to the black hole that was my everyday life at work. Because I had finally decided it was going to happen. I had finally decided it was time to leave this place. But the job wasn't the only thing I had decided to leave.

I had staked claims to my friend and coworker Torry that I would reset my life. I had said to Melody, "I don't care if I find a job when I get back! Maybe you and me will run off and live on the trail together forever!"

While they were happy thoughts, they were unrealistic ones as well. You couldn't finance a future together on dreams alone.

You needed some kind of income.

Dropping everything and just going was slowly losing its bold and brash appeal quite suddenly.

And while she hadn't known it in that moment, still I had made the decision all on my own.

Something was no longer *telling* me to leave.

It was demanding it.

On our hiking excursions together, I began to open up more to Torry than I had ever dreamed of doing with a coworker before. In doing so, he became more than just an acquaintance or a close friend.

He became like the *older brother* I never had.

I began to talk about my dreams and relationship issues as we sat on some edge of the earth on some distant mountain range overlooking some great expanse and sea of clouds that led into oblivion. He had become a counselor and wise figure to me.

I sort of had a guilty conscience during these times together because I began to plan some grand trip with him that I ultimately knew Melody would never agree on. In a sense, I felt like I was mentally cheating on her for wanting to make this theoretical hike a reality. And Torry had become my outlet. My vent.

I had entrusted my thoughts and feelings on the subject to him, who as the great friend he was, stood back nonjudgmentally and only interjected his personal thoughts or opinions when I asked. And it was here that I had learned he too, wasn't enjoying what he had thought life essentially was either. His marriage to a woman he had at one time "loved more than life itself" as he had put it, had started to fall apart.

But he explained that things change over time. And he would go on to tell me that *time itself* was something that could ultimately distort the person you *thought* you knew better than yourself.

That was why he and his wife had separated.

As we hiked together more often, there was this "third person" he and I both came to fall rather unapologetically in love with.

Her name was Mother Nature, and I had started to feel that the people standing in the way of that love should have been the very ones *supporting* it.

I wanted to understand why I felt suffocated in this world. I was tired of my predictable days, knowing when I was going to eat, when I was going to work out, when I was going to an appointment, and when after every romantic dinner between Melody and I, we were going to make love. Almost as if on cue, without the slightest inkling of spontaneity.

Nothing felt random to me anymore. Everything had become routine.

As Torry and I secretly planned this theoretical hike, ultimately, in the backs of our minds, we kind of felt as if it was actually going to happen. We relayed information we had learned to each other over text messages and hid our phones away from our partners like gossiping old hens.

I had recently read in online hiking forums that to comfortably thru-hike, you needed anywhere between $3,500 to $5,000 dollars for the entirety of the trip. These expenses were to cover anything from staying at hostels or hotels to going into towns and paying for laundry, repairing or purchasing new equipment, and so on and so forth.

Torry in turn relayed something to me called a "mail drop" system he had read up on in which you boxed premade foods and had a friend or family member ship them out to you in towns you came across along the way. This way, you avoided the exploited costs of "trail food."

I borrowed my father's dehydrator and vacuum sealer, and Torry and I began to get to work on prepping our meals for the six months we would be gone. That is to say, if our plans ever came to fruition. Our prepared dinners and breakfasts consisted of cheap but effective carbs, fats, and proteins. We collectively bought strawberries, bananas, blueberries, or whatever other kinds of fruits we felt a liking toward and dehydrated them. I then added them to vacuum-sealed packs of oatmeal, with several teaspoons of dehydrated powdered honey and a couple of tablespoons of cinnamon. Upon completing that, I sealed them up and— *ta-daaa*!—Torry and I now had a single, two-serving breakfast that was cheap to boot!

You had instant mashed potatoes that you could add bacon bits, garlic, dried chopped chives, and powdered butter or cheese to and then vacuum seal it. Once again, cheap and effective meals. You could even utilize this exact recipe with grits or powdered eggs mixed in if you wanted.

As our items and gear began to mount up, we poured hundreds of dollars into prepping enough meals to carry us all the way from Georgia to Maine. I had fifteen three-gallon boxes filled with pre-made meals hidden in my closet out of Melody's sight that we would later ask my parents to ship out to us if we ever truly made our dreams a reality.

Finally, as Torry and I shared a beer on my balcony under the simplicity of the sun's afternoon light, I said to him, "We've done a lot of prepping."

"Well, you were prepping long before I even came along," he said.

"What I'm saying is, I don't want this to be something that we just give up on."

Torry took a swallow of his beer and tilted his head.

"I don't *enjoy* my life. I *should* be happy. I *know* I should be happy. But for whatever reason, I'm not. All of that…" I said, waving my arm to the boxes of food we had spent over $400 on, "can't be for nothing."

I desperately needed him to understand the urgency in my voice.

He nodded his head, taking another sip from his can of beer. "Have you told *Melody* that yet?"

I looked down at the ground, defeated. I shook my head.

"She knows I want to go. She thinks that by telling me she's going to leave me if I do that maybe I'll change my mind," I replied.

"Isn't that just like a woman." he said, laughing and shaking his head unbelievably.

I began to reminisce about when I had met Torry's ex-wife. He had spilled the beans to her, explaining that she'd not only become a couch potato but that she had borne down with a vengeance on any ideas he had ever talked over with her about his joining me on the AT.

I remembered the way she had looked at me with a subtle, underlying anger, as if I was taking her husband away from her. The seeds of change I had unwittingly planted in Torry's mind had started to grow, and his former wife knew it. It had been an awkward meeting because of that. Ultimately though, in the months to come I would wonder how long their relationship had been falling apart for him to so readily decide upon joining my side.

"So we're really going to do this, huh?" I asked, still uncertain of my own wavering stance.

"I believe we are."

"Promise me something," I said, setting my empty beer can down on the table.

"Sure, what is it?"

"If I ever start to want to turn around while we're out there and decide to go home, promise me you'll punch me in the face."

Torry laughed hard and shook his head. "The hell are you talking about?" he asked, clearing the tears of laughter from his eyes. My face was dead serious though.

"I'm *not* playing, Torry."

"Why's it gotta be like that? I'm not going to promise to hit you. If you wanna go home, you wanna go home. I'm not going to force you to be there."

If it wasn't evident up to this point, then let me explain to you that I am quite the dependent individual at this stage in my life. I'm not sure how weak that makes me appear, but I'm confident enough to acknowledge it. I liked the idea of someone essentially telling me to suck it up if I felt like quitting. Only because I knew I didn't have the willpower to do it myself.

Torry had unknowingly become my support beam in this crazy idea that we tossed around. I only felt I could go through with it because he had agreed to do it with me.

We were still short of food though.

Of the fifteen food boxes we actually needed, that day we only came up with twelve. Furthermore, six of those boxes of food only had seven days' worth in them instead of the ten days that were in the other six boxes. Our hiking itinerary at this point was completely shot and would have to be redone entirely.

Part of the adventure was figuring out this stuff on the trail, and that "chaotic unknown" could be exhilarating at times. But that didn't mean I wasn't scared.

Ultimately, as we looked upon the boxes and realized how far behind we were, I looked to Torry, who said, "The hell with it. We'll buy whatever we need when we get into the towns we pass by."

He smiled and I laughed, "It's more fun that way. Right?"

Torry, utilizing his smartphone, hopped online and in a final act of ensuring that our mutual decision was set, purchased two train tickets going from Greensboro, North Carolina, to Gainesville, Georgia.

We weren't sure how we would get to the trail after getting off of the train, but once again we laughed as we both agreed and shouted in unison, "We'll figure *that* out too!"

I couldn't believe the excitement running through my veins at that moment. This was all real. Everything was actually happening.

As a result, only two days later we both went to our project manager and informed him—four months ahead of time—that we were quitting our jobs as of March 14, 2013.

And I chose to keep that fact hidden from my partner.

"Why are we talking about this again? If you leave…then I can't say I'll honestly wait around for you," Melody said, rather angrily.

"Why? Because I want to live my *dream*? How selfish are you being right now, honestly? For Christ's sake, you make it sound like I'm never coming back!" I said with awe.

"You only want to go out there and party. Probably just want to meet other women too, and I know Torry.

He's irresponsible, and he's a drunk who can't even keep his own life in order. And you're calling that guy your *brother*? Get outta here!" she shouted back, waving her hand dismissively at me like I was a child with a wild imagination.

"You don't know the whole story. He's not irresponsible. He's fed up, like I am. We both want to go find something out there about ourselves, whatever it is that may be."

She had an express need to let me know how much she distrusted Torry.

Quite often she hinted her concern to me that she didn't believe him to be serious about the trip at all. It regularly felt as if she was attempting to fill my mind with self-doubt and some underlying deception in his plans. If he was to go at all, she was very sure that he would be solely looking out for himself instead of us collectively.

"Aw, isn't that magical? Why don't you get married while you're out there too?" she spat sarcastically.

"You really think I *want* anybody else, Melody?" I asked, placing my hands on her shoulders. "I love *you*. I'm not going out there to find a piece of ass. I'm going out there because I love nature and I want to seek true freedom."

"I see…" she said, nodding her head slowly, with a knowing look on her face. It was a face that was only seconds away from bursting into tears.

"You don't love me like you said you do anymore. You'd rather go be with your friend Torry on some fucking trail than to be in a relationship with *me*," she said, shoving my arms away from her shoulders.

"Funny, you giving me those options. Because it can't be *any* other way, can it?" I asked. I had to get out of there. I grabbed my coat and walked out of her apartment at that very moment, slamming the door behind me. I was livid, and being there at that time wasn't conducive to a working relationship whatsoever.

And in a sense, she was right and I knew it. I was a hypocrite.

How fair was it to essentially put our relationship and moving in together on hold while I went to clear my mind of the depression and feelings of worthlessness I felt inside day after day? And while I could have told her the truth—which was that I simply was not happy anymore—I knew I didn't have the gall to do it.

She called just as I was driving out of her apartment complex, all the same.

"You're *really* going to let this ruin your next four days off work with me? Why can't we talk about it later? Just come back," she asked, more calmly than she had been speaking to me before.

"Melody, I can't talk about it later. You want to know why? Because I already told my job I'm leaving in March. I've stored up food. I've saved money. I bought the equipment and made the plans…and Torry has already bought the tickets," I said, just before realizing what I had just blurted out.

"You've been *lying* to me then?"

I had just realized in that very moment that I *had* in fact been keeping all of that information from her.

"Not lying…really…" I wavered momentarily. "Just not telling you because I knew you would overreact."

She wasn't willing to accept that answer though.

"I can't believe I've been dating a liar this whole time," she said over the phone, her voice beginning to break. I realized in those seconds to follow that I was in fact at *fault* for all of my actions. It was wrong of me to keep such a life-changing decision from her.

But I tried to justify it selfishly with my own reasoning at the time, that if she truly loved me, she would have supported my desire to clear my mind and take control of my ever-growing mental struggle with depression.

"Melody, you have to realize that you aren't being fair to me. I don't want to break up with you. Do everything you can in this moment to believe that. But if you can't support my dreams, then how can you say you love me? How?" I pleaded with her, begging her to understand.

"I know you want to go hike. It doesn't make any sense to me, and it probably never will. I just want to enjoy the little time I have with you while you're still here, John. Can you give me that much? We can talk about what happens when you leave later," she explained, doing a rather immediate turnaround over the phone. It not only told me that she didn't take me seriously, but that she believed she could make me change my mind within the four months to come.

I sighed and did a U-turn on Flagstaff Avenue, driving back toward her apartment complex.

There I spent the next four days in a zombie-like state where she talked about our future together but always in a way that expressed indeterminable consequences should I ever make to leave for the Appalachian Trail. In a way, I completely understood where she was coming from. Had I been in her position, I wouldn't readily want to see her leave for six months, just to head out into the middle of nowhere either.

But I wouldn't break up with her for doing it either, if I understood *why*.

If she wanted to physically and mentally challenge herself, then why would I ever want to hold her back from that?

If it was something she'd always wanted to do, how was it *my place* to tell her otherwise?

I had been twenty-three years old when I had started working there.

I had just been a kid. Now, at almost thirty, all I could think of was all of that wasted time.

So much wasted time… I thought miserably.

The job—with all of its inconsistencies, all of its technicalities, and all of the micromanaging that took place—had in fact supported me quite comfortably over the six years I'd been employed there. When I thought of what I had left behind, it wasn't experience or fond memories of an interesting or mentally challenging job.

It was the friends that I had made there.

It was the good officers, the good sergeants, lieutenants, and captains that had come and gone.

That was *all* I would miss.

The people I considered friends.

It was cold that morning. No clouds clogged the skies, but still the stars failed to shine within the light pollution emitted from the plant. A somber morning to match my detached feelings. You would have thought that I'd feel ecstatic about leaving a job that everybody hated. But there still existed that ultimate uncertainty.

Am I really ready for this?

My company cell phone began ringing suddenly. "It's time, man. Montgomery will take your radio," my sergeant said over the phone.

"En route now," I replied, and hung up.

I took a final drag and put my cigarette out, making my way to the rad waste-processing building slowly. I was milking the clock. I was in no rush, as I couldn't make my departure for the Appalachian Trail come any sooner.

When you quit working at the nuclear plant, it was required that you receive what is called an exit count. This is includes a final whole body scan and a calculated measure of the radiation dose you picked up while working there over the years. It was also relative practice that you complete an exit interview and an officer checklist given by the project manager of security.

The latter, I never received.

"I'm here for the exit count," I said, approaching the health physics workstation counter.

The individual giving the count looked me over in surprise. He knew me from the years of work I had put in there, and he knew my father, who had worked at that very plant since it had opened.

"What are you going to do after you leave here?" he asked as he stood and left the front office desk and came out into the hallway to greet me.

I shrugged nonchalantly, distant in my thoughts. "Maybe I'll go for a walk?" I responded.

He gave me an uncertain and confused look, clearly unaware of what I was talking about, and then directed me into the exit-count machine.

When I was done, I was disarmed by my captain. I was then escorted by my lieutenant toward the exit turn-stiles since my site badge had been deactivated once my weapons had been returned to the armory. I smiled at the ground as I walked, remembering the many times I had done the exact same thing for other officers when they had been fired or quit. It felt so odd to be on the receiving end for once.

As I exited the plant and headed out of the turnstiles, a huge weight lifted from my chest. I felt years of regret and depression evaporate. I felt anger and disparaging thoughts begin to die like some kind of cloud dissipating over me.

Why?

Because I had options. I never had to go back there, if I didn't want to, ever again.

And as I drove away, I watched the cooling tower vanish into the wood line from my rearview mirror, not just for the day, but for the last time.

The only difference was that for the first time in a long time, I actually felt free.

There was an urgency between us.

The last twenty-four hours together played out perfectly, if only because of the knowledge that by the end of that day, I would be gone.

I had a knot in my throat that was undeniably apparent every time I swallowed. It matched the fear I felt in my heart. Was this all *really* happening? Surely this had been a dream. Tomorrow morning I was sure to awaken from another drunken haze, half hanging off of the couch and probably late for work.

Only it *was* real. I *had* made it happen. Through all of my fears and feelings of self-doubt, I had overcome all of it to make this a reality.

We had made the most of it, Melody and I. We enjoyed each other's company with what little time we had left, and in doing so we had managed to last an entire day without a single argument.

After a proper send-off from friends and family, Melody drove Torry and me to the train station. Overcome by fear, excitement and exhaustion from the festivities, we both slept most of the way in the car and only awakened when we came within a few miles of the train station.

Inside, after Torry retrieved our tickets that would have us bound for Gainesville, Georgia, we met a fellow thru-hiker by the trail name of Bubblegum awaiting the same train we were.

He spotted our packs and, while reserved at first, finally approached and asked if we too were in fact headed to Springer Mountain. I wondered how transparent we looked with our massive backpacks on. When we said we were, it didn't take long for me to spill out the question.

"Are you thru-hiking?"

"Sure am. How about you guys?" Bubblegum asked us.

I stood proudly as I clapped Torry on the back. "Yes sir! All the way!"

It turns out that the sixty-three-year-old gentleman from Richmond, Virginia, who, despite undergoing recent knee surgery, was still taking on the 2,188-mile challenge, much to the disagreement of his doctor.

Bubblegum was definitely blunt enough to inform Torry and me that only 17 percent of the people who had attempted it the year before had actually completed it.

I became a bit disheartened once I heard that.

I had done a lot and given up so much of myself and my life to be there at that train station in that moment, to take a shot at doing what so little seemed to ever do. I was determined to never *willfully* quit. I had sold or given up everything that I owned. I had quit my job and left family and friends behind in this journey to be free.

But what he said troubled me all the same. With such odds stacked against me, I wondered if I'd be one of the many that gave up along the way.

Suddenly, a message over the public announcement speaker above our heads explained that our train was going to be late by almost thirty minutes. Meanwhile, Melody was growing more and more weary as we passed time, anxiously awaiting our ride south, with conversation about things she found no interest in.

"I think I'm ready to go," she said, rubbing her blood-shot eyes. I wrapped my arm around her shoulders and kissed her forehead lightly.

"Don't," she said, slightly pushing me away in exhausted annoyance. Till the very end, she was embittered by my leaving.

I asked Torry to watch my pack as I walked her back to her car.

"Sure thing. Oh, and Melody, thanks again for the ride," he called out to her.

She smiled weakly. It was a false smile, of course, and even in the last few moments of our time together, it seemed she couldn't give the guy an ounce of trust.

Outside, the air was cool and the night loud. Techno and electronica music played from a dance club far away, and the screams and laughter that mixed in and out of it let the sleeping world know that somebody, somewhere, was still up this late and having fun.

"This is going to be the hardest part of my trip, you know," I said to her as we walked through the desolate parking lot. The pavement was moist from a misting rain that had started to come down and gleamed brightly beneath orange sodium lights.

"Why?" she asked.

Maybe she was fishing for the response. Maybe amid the recent battle of words she had forgotten. Regardless, I had no problem telling her again.

"Because I love you," I said as we reached her vehicle. I looked down into her dark brown eyes, taking a picture with my mind. Whatever was to come of us while I was gone, I wasn't sure. But I didn't care because in that moment I didn't want to forget *what had been*.

We kissed for a few minutes, holding each other there in that empty parking lot.

"This…just all seems so stupid, John," she said, running her hands across her tired face.

"Melody," I began slowly.

She dropped her hands and looked up at me tired and unyielding.

"I don't have to worry about *us* while I'm out there, do I?" I asked. I was still unsure of where we were at this point. Had we broken up? Did she *want* to keep the relationship going? Every argument about the subject had always ended with "We'll figure it out later." Well, now "later" was here, and what the hell had we decided?

Melody sighed and looked away before replying. "I don't know what you want me to say. It'll be hard, and I don't know what will happen to us while you're gone. We'll just have to see." She unlocked her car and sat down in the driver's seat.

I closed the door for her as she rolled down the window.

"What if I got back into the car right now and ended this journey before it ever started?" I asked, with some small piece of me actually wanting her to convince me to do it. Maybe love was what I was searching for, but I had been blind to it by my own stubbornness and determination for change. Maybe I didn't have to walk thousands of miles to clear my mind and reset my life. Maybe all I had to do was start over with her.

"Go," she said, her eyes bloodshot and teary. "It's your *dream* or whatever," she said sarcastically. It hurt, the way she said that. Rather deeply, to be exact, in a tone that made it sound as if everything I was doing was pointless. But I washed it away from my mind to keep from letting that hurt turn to anger.

"I love you," I said as I stepped back slowly from her car door.

"I know you do, John" was the only reply I received as she backed out of the parking lot slowly.

I stood outside watching as she drove away into the night.

In my last few moments in Greensboro, North Carolina, I posted the following message on her Facebook page, if only to salvage anything that might remain of our relationship:

To Melody:

This world in which we live is filled with uncertainty. It is that thought that at times…

…can leave us in doubt. We've made no promises other than to try again someday when the shadow of my departure no longer looms omnipotently above us.

Before you lays a future, new responsibilities, and success, simply waiting for you to claim it and make it yours.

And you will…

…because you are strong. Your willpower is undeniable. Your courage, inspiring.

Your heart, endearing.

Our battles have been but a stepping stone to what I believe can be greatness should we overcome the obstacles and pitfalls that encompass our everyday lives.

We weren't meant to fail. I do not just think that, but I KNOW IT. We weren't made to give up just because things got hard.

It is not in our nature.

Within you, I see a determination that is awe inspiring. If only I could mirror it for a moment, I could do, say, or become anything or anyone I aspired to be.

But only because of you.

We aren't sure where six months apart will place us. We both may be completely different individuals when my journey is over and I stand atop Mount Katahdin looking down upon the world, and you watch the world distantly from within your office.

But you will be my inspiration to try.

You will be the warmth I so desperately search for on the nights that snow, ice, and rain are the only bed I can find.

You will be the sun on my face as I traverse narrow ridges thousands of miles away from you.

But most importantly, you will be the dreams that chase away the nightmares of fear and doubt.

And I will love you.

I will always love you.

And one day…

…we will find each other again.

Amicalola Falls—March 17, 2013

CHAPTER 3

The Chaotic Unknown

A FAST, METALLIC VESSEL CHARGED along, seven hours south, cutting into the night like a knife.

That vessel carried two individuals with monumental dreams and left them absorbed within their own imaginations and excitement in the hours to come. And while I tried to sleep, I found myself more often than not thinking about Melody and how she had so distantly said good-bye to me back at the station.

Outside my window, the trees whizzed by in blurry silhouettes created beneath a brightly lit moon. Orange street lamps appeared and dotted the distance like illuminated last bastions of light. Little islands in a sea of darkness.

That's all they were.

I began asking myself questions that Torry and I had never answered back at home, when we had been laying out our journey with nubile excitement and ignorant bliss masking our realities.

How will we get to Amicalola Falls once we arrive at the Gainesville train station?

What'll we do if we can't hitch a ride there?

And while the simple answer ultimately was *walk*, part of me knew that there would be *more than* enough of that in the months to come.

I began to drift off slowly as the heat within my row kicked on full blast. I snuggled down into my tin can corner and placed my toboggan between the glass and my face. This was done if for no other reason than because of the dried saliva specks on the window pane from the thousands of other passengers that had preceded me.

A lot of people must've sneezed here, I thought to myself as I eyed the window warily.

I closed my eyes, watching movies in my mind, and dreamed of being *somebody*. By that I meant I was finally beginning to take pride in myself for the first time in my entire life. Because hadn't the *hardest* part already been done?

I had left a comfortable niche. I have given up everything to make this all come to fruition. And while some of those things I'd lost hadn't been by choice, all the same I found pride in the fact I had kept headstrong with my decision.

I adjusted uncomfortably in the cramped sardine cans they had the gall to call seats.

When we arrived many hours later, I was kind of confused as to whether we had arrived at an actual train station or we'd been dropped off at some dilapidated abandoned warehouse and left to die. The Gainesville station was in fact positively falling apart.

As Torry and I walked about exploring, I made my way towards the restroom. Seven hours of needing to use the toilet and holding it in seemed rather detrimental to your health, but I had done it all the same.

Well wasn't it my luck then that there wasn't a shred of toilet paper upon arrival?

"Guess I better get used to that," I said to myself as I looked over at the rough paper towels available. I began to reflect on that rather instantly. Months from now when I was in the middle of nowhere and I had to use the restroom out in the wilds, how happy would I be to have that rough paper towel over a handful of leaves?

When I was done, I sat down on one of the ancient orange bucket seats that had clearly been left inside the lobby since the 1970s and began looking through the *A.T. Guide 2012*[2], which had been put together by David Miller (Author of *AWOL on the Appalachian Trail*).

Within the guide, meant to keep me informed all of the way to Maine, I was looking for any information I could find about a way to reach Amicalola Falls, such

---

[2] Miller, David. The A.T. Guide 2012. Northbound ed. Jerelyn Press, 2012

as cab companies or shuttles in the town of Gainesville. Meanwhile Torry was outside the dilapidated structure, beneath a crumbling awning covering an abandoned loading dock, smoking a cigarette and looking on his smartphone for local taxi cabs.

"That's a fancy li'l book you got yerself dere," a young, gangly looking kid with a scraggly thin patch of reddish hair on his chin said to me suddenly. He had a rather thick hillbilly accent that was so strong at times, it made his sentences indiscernible. I looked up slowly at him and then trained my eyes to the older, external-framed backpack he had leaning against his seat.

"You a thru-hiker?" I asked, averting my eyes back down to my book.

"Could say that I 'spose. I've done the trail prolly like seven er eight times…but neva made it past Virginia," he explained, as if that made perfect sense to me.

"So you've never *completed* the trail?" I asked, setting my guide down in my lap.

"Well, if you added up tha mileage I've already done, then like I's was sayin', I've done this trail several times over. Gone up and down to Virginia more times than you can count on both hands."

For some reason, I had a hard time believing the kid. His clothes were rather ragged, and he looked just a little malnourished. Then again, maybe I was the one being too judgmental. But if he looked like anything to me, it was *homeless*.

"Where are you from?" I asked as I stood and offered him my hand.

"Kentucky. What's yer trail name?" he asked as he shook my hand. His fingers were absolutely frozen, and his palm sweaty. I quickly wiped my hand against the back of my pants.

"I, uh, well I'm not too sure. I guess I never thought about it that much. I kinda gave myself a name back at home. Went by Morris the Cat." In truth I hadn't really thought that much of it. I thought the point in being out here was to be given a nickname or earning one for something unique about *you*. Everyone at work had called me Morris the Cat. My mother had called me that as well a couple of times in my life only because our last name was in fact Morris.

"Yous like dem cats a whole's lot er somet'in?" he asked, cocking his head. Truth be told, I hated cats. But I didn't mind the name, I supposed.

I only shrugged though in response to his question as he smiled softly.

"Cool, cool. Well, I'm Robert, but people called me Candy Cane last yeera. I think it t'was a joke er somet'in. I don' wanna be called dat no mo'," he explained as his gaze shifted dreamily across the room.

I began to wonder by how slow he spoke if he was "all there" upstairs, but regardless, he seemed to be a kind enough fellow.

Robert went on to tell me that he had attempted to thru-hike the year before but had run out of funds and water sources along the trail. He'd gotten ill from drinking straight out of ponds because he hadn't had the money to afford a filter.

As I walked outside to find Torry, Robert followed along and stood beside us, talking and contemplating how we were going to get from the station to Amicalola Falls State Park.

"Robert, if we called a taxi, would you want to split the fair three ways with us?" I asked. He didn't think on it long.

"Sure, sounds great."

"Well now I feel like a *real* hiker!" I exclaimed cynically before laughing.

"Why waste money on a taxi when we could just walk?" Torry asked suddenly.

My mouth dropped, and I glanced over at him. "Where are we gonna sleep?" I countered.

"Who cares? We'll get a hitch! Wasn't the point in us coming out here to be *spontaneous*?" he asked. I guess he sort of had a point, but I hadn't thought that after seven hours on a cramped train with no real rest that I was going to have to start hiking immediately for the next forty miles upon arrival.

Still, Torry was looking rather impatient, and he clearly wanted to just get out of Gainesville all together and hop onto that trail that we had dreamt so much about for so long.

"Robert, what are you gonna do?" I asked.

"Prolly jest hang 'round heerya...till someone comes 'long..." he replied, scraping dirt from beneath his fingernails.

"Well. I guess we go *this* way," Torry said, looking at a map on his Droid and indicating toward the west.

"Hope to see ya'll lata..." Robert said as we started to take off. Just as we did though, a white '83 Toyota Camry pulled up with Spanish words spray painted on the sides of the door in stencil.

The driver reached over from inside the car and manually rolled down the passenger's side window. He then began asking us a question in Spanish, which I didn't understand. I looked at Torry, who shook his head from side to side.

I then looked back at Robert, who only shrugged and muttered, "I don't speak no Mexican..."

"Let's just take the cab," I whined to Torry, who rolled his eyes.

"All right, all right. Let's just go. I'm sick of hanging around here." he complied resentfully.

"Robert, you still in?" I turned to ask, but he had already hopped into the backseat with his pack sitting in his lap.

After several communication errors with the driver about where we were actually going, we finally arrived in the Amicalola Falls parking lot, where the three of us pooled sixty bucks in cash over to the driver.

Robert had become quite the talker along the way. Even more so once we'd reached the park. He had started chattering on and on, asking how much we had paid for this piece of equipment or planned on spending for that hostel stay…how much we'd laid aside for the entire trip and then about our backgrounds back at home. Only whenever we would begin to answer him, he'd cut us off and start in on wild stories where bears had chased him down the trails the years before and how he'd had to fight them off with a stick.

I wanted to say to him: *You're making this up, right?*

But he looked as if he was quite desperate for attention. He couldn't have been much older than twenty-two, and if he had in fact been out here as many times as he said he had, it sort of made me wonder what kind of life he was *running away* from back at home in Kentucky.

So Torry and I passed glances at each other with every high tale Robert had to give us.

At one point as we were looking around at the gift store inside the visitor's center, Robert began to rush us impatiently.

Hey guys, how long do ya'll think yaw be?

We should probably get goin' soon. I think it's 'sposed ta rain.

One time, I found this ol' yellar jacket nest in the side of a tree and—

Finally I cut him off. "Hey man, how about you head on down the way and we'll catch up to you or something at the first shelter?"

He shrugged before replying. "Naw, it's all good. I can jest wait on y'all. Ain't got nuttin else ta do…"

Another glance passed between Torry and I.

Outside, I searched for a restroom and came upon a frog hanging out beneath a water fountain and snapped his picture.

In the distance you could hear the waterfall that I had heard so much about.

In Cherokee, *amicalola* means "tumbling waters." These falls were the tallest that you would find east of the Mississippi River.

The Cherokee Tribe once owned the falls and the land surrounding it until gold was found around Dahlonega and they were slowly pushed from the area.

After the Treaty of the New Echota forced them from their lands in 1832, it remained uninhabited for almost a hundred years.

At 729 feet in height, the falls were quite a climb. They were accompanied by a winding wooden stair that crossed at a bridge almost halfway up to the adjacent side of the stream.

Torry and I, along with our new tagalong friend Robert, had decided to sign the thru-hiker registry and then take a few memorable pictures next to the trail's approach arch.

Before I had ever even started my journey, I had posted tidbits of my prep hikes and determination to traverse the entire length of the AT on a hiking-enthusiast website titled Trailjournals.com.

As a result, I had a few followers long before I'd ever even started the trail, one of which was going to be a thru-hiker that very year herself.

After Torry and I had weighed our packs on a hanging scale beneath the porch awning, (mine was in the neighborhood of fifty-five pounds) we were on our way toward the approach trail when I suddenly heard a young woman ask, "Are you Morris the Cat?"

I turned slowly, unsure of who had asked it. I'd never seen the woman before, but she obviously knew *me* from my pictures.

"I'm Stephanie," she said, but I only gave an apologetic face, drawing a complete blank.

"Brown Squirrel, from the Trail Journals website? Come on, dude," she said, shaking her head as if I was a complete moron.

"Ohhh! Hey! How are you doing? Didn't you leave a comment on my guest page or something? Yeah, I remember you now!" I said excitedly as we hugged each other. Man was this a mindblower. I *never* thought I'd actually get to see somebody I'd been chatting with online that lived all the way in California. And what do you know? Here she was as if by fate itself.

She was within a sea of other thru-hikers wearing green shirts with logos of a soldier hiking with full gear and a rifle in hand. On the back, beneath a picture of mountains, it said "Warrior Hiker."

"I promise I'm not being stalkerish," she said. I laughed. The thought had never even crossed my mind.

"Well, how are you? Excited about all of this?" I asked. I wasn't sure what to say and felt kind of stupid for even asking *that*.

"Yeah, you could definitely say I'm excited." she acknowledged. I introduced her to Torry then. I didn't call him by the trail name he had decided on giving himself.

Torry had explained a month before that he had wanted to be called Stupid, even though that wasn't how he existed to me. As a result, people found his name funny, and he used it quite regularly in the months to come as an icebreaker.

"Well, I guess we'll be going in the same direction. I'll see you down the trail," I said, and she wished me well.

"Who was *she*?" Torry asked as I looked back at him. "Spare girlfriend or something?"

I rolled my eyes.

"Yeah, sure. Met her online and we decided to go out on a six-month date across the Appalachians." I responded. "She was somebody I met on the Trail Journals website. She had been reading all our prep hikes, like the ones back at your house and then my crappy hikes up in the Uwharries. She's really nice," I said.

"Cool."

And we were on our way up our first obstacle of the trail.

Six hundred and nine steps may not sound that bad, but let me tell you, it was vicious. That was how many steps it took to get to the top of Amicalola Falls.

It would definitely take a lot of oomph out of your initial "get up and go" enthusiasm.

Once we reached the top, we were already resting again in the grass by nearby benches at the overlook.

"Christ, do you think the rest of the trail is going to be this bad?" I asked Torry between gulps of air.

"If so, it's gonna take a hell of a lot longer to get to Maine than I thought," he replied, wiping sweat from his brow.

I tried to think a bit logically if only to give myself *any kind* of an excuse other than I was just plain out of shape. To be fair, we had come from a party the night before where we had both drank until we had blacked out in Melody's car. We had then hopped a seven-hour train to Gainesville, where we had both been cramped into metal cans called seats without anything resembling sleep.

Now here we were, without any rest in over twenty-four hours, nursing hangovers, and trying to hike up to Springer Mountain as alcohol seeped from our sweating pores. Our groggy, pale faces made us appear rather pathetic and sickly, and already I had started to stink.

I broke out my AT guidebook from the brain of my pack and opened it only to see that we had done a breath of the distance we needed to do before reaching camp at Springer Mountain Shelter.

"Wanna read something depressing?" I asked, offering the guidebook to Torry. He only shook his head and fell back into the grass with the sun beaming down upon his exhausted face.

As I looked toward the stream cascading down the falls before us, I quickly had the urge to look inside the front face of my backpack and purify some water. I set the guide down slowly in the grass beside me, suddenly aware I had the same feeling I'd had before when I had done my prep hike back in the Uwharries. I felt my stomach roll with nervousness as I began to obsess about something I was going to be in need of dearly along this journey.

Just a little over a year before, I'd been hard up in the wilds without a change of clothes after getting soaked by the rain. Now as I tore open the front zipper of my pack and as Torry sat up slowly with a look of concern on his face, I realized what I had done.

I had left my water filter back at home.

"Damn!" I shouted, shoving my backpack over angrily.

"The hell's wrong with you?" Torry asked, half laughing at my theatrics.

"I left the water purifier at home, like an idiot." I said dejectedly. Suddenly he was no longer chuckling.

"You *what?*"

"I thought for sure, *for sure* I had put the thing into the front pocket of my backpack. Do you think it was stolen or something?" I asked frantically.

"How, moron? You've had that backpack with you ever since you left the party last night. It hasn't left your sight," he returned irritably. And while it wasn't completely the end of the world, it *did* however mean we would have to use more fuel to boil our water and the bacteria probably seething inside it. It also meant hot drinks instead of cool ones unless we waited for the water to cool down.

"Well, better conserve what you have. I don't know when we come across another water source," he said, standing up slowly and dusting off his ass.

"Should we go back or something? I mean I don't want us to die of dehydration or something," I said as he gave me the most convoluted look I've ever seen before in my life.

"Die of *dehydration*? This is Georgia, John, not the fuckin' Sahara Desert. Get a hold of yourself," he said, shaking his head as he threw his backpack on again and took off angrily.

"Well, I didn't do it on purpose! You don't have to be a jerk!" I shouted after him as he simply shook his head without turning back.

Throughout the day, we would both play leapfrog with hundreds of other hikers who, like us, had planned to go all the way to Maine. In what little studying I had actually done on the trail before stumbling out there like an idiot, I had read that anywhere from one to two thousand people attempted to hike the entire trail every year.

I guess I hadn't expected so many of them to all be starting the same day as Torry and I were.

Of course you could always look at somebody and sort of *tell* whether they were going all the way or if they were simply out for a few days to the next road crossing or gap. Their faces were usually in the same painful contortions as yours, scrunched expressions that spoke of their physical ability early on, while absolutely dripping in sweat. Only difference was, they were less hopeless in their facial expressions because they weren't going to be out there in the woods for the next six months.

They wheezed just as heavily as you did, as they opened more pockets in their lungs to air than they had since they were teenagers.

But even by judging the size of their backpacks alone, you couldn't even really tell if they were out for a weekend stroll or balls-to-the-wall serious about giving the two-thousand-miler ago.

Not these days.

"Ultra-Lighters[3]," as they would be called along the trail, tended to carry less than thirty pounds on their backs at any given time. These people had tents that weighed less than a pound and only one change of clothes. Sometimes only what they were wearing on their

---

[3] Ultra-Lighter: An individual who chose the monetary expense of lighter gear and less bulky synthetic apparel. They typically kept less food and non-essentials at any given time on their journey than most. This is because of a stricter and well thought out itinerary.

bodies at that very moment to be exact. Everything they owned was relatively expensive and super-efficient, but more than that, these people had actually *planned* an itinerary out. By that, I mean they weren't carrying two weeks' worth of food in their packs like Torry and I were. They normally didn't have more than four days' worth of sustenance at any given time.

My shoulders were already screaming at me in pain, and I hadn't even gone a mile. Part of that was due to bad planning, but also I hadn't quite learned what I truly needed and didn't need out in the wilderness at that point.

I'd taken a lot of luxuries from home, and individually they weighed close to nothing. But built up and stacked upon each other along with everything else that had *weighed close to nothing*, and now I was crying as I drug my half-ton backpack up thousand-foot climbs.

The trail became a clogged artery at times as you awaited slower people in front of you trying to take a break in the middle of the trail. This was of course while some sweating old man or stranger behind you breathed his sour breath upon your neck, waiting for you to move forward.

Are you thru-hiking too?

The very question that I had asked, and others had now started asking *me,* became a little irritating, to the point that I had started to give grunts as responses. It was all anybody asked as we trudged along like some lost group of well-equipped refugees.

When Torry and I reached the summit of Springer Mountain, we were greeted with a plaque showing a man hiking mountains and the year 1934 inscribed into the bottom left of it. The plaque read: "A Footpath for those that seek Fellowship in the Wilderness."

The words couldn't have hit any closer to home.

The summit was little more than a crop of pine trees dotted by scant underbrush that had been trampled almost out of existence by humans walking about off-trail and setting up for picnics or pictures. It made for a small breathable opening at the pinnacle, which offered a view from the rocky outcropping that had accompanied it.

I told Torry he could go ahead and that I'd catch up with him a little later.

"Why? What are you going to do?" he asked.

I removed my smartphone from my side pocket and waved it back and forth in the air.

"I'm calling my pops, to get him to search for my purifier."

Torry nodded and waved good-bye as he headed on down the other side of the mountain.

I then sat atop the summit making a phone call with a dying signal and asked my father to ship my Katadyn Water Purifier on ahead to some place marked in our guidebook called The Blueberry Patch Hostel. I also made sure to gush about how excited I was and how this "easy little climb up Springer" had been a breeze, when the truth was that I thought I had been suffering from a stroke at least three different times on the way up.

It had taken Torry and I quite a while to get this far. At a little over eight miles, with almost a two-thousand-foot climb, it had taken us six hours to be exact.

"Hot dogs at the shelter tonight, dude," a passing hiker said to me out of nowhere as I wished my father well and hung up before he could grab my mother and put her on the phone to shout at me for leaving home.

She still wasn't very happy I had left, being the over-protective mom that she was.

"I'm sorry?" I called out after him, slipping my phone back into my pocket.

"Me and some buddies are doing trail magic[4] at the shelter ahead. We're gonna have some beer and hotdogs if you wanna join us," he said.

I started to thank him, but he had already begun to descend Springer Mountain.

"Hot dogs and beer sound nice," I said, nodding my head with approval.

At the summit, while curiously exploring, I had found a metal door with a handle built into the side of

---

[4] Trail Magic: It could be defined as 'little acts of kindness' that strengthen your willpower and resolve along your journey, reigniting your belief in the kindness of humanity mostly given to an individual in the form of food or snacks.

some rocks. I opened the hatch to find a little logbook and opened it. I quickly thumbed through it and looked up at the fading light in the sky before placing it back.

I wasn't sure what the purpose of it was at the time. Months later, after meeting southbound hikers, it began to make sense. It was a finish line for those who had hiked from Katahdin, Maine, to Springer Mountain, Georgia. A way of saying, "I made it all the way here!"

I wondered then, how exhilarating and monumental their finish line was when they could scrawl in fading ink upon moist paper: *I made it all the way from Maine!*

A quarter mile down the summit, I reached the shelter as it pulled off toward the right. Already, there had to be almost a hundred people in the campsite area. I walked over to the shelter, which appeared to be overflowing with bodies, and saw a small fire had been built out front of the structure.

I walked back and forth, unsure of myself or what I was going to do, despite the fact I had a hammock tent in my backpack and I could've set up *anywhere* else.

"Yo, what's up, man? You lost?" a heavier fellow—with a scraggly black beard he had shaved everywhere but his neck—called out to me from inside the building.

"Nah, was just checking out the shelter," I said as everybody inside turned to look at me.

"Oh, OK. Water is over *that way,* bro, if you're looking for it. It's coming out of a PVC pipe. You can't miss it," he said.

I thanked him.

Too bad I didn't have a filter.

I sighed and walked over, filling my camelback[5] and cringing every time I saw a black piece of debris floating in it. It could've been bird poop, worm poop—hell, I was finding leftover ramen noodles in the water supply out here from lazy hikers.

I wasn't discounting anything as I meticulously tried to filter every last oddity out.

As I walked back past the shelter, I took pictures of food bags dangling from bear cables. I wasn't sure how the whole process worked, and the idea of someone running off with my food at any given time after having left it there, seemed more angering to me than losing it to a bear. Because of this possibility, I didn't bother to hang mine.

"Yo, man, come back over later, and we'll have some beer and hot dogs out. We're doing some trail magic," the neck-beard guy explained. I thanked him for the information again and made my way toward Torry.

"Hey, dude, free hot dogs and beer over there later," I said excitedly to him. He had set up his own hammock tent already during my dilly-dallying.

---

[5] Camelback: Hydration water packs, which have a protruding tube leading to a mouth piece. Typically found amongst hikers, this device can be hung or situated within a backpack with the protruding tube leading down the shoulder straps. This is done for quick access to water without the need to stop and unpack bottles or to remove your backpack.

"Not really hungry, but I'll take a beer," he said.

"And who's gonna get it for you?" I asked with a scoff.

He simply grinned and fell back into his tent.

After setting up my tent, I stood proudly over it in astonishment. This would actually be the *first time* I had ever set up the hammock and had been *proud* of how decent it looked.

I sat down in it slowly and felt the ropes tugging just enough and slipping if only a bit to make me fearful it was going to snap at any moment. This hammock hadn't been made to support more than two hundred and fifty pounds, and I was easily pushing thirty pounds past that limit.

I adjusted slowly as the graying skies above warned us all of rain.

When I began falling asleep, I simply let it take me. Torry was in his own world, smoking and texting and playing on his phone, so I didn't want to bother him. It would be two hours later when I awoke starving, and I went back over toward the shelter, only to find the hot dogs were all gone. There was only *one beer* left as well.

"I'd give it to ya bro," a lanky shirtless guy I'd never seen before with red basketball sweats on said as he hopped down and began to whiz on the side of the shelter right in front of everybody. He then popped the top on the beer can one-handed. "But I'm a li'l thirsty," he said.

A few of his friends laughed as I smiled at the crude gesture and thanked them all the same. I didn't hear what somebody had said to him completely, but I heard the guy in red basketball sweats reply with a "I don't a give *fuck*, dude."

I didn't wake again until three, but that was only because the rain had rolled in and began pouring down heavy enough to bring me out of my sleep. I had to pee so bad that I thought my bladder would explode. Looking out from my hammock tent, I said to myself, "I'm too cold, I'm too tired, and I'm too sore to go out into that," and somehow managed to fall back asleep.

I awoke again at ten to more rain steadily pounding upon my rainfly. This time I couldn't hold my bladder any longer and jumped out of my hammock as if a fire had been lit beneath my ass. I managed to make it three feet away with my feet submerged in two inches of mud and rainwater when I felt myself on the verge of releasing everything into my pants.

Luckily I was able to drop them in time.

I sighed in relief and saw Torry stirring in his tent because of doing this so loudly. I tried to hide the magnificent feeling of letting loose what felt like gallons of water from my body after holding it in for so many hours.

After I had finished, I walked back over to my tent and began to crawl into my sleeping sack, only as I peeled open my bag, I groaned at how wet it was inside. I hadn't even noticed throughout the night, I suppose. It was funny how exhaustion could essentially make you nap through anything.

There was an inch or more of collected rainwater in the base of my hammock, and my sleeping bag had become soaked through. Upon further inspection, I found that the asymmetrical rainfly had been hung off by about half an inch whenever weight had been applied to my hammock. As a result, the heavy downpour that awoke me earlier in the evening had managed to sabotage my bed for the evening.

Yet all the same, my synthetic sleeping bag had done a damn good job of keeping me warm during the night despite this. I dragged out the sopping material within the foggy, moist morning. Everything was wet or dripping outside, and even my clothes had gotten damp as my clouded senses slowly brought me back to reality.

I unsuccessfully tried to wring as much water from the bag as possible. Already it wasn't looking to be a good start to the day.

Packing wet equipment is never very desirable. I had learned that the hard way back in the Uwharries. Here though, I didn't have the option to go home and dry my things.

Instead, I got to smile with dissatisfaction knowing that when I unpacked my equipment later that evening, my things would *still* be wet.

I opened the 2012 guidebook and looked at our proposed trek for the day as I sat on a nearby tree stump and smoked a cigarette. Torry was still asleep inside his hammock, only occasionally stirring when his own snoring woke him up. As he and I had made no real plans on where we would meet the other person if one of us had decided to hike ahead of the other, I hung back from carrying on if only for that very reason.

Also, Torry carried our shared cook kit and my job (if I had remembered to bring it) had been to lug the water purifier.

My intentions all the same, were for us both to make it to Hawk Mountain shelter by that evening, which would have made for a nearly eight-mile day. But at the rate we were moving, that wasn't looking very promising. I took the opportunity to attempt to wrench as much water as I could from my items again and walk around the nearby shelter.

It was insane that at ten o'clock in the morning, more than *half* of the people who had camped there the night before had already left.

It seemed as if they were far more determined than either Torry or I had been.

The now-abandoned grounds looked so used, and the earth so packed down and scarred where people had created a tent city just the night before, that the fog resting over scant pieces of trash and broken limbs and smoldering fires made it appear as if a battle had taken place there the night before. There were still a few hikers who looked as if they were nursing hangovers stumbling about camp like zombies, with no clear direction.

I grabbed some water from the spring and quickly made my way back to our campsite.

"Ahem," I said, if only loud enough to stir Torry. He didn't reply, so I began packing my things just a bit obnoxiously, coughing when I didn't need to cough and "accidentally" dropping things that clanged or made noise.

Eventually he stirred and lifted the flap of his rainfly and peeked out at me. He flickered his red, bloodshot eyes momentarily.

"What's up?" he asked, rubbing them with the back of his hand. I wondered if he'd gotten any decent sleep.

All the same, my miserable night called for me to sigh overdramatically and proceed to whine in contempt of my father's decade-old hammock.

"Stupid thing *sucks*. Maybe when we reach Neels Gap, I'll look into buying a new one," I said as he offered a sympathetic face and lit up a morning cigarette.

"So you know how many miles you wanna do today?" he asked, taking a slow drag. I shrugged slightly, not really feeling like walking that much at all. When I thought about my reasoning for being out there on the trail though, that seemed quite amusing in an ironic kind of way. I laughed only because when I saw him smiling, it was almost as if he could read my mind.

"Not many, I can tell you that much," I responded drearily. He laughed in understanding and swung his legs out to sit upright in his hammock. He then stood and came out.

"Any leftover beer or hotdogs?" he asked, looking around and scratching his stomach with both hands. I only shook my head as I tightened the brain on my backpack and set it up against an adjacent tree trunk.

"Shit, you're already packed!"

I leaned back against the tree and crossed my arms over my chest proudly. "Yeah, I am. So what the hell's taking *you* so long?" I asked.

We took the day easily, and it was quite a gentler walk than the approach trail had been. I only suppose this might have been the case because for the most part we were up on ridgelines as far as the terrain was concerned.

The first two and a half miles fell beneath our feet in just a little over an hour. Along the way, we heard more rumors of rainstorms coming in from passing hikers heading south, and even thru-hikers that had already decided after one night of rain that they no longer had the urge to go on.

Don't wanna be out here in a downpour. People get lost and die that way.

Better hope you can snag a spot in Hawk Mountain Shelter because it's gonna be a tight fit and everyone *will be racing you for it.*

Trying to climb a mountain in a thunderstorm is like trying to go on a date with an electric chair!

Everybody was an expert, and everybody had information to give out. Now that wasn't to say that Torry and I weren't appreciative. But after a while it began to be condescending in tone. It was sort of like, "Wow, I got it…you've hiked the trail before. Could you please stop interrupting me every time I'm in mid-conversation with somebody to correct me about mileage and water sources and towns?"

In all honesty, the first few days would become so littered with people that I began to grow tired of it rather quickly. In a sense, I had come out here to *get away* from people and instead found myself drowning within the crowds.

After crossing a bridge in a clearing of rhododendrons, Torry and I stopped for a break and broke out some power bars.

This was the first time I realized my backpack made a decent seat when laid down on the ground. The skies above us were struggling with passing moments of light, and still the rain descended on us sporadically without pattern or reason.

It was here that we officially met a fellow thru-hiker that went by the name CookIN. I say *officially* because we had passed him several times on the trail, and after taking a quick break, we'd come to see him tottering along just in time for our departure. But it was here he had caught up to us, and so we decided to converse with the guy.

"I know you've heard it a thousand times, and I hate to ask. But I'm guessing ya'll are goin' all the way?" he asked us.

I smiled at his apologetic tone, not nearly bothered by the gentleman. You could just look at some people and tell they were kind. He was definitely one of those individuals.

"Yeah, I am. You?" I asked in return.

"We *both* are," Torry corrected proudly. I glanced to my hiking partner rather quickly and caught the expression on his face. He was tired and maybe just a little bit out of shape at forty-four years of age, but he looked more *alive* than he had in the years I'd known him before. He looked like he was ready to take on the world at this point, and the pride that went along with the moniker "thru-hiker" felt as if it was a name attributed only to the strong and the dedicated.

"Morris the Cat," I said, offering my hand.

"Alan, or, well, out here I go by CookIN. Nice to meet you," he replied.

"Stupid," Torry said, referring to his own trail name as he held out his hand. I only rolled my eyes and laughed.

"I can't call you that," CookIN exclaimed, shaking Torry's hand as well. "How did you even get that name?" he asked, with a bemused expression.

"I gave it to myself. Thought it'd be funny," Torry replied assuredly.

"Now all you need, Morris the Cat, is a shirt that says "I'm with Stupid" and an arrow pointing to the side." We all chuckled.

CookIN had been a shop teacher for three decades back home in Indiana, where he was from. He explained to us that he had never hiked a day in his life until he hit Springer Mountain. I wondered how you went from being a shop teacher to wanting to walk a 2,188-mile trail up the eastern coast of the United States. But I never thought to ask him during the times we spent together.

"Everyone's been telling us that storms are coming in," I said.

CookIN nodded, knowing. "You think there'll be any room in that next shelter?" he asked us.

Several hours later, I was looking at a mess of people looking back out at me from inside the Hawk Mountain shelter with miserable expressions on their faces. It was pouring down rain, and Torry and I stood dripping in the elements. Still, somebody had somehow gotten a fire started, and it was smoldering beneath a rusted sheet of tin that had been thrown atop to save the coals.

The ground was a muddy massacre, and brownish yellow runoff streamed out from beneath the back of the shelter and downhill toward the privy like a sickly diarrhea.

"Any way we could fit two more in there?" I asked, quite awkwardly. I didn't initially get a response, as mostly everybody was within their own little worlds. There were a row of people cooking on anything from denatured-alcohol stoves to little wood-burning stoves to Jetboils and MSR cans that people called pocket rockets. Impatient with their lack of response, I began to step up into the shelter when I was suddenly shouted at by a man who called himself Bismarck.

"Hey, bro, what the hell are you doing?" he shouted as other people chimed in.

Dude, get out!

Don't bring your wet shit in here!

I slowly stepped back down into the rain and looked in at them apologetically.

"OK," I said, turning and beginning to walk away.

"No, it's not that you can't stay in here. But you need to remove your boots. People *sleep* in here," Bismarck said to me, while a woman calling herself Hopper parroted what he had just said. The whole of the packed structure was looking down at me as if I was a dog who had just shit in the middle of their floor.

I sat down without much response other than a nod of acknowledgment and slowly began removing my boots.

I set my wet backpack down against the inside wall, which I was quickly scolded for doing so as well because it was soaked and dripping.

Clearly I had no idea of shelter etiquette.

Hopper, who had hiked the trail in the years before, explained to me, "We were all newbies at some point. You'll learn, *if* you make it."

Her comment was followed by a few snickers.

The snide remark made me smile sarcastically at her when she wasn't looking.

I quickly unrolled my sleeping pad and began to set up next to a heavier fellow in a red T-shirt and black gym shorts whom I had seen hiking the day before up the approach trail. He had been struggling with the physical portion of the trail just as badly as Torry and I had been, going up the "Amicalola Staircase to Heaven" as I had donned it.

"I'm sorry if I snore. I just want to warn you, and I have some earplugs if you need them," he offered quite apologetically to me as I sat down against the wall beside him. I felt odd practically sitting in the guy's lap due to the lack of space.

"Nah, don't worry about it. I have some earphones. I planned for this occasion. I knew I'd have to share these little sheds with others, so I'll just drown you out with music." I replied, smiling.

Having made it so early, Torry and I were surprised to have found that there were almost fifty people already there in camp upon arrival. But most of them had opted to sleep in their tents as opposed to staying within the cramped quarters of the shelter.

As I went about my chores, using the privy or carefully gathering water, I had to remember that I was in a completely different culture now. Out and about I'd sometimes glance in the wrong direction only to see a woman bare from the bottom down, standing to pull her hiking shorts and underwear back up after peeing just twenty feet into the wood line beside her tent.

Other times, I'd hear moaning and the sounds of couples having sex mere feet from other people as I tripped and fell clumsily over their tent-support lines.

"Jesus Christ…I'm so sorry!" I would say, completely mortified, but the only replies would be those of their moans getting louder.

When I got back to the shelter, I began to attempt to hang some of my items carefully and safely among a litany of exposed nails crudely hammered into the walls and wooden hangers people had made with twigs. Hanging them up to drip was an attempt to dry them, which ultimately felt hopeless within the humid, moist air surrounding us.

The rain steadily began to get worse as evening progressed, and a lot of the people I had seen back at Springer stumbled in with sad, wet, dreary faces.

Their questions were always the same.

Any more room in that shelter?

There was guilt within our voices as we regretfully answered no, and they expressed sad smiles before walking off into the drizzling dusk.

When CookIN arrived at the campsite, he made a beeline straight for the structure.

"Any room?" he asked, like the dozens before. I began to apologize, until I looked up at the second-floor loft.

I hadn't physically checked the upper level, and neither had anybody else really. Every time somebody had asked if there was room, they normally shouted no from up top.

Only this time, I stood up and climbed the ladder to look.

There were four people up there with their things thrown or spread out all over the floor. Suddenly I realized *why* they had been yelling, "No room."

They were greedy hikers that wanted as much space as they could possibly get to *themselves.*

Meanwhile, downstairs, I was practically spooning with the stranger next to me who had warned me about his snoring. We were packed!

"Do you think I could fit up there?" CookIN asked, looking up.

"Not really" or "I don't know" were the only responses he was getting. Torry *finally* spoke up after reading the trail guide and stated out loud that the shelter was created to house at least fourteen people.

That meant there was *more* than enough room up top.

But CookIN was too nice to say, "Well, get your shit outta my way before I throw it in the fire," so I began to speak up, along with a few others that chimed in.

"Yeah, there's room up there. Get yourself a spot, buddy!"

At that point it was almost mandatory that the greedy hikers move their things to make room for him. And while their expressions weren't happy, they moved aside all the same.

As I settled into my own spot for the evening, I typed my notes from the day into my smartphone. I asked the guy sleeping beside me what his name was.

"Why do you wanna know?" he asked in jest as he glanced over at my phone screen.

"I gotta add you to my journal."

"What are you going to write?" he asked.

"Oh, nothing really, except that this will be the first time I have ever spooned with another man before," I said, laughing, as he joined in.

"Woodstock," he replied, offering me his hand. He was writing about his day's events as well, only on paper while utilizing his headlamp. I shook his hand and gave him my name as well.

"How'd you get the name Woodstock?" I asked him, settling back against the wall.

"I met a woman hiking who said my yellow rain jacket reminded her of the little canary from the Peanuts comic strip," he exclaimed.

"Ahh…" I said, more into my phone screen than in his general direction.

"I know, stupid, right?" he asked, almost looking for confirmation.

I shook my head as I looked over at him. "Sounds good to *me*. Look at it like this: at least it wasn't something like Smelly Ass or Loser Face," I replied with a chuckle.

He joined in.

"You wouldn't wanna be known as good ol' Smelly Ass, now would you?" I asked. He nodded his head agreeably.

"Look, I've hiked this trail probably three or four times now, so before you go off givin' bad information to others, try shutting your mouth a moment and look for an adult next time something like this happens. I don't want Jason burning down the forest," the angry older gentleman said to what I presumed was one of his Boy Scouts.

"Well, which was it?" the kid asked the man with a hint of annoyance in his voice.

"Which was *what*?"

"Did you hike it *three* or *four* times?" he inquired.

"I mean…what does that have to do with anything?"

"Well it just seems to me that to hike such an incredible distance from Georgia to Maine—it wouldn't be so easily forgotten. Oh, three times here…four times there. I wouldn't imagine it'd be *that* hard to remember," the kid responded sarcastically.

"Don't get smart, kid. Go wake up the others. We're leaving soon," the man replied angrily as the young boy walked off, confused and clearly unsatisfied with the conversation.

I slowly stood from the spring, keeping my eyes averted from the whole discussion. Apparently one of the kids in their troop had been getting teased, and he had gone off into the woods on his own—setting up his own fire—and there had been the potential of a raging forest inferno as a result of some out-of-control embers. I didn't find that very likely though, with the downpour we'd had the day before and overnight as well.

I picked a few black flecks of floating debris from out of my camelback and returned to the shelter.

Exhausted, I had awakened several times during the night simply because I wasn't used to being within such close quarters with complete strangers. I kept wondering to myself, *What if one of these guys is a bed wetter?* Or even worse, *What if I woke up with somebody's morning woody jabbing me in the back?*

How awkward would that have been, for me to accidentally elbow that guy in the throat?

Though as night started to slowly draw in the evening before, hikers had huddled around the fire despite the drizzling rain, drinking cans of Yuengling and eating cosmic brownies that a former thru-hiker had packed in as "trail magic." This would effectively be the second time I had received such an incredible piece of luck.

Former thru- or section-hikers all told stories about where they had come from or strange experiences with people or wildlife that had occurred while hiking the trail in the past. A hiker that went by the name Twizzler (which he was not ashamed to inform us was a reference to a body appendage of his) told fascinatingly bad stories of *all the women* he had hitched rides with and simultaneously managed to sleep with when hiking back in 2010. He spoke of something called the Fourteen-State Challenge, where you got a different woman to sleep with you in every state.

"Sounds more like the STD challenge to *me*," I said, trying to make the group laugh. Instead I only got grunts and insincere nods of acknowledgment before they all went back to talking about the women they'd slept with while on their individual adventures in the past. I cleared my throat and shut my mouth after that.

Farfetched as they were, I was nowhere near intrepid enough to call Twizzler out with my disbelief of his adventures in bagging women.

There were a few times though that I had actually wanted to ask him if his story had come out of a movie I had seen in the past.

As the evening had progressed, everybody began turning in for the night as soon as complete darkness had set at around six. It also surprised me at how quickly the marijuana had been broken out of hiding as well. It was almost as if it was as normal as somebody pulling out a stick of chewing gum from a pack.

Now I wasn't one to discriminate, but I certainly became aware of the prudish looks I received when I declined taking a hit from a pipe being passed around the fire.

First and foremost, I can be a human germophobe.

Some of these people looked gaunt or had yellowed eyes and sores on their skin. I didn't want to grab a bug these people were carrying on day two of the trip. Furthermore, I simply wasn't interested in smoking weed.

Plain and simple.

"Dude, you're *never more free* than when you say *fuck you* to the world and put into your body whatever the hell you want to," one of the hikers standing around the fire said to me after I had passed up the pipe. I smiled and nodded agreeably while inside I thought to myself, *I feel* completely *free actually, because* you *weren't able to* persuade me *to smoke weed when I clearly* didn't feel *like smoking it.*

I had experimented with the stuff when I was in high school up into my early twenties and hadn't enjoyed it that much.

The end.

But it didn't stop Torry from taking a couple hits. As he did, I glared him down, and he simply smiled in return, making it clear by his expression alone that it wasn't *my place* to tell him different.

As people started to shift away from the fire, I found it funny how part of me had actually believed we would all be up and talking into the wee hours of morning.

But people were serious about getting their rest out here.

Woodstock hadn't been kidding either. His snoring was loud enough to shake the floorboards of the shelter. Drowning him out completely with music packed into my ears all night was damned near impossible as I shifted from side to side, painfully aware of what little room I actually had in the process.

The next morning I awoke on the back of a mere two hours of sleep, only to find the other hikers had already begun to pack up and leave the shelter.

Torry and I set off at around ten in the morning, with plans to push either to the next shelter or to Gooch Gap just beyond it.

The trail was riddled with mud patches and fallen branches. Our feet sunk into the earth, soft from the hundreds of people who had set out before us that morning, all of them stomping into the ground with their hiking boots like herds of cattle.

"Excuse us," I heard a soft voice call out from behind Torry and I unexpectedly. A young woman in her early twenties, with short brown hair no further down than her ears, looked up at us with astonishingly green eyes.

"I...I'm sorry..." I stammered, stepping aside. Torry initially didn't hear her, so I smacked him on the back of his head.

"Ow! The fuck did you do that f—oh, hello," he said, quickly changing his angered tone once he'd seen the woman within our presence. We had been playing leapfrog with her throughout the day, but each time we saw her, she became just a little more beautiful.

Her name was Lindsey, and she had been traveling along the trail with her friend Jenna. As Torry and I had conversed throughout the day with her at random rest stops, we learned she too had planned to make it all the way to Katahdin. Sadly, we became *more* impressed with the fact that she was a young woman taking on such an incredible adventure.

And not to sound sexist or chauvinistic, but the male-to-female ratio out here was astoundingly different.

I wondered how long it would be before she unintentionally had a trail of male hikers tagging along "protectively" beside her, you know, *to keep her safe*.

You could find the male libido to be a rather funny and a sad thing at the same time.

"Where do you guys plan on staying tonight?" I inquired, only realizing immediately after how creepy I had probably sounded by asking.

"Probably Gooch Gap shelter…we aren't sure," she replied, stopping and taking a deep breath as she rested her hands on her hips.

"Well, we don't wanna keep you," Torry said as I stole a quick glance at him in confusion.

"You aren't," she said, catching the non-verbal exchange between Torry and I.

"Yeah, Torry, *we aren't,*" I stated almost as solid as fact.

"Unless you *want* us to move on," she offered cautiously.

I began to think how weird this was all starting to appear. I apologized and said that we hadn't had much rest and were just looking to get to our campsite for the night and that we would probably see them on down the trail.

"We'll see you guys later then," she said, with an awkward expression on her face.

After we had let both her and her hiking partner, Jenna, pass us, I called Torry out.

"The hell's your problem? Why'd you scare them off?" I asked irritably.

"I have a girlfriend. Besides, so do you," he said, hiking on.

It had to be explained at this point that before Torry had set out to the trail alongside me, he had found himself a girlfriend. Ironically, they had met on the very dating website I had condemned prior to meeting Melody.

He often spent much of his free time after chores or during breaks from hiking, texting the new woman in his life.

I hadn't yet told him about Melody's *good-bye* in the parking lot of the Greensboro Amtrak station. I hadn't really even wanted to talk about it. While she hadn't officially left me, she also hadn't sent me a single text or words of acknowledgment either. It was as if she had simply dropped off of the face of the planet once she had driven out of that parking lot back home. And for somebody that had been calling herself my *girlfriend,* I found that very odd.

"What's the harm in just trying to make new friends?" I asked.

He stopped and turned to face me. "Oh? So that's all you wanted to do, huh? Have a picnic or two with her? Maybe grab a coffee sometime or hang out at a concert together?"

I sighed, growing annoyed rather quickly.

"So sorry. Forgot that I can't talk to another woman without trying to *sleep* with her too. Guess I let that fact slip my mind," I spat back sarcastically.

"Look, I'm just saying she's not worth your time," he said, turning around and continuing to hike.

"How about your time? She worth *that* much?" I called after him. Only he never answered, just grinned back at me.

So I decided to change the subject.

"So when are we gonna want to stay in a hostel?" I asked as we plowed up one of many identical Georgia Mountains that offered only a miniscule view of the depressing dead trees we had been surrounded with.

He only shrugged, with a cigarette dangling from the corner of his mouth.

"How are you breathing right now?" I asked.

He looked back at me with that same grin on his face. "What do you mean?"

"You're smoking and hiking at the same time. I'm practically *dying* here just breathing this humid air." I relayed, gasping for breath.

"Well, I don't want to point out the obvious," he began, gesturing toward my stomach.

"Ohhh, OK, OK. Sorry, 'lard-ass' here is struggling up the hill behind you. Got it. I'm fatter than you. I mean seriously though, your lungs don't feel suffocated or anything?"

He only shook his head no and kept on hiking up.

"Comin' through," I suddenly heard behind me. It actually scared me, despite the fact it was the voice of an elderly woman.

"Sorry," I offered as I stepped off the trail for her to pass.

"Always keep an eye out behind you. That way people can pass," she added as she practically flew up the hill ahead of both Torry and I.

I guess I still had a little more trail etiquette to learn.

"You guys going all the way?" she asked without even looking back.

"Yeah, why?" I breathlessly called out after her.

"Well I'm headed to a hostel once I reach Woody's Gap if you wanna come along," she offered. At the summit of some unimportant and viewless Georgia mountain, Torry and I asked her for the details.

It turns out that her name was Diet Coke, and she had been the same woman who had officially named Woodstock on the trail the day prior. She was headed to Woody's Gap, where she had planned on getting a shuttle to some place she called the Hiker Hostel. When we asked if we could hitch a ride with her as well, she explained that the people picking her up would possibly be able to take us with her as long as we were there by three in the afternoon. As it was 10:23 a.m., that meant a five-hour scramble, which wasn't as simple as saying "OK, let's go!" when you saw the terrain we had ahead of us. And while this old woman might have been in physically better shape than we were, she was also slackpacking[6].

She was bouncing up the trail like this by having the Hiker Hostel shuttle take her backpack further up trail while she only carried the essentials on her, like a snack and some water.

Now I may not have been an avid hiker, but I can tell you the trail is crazy at times and damn near dangerous as you traversed algae-covered water streams that cascaded off the edges of a mountain or cliffs at random times. It took time traversing these areas with huge packs on. Far too much time to keep up with Diet Coke's speed.

Further up trail, during one of our breaks, we met up with CookIN and Woodstock, whom we forwarded Diet Coke's information to.

They expressed interest as well, though the timeline seemed insurmountable. In a sense though, it still made me feel good to know that after two days I wasn't the *only* one that was hankering for a shower and a *real bed* to rest in.

So our plans were set, and the four of us were *all* moving, almost in tandem, just to try and make it to

---

[6] Slackpacking: A "slack-packer" describes an individual who takes only the bare essentials such as food and water and completes sections of the Appalachian Trail unencumbered by the full weight of their backpack. This is usually achieved via local hostel staff in the area offering the service to thru-hikers or by shuttling their backpacks ahead of them as the hikers walk to retrieve it.

the three o'clock deadline with anywhere from thirty to fifty pounds of gear on our backs. As Torry and I pulled ahead, we stumbled on a brief moment of luck from a phone signal that popped in and out of service, which we used immediately to call the hostel.

Unfortunately, as Torry and I stood there, I watched as his face began to drop as he looked up at me.

"Quick, ask about tomorrow!" I offered, already reading by his face that today was a no-go for whatever reason. But Torry simply shook his head. As it turned out, they were booked then too.

I sighed, clearly irritated as Torry thanked them all the same and hung up.

"Now what are we gonna do?" I asked, as if our entire world had come crashing down. Truth was, I didn't even really need a day at a hostel, having only started two days before.

"No room at the inn, guess we push on to Neels Gap," he said, relighting his cigarette.

"This sucks," I whined.

"Why?" he asked.

"I really wanted to get a room in a hostel," I complained childishly.

"So you quit your job, sold everything you owned, and left your relationship on the rocks with a woman you loved…just so that you could come out here and get a crappy fifteen-dollar room in the middle of nowhere?" he challenged wisely.

I didn't have a good retort to that.

He tilted his head, egging me for a response.

Torry was smart and a lot more calm and collected than I was at times. I could see my spontaneity as being fun but immature as well. And in reality, I had actually begun to cling to him for mental strength in as little as two days.

He had taught me a few things that he'd learned in the army. He had showed me how to start a fire with wet wood. He had also shown me how to gather good kindling when I thought none existed. But most importantly, he made our denatured-alcohol cooking kit out of soda cans all by himself.

I nodded regretfully but understandingly. "Yeah, I guess you're right," I muttered.

The terrain began to ease up some from going straight up and down to winding gently around the mountains.

We stopped at Coopers Gap, where I took out my Leatherman and shaved thick hunks of dead skin and calluses off of the pads of my feet. Beneath these calloused sections of skin were painful blisters. It eased the pressure, but the pain was still there, even after only two days. It seemed that the calloused flesh was being pulled and tugged on by my weight plus the added pounds resting upon my back. Every step had been irritating the sensitive flesh beneath it.

But there was nothing I could do about it, other than take the pain and hope I'd get used to it in time. I was putting my socks back on when Torry gave me a heads up that we had company. Jenna was quietly clomping along and gave us a glance without much acknowledgment as she continued hiking on.

"I think she likes you," I said to Torry, who only rolled his eyes.

"I think *you're* an idiot," he replied. It was maybe two or three minutes later that her partner, Lindsey, came behind and sat down to talk with us for a few moments.

Torry pulled out a cigarette and offered her one, but she politely declined. I had started to light one up myself but stopped once I heard her response, as if trying to impress her for some reason.

She looked over at me and tilted her head to the side.

"Can I tell you something without trying to sound like a jerk?" she asked me.

"No, just be honest with him. He looks like a sea manatee out of the water right now. Right?" Torry said, laughing on my behalf as Lindsey joined in.

"Ha ha ha ha!" I replied sarcastically. "Hey gramps, grown folks talkin' here. Get your old ass on down the trail." The laughter died off, and I realized my comeback wasn't that funny.

"I was just gonna say, you don't look like a hiker." Lindsey exclaimed.

"Well what's a hiker supposed to look like?" I asked.

She only shrugged, and then jutted a thumb at Torry.

"*That* guy? Seriously? He belongs in a rest home, lady. Not stumbling around in the woods with silver alerts ringing off left and right back in cities and towns across the nation." I said, shaking my head in disbelief.

"Oh, here we go," Torry said, shaking his head from side to side.

As we talked we learned that Lindsey was a psych major but hadn't known where she wanted to go with her degree back at home.

"I figured I'd come out here and maybe have a better idea of where I wanted to be, at the end." she explained. It seemed as if there were a lot of people just like her out here. Looking to figure out where they wanted to be down the road of life. As if walking this extended path would somehow make it all clear for them by the end.

Her plans that day had been to reach Woody's Gap by evening, but she didn't feel her friend Jenna could make the long haul.

Day three, and the hikers were already trying to push themselves farther than they were sure they could actually go (us included).

We invited Lindsey and Jenna to join us at Gooch Gap, but she was adamant about sleeping inside the Gooch Mountain Shelter which was a mile and a half before that campsite, because she had been unable to snag a spot inside Hawk Mountain the day before.

"I have some things I still need to dry out," she said with a sad frown. I thought about my own things, knowing I needed to air them out as soon as possible before mildew set in.

Upon reaching our campground, we crossed Forest Service Road 42 and set up in a clearing on the opposite side. It was there that I learned more so than anywhere else that after sweating all day, when you stop to rest, that wind blasting about around you turns cold, and it becomes imperative that you start layering up.

When Woodstock and CookIN appeared, *everybody* immediately set to work on their chores. I was chatting away, not even paying attention to the fact that there was a *reason* why they were doing that.

Because setting up can become quite a long process.

"Water is quite a hike downhill if you guys are thirsty," Woodstock said, slowly walking back into camp after making a run down to a nearby stream.

Woodstock was short and stocky with legs like tree trunks. He was top heavy and had dark-brown hair that he had shaved completely down to nubs atop his scalp. He had grown a thick, bushy beard with two streams of gray hairs that lined down to either corners of his mouth.

Back in Minnesota where he was from, he had worked as an accountant for a closed-captioning television station. So in this camp you had two former nuclear security guards, a high-school shop teacher, a closed-captioning station accountant, and later in the evening, we'd come to find we would be joined by a former truck driver from Austin, Texas.

You truly met people from *all* walks of life out there.

"How far is it?" I asked Woodstock as I picked up my water bottles.

"Maybe around half a mile," he said, pouring some of his water into a Sawyer filtration bag he had.

"You can use some of mine if you want," he offered, holding it up. I thanked him but didn't want to be rude after he'd done all the work to retrieve it.

I trudged down the hill, trying to find happiness if in nothing else than the fact that I was no longer carrying my pack. The wind was horrendous all the same and cut through my thin, sweat-dampened synthetic shirt, chilling the flesh there almost painfully. I hadn't thought I was going to need cold-weather clothes this time of the year, and this far south. Then again, I hadn't been thinking about the terrain I'd be walking on a day-to-day basis and how it differed sometimes by as much as thirty degrees or more just based on varying elevations.

As I neared the water source, I found gravestone markers for two dogs beside the stream.

Surely nobody had been stupid enough to bury them *that* close to a water source, right?

All the same, I walked upstream about twenty feet to gather *my* water, wondering what the history was behind those two gravestones. When I reached the camp again, I was surprised to find somebody I hadn't seen since Gainesville, Georgia. But really, even further back than that.

It was Bubblegum! Having initially met him back in Greensboro at the Train station, he had done *twice* the distance in the past day along the Appalachian Trail than Torry and I had in two.

As we sat down around a blackened coal pit where flames once blazed, we all exchanged stories of our experiences thus far, just before Torry began building us all a fire.

As evening rolled in, the mystery hiker from Austin, Texas, joined us after crawling out from his tent to see what the commotion was.

I shook his hand. "Didn't catch your name."

"Ryan. Nice to meet you," he responded kindly.

Woodstock had brought out some alcohol for everyone, taking cap-sized sips and passing it around.

"Do any of you guys like whiskey?" Woodstock asked us. I shrugged, not really a fan or a hater. I was actually indifferent, but out here for some reason, beneath the stars and while surviving in the elements, it just seemed *right* to have some.

Some whiskey with a little bit of tobacco while talking around the fire had some ancient meaning to it, which ultimately felt *primal* for some reason.

The whiskey that Woodstock broke out from his pack had been aged in a cherry barrel and given to him by his friends as a departing gift. We all took nips off of it (though as the germophobe in the group, I had my initial reservations) while we talked about our former lives, soaking in the heat from the blaze before us.

The best feeling of all though was the fact that tomorrow—hell, even the day after and even still *months from now*—I didn't have some soul-sucking job to go back to.

During the night the wind had been so incredibly cold and unrelenting, offering no mercy as it cut through the meager material of my hammock. The wind even managed to tear through my sleeping bag as well. As I rolled from side to side within it, I realized I was only prolonging freezing one side at a time until the utter discomfort had forced me to switch to the other.

I pulled my phone from my pocket as I rolled onto my back and shivered. It was hard to believe that a $180 sleeping bag was failing on me already. I used the light from my phone to inspect the tag. Strangely enough it read that it had been rated for seventeen-degree weather, yet here I was freezing in temperatures above forty outside, even with my thermals on.

During the night I had also been stirred awake by scratching noises on something metallic outside.

Annoyed, curious, and unable to sleep, I crawled out of my semi-warm bedding to see what it was.

As I stumbled about in the dark, I felt around on the grass for my pack as the wind howled and tossed my hair listlessly. I managed to find my headlamp dangling out from the left side of my backpack's front pocket and clicked it on. As I concentrated my beam upon my cooking pot, I saw the lid raising and lowering sporadically, so I begrudgingly limped over on painfully swollen, sore feet. When I kicked the pot over, a field mouse scrambled back and forth not knowing which way to go in the spur of the moment—before it scurried out over the top of my foot.

"A mouse," I muttered. In my few days in the woods, I hadn't even seen squirrels. I had seen a few birds here and there, but other than that mouse, I had yet to see any other form of wildlife whatsoever.

I looked inside my pot to find the little bastard had left a few turds for me to choke on as well.

"Nice," I grumbled, flicking them out.

Lesson number 1,392 learned. Clean your food pots out before going to bed.

March 19, 2013—(from left to right)
Woodstock, CookIN, and Torry

CHAPTER 4

The Camaraderie of Thru-Hikers

"Anybody want some of this? I brought way too much," CookIN called out to us, while clutching a Costco-sized, two-pound bag of flat sandwich bread.

As I glanced up from my backpack at him, I suddenly remembered that I had a jar of peanut butter in my food bag. It would go perfectly with all that bread. So I gladly took several pieces, as did Ryan.

The morning was bitterly cold and the wind unrelenting as we set out early, ready to rid ourselves of the cold. We all began with achy bones and tired muscles, which were still adjusting to this new lifestyle we had forced them into. What would essentially be our way of life and the main means of transportation for the next six months or so. And while I had only just begun adjusting, that didn't mean it had gotten any easier. I was still waiting for something called "trail legs[7]" to kick in as early as day three of my hike.

I suppose my naiveté kept me in constant anticipation, which was not a bad thing. It actually drove me forward.

We climbed 3,200 feet up Ramrock Mountain and had a stellar view of Georgia. Believe it or not, you could actually spot the Atlanta skyline in the distance.

"Not that impressive," Torry remarked with a matter-of-fact expression.

"What, the view? Or Atlanta?" I asked, puzzled. I thought the view was amazing.

"Both, actually. Atlanta doesn't look that amazing, and this view isn't that stellar to me." He shrugged as he kept hiking along.

I glanced back the way we had come and then toward Torry as a young woman started to approach him heading south.

"So this is what I'm going to need you to do," she explained, handing Torry a potato out of nowhere. Torry glanced down at the spud with googly eyes pasted to it and then to her again with a confused expression.

"Now, hold up Edward and smile!" she said, breaking out a camera and directing it at him.

---

[7] Trail Legs: is a term used to describe the eventual adjustment and ability to hike long-distances where once limited by physical fitness or lack of stamina early on in a person's thru-hike.

"Uh…Edward?" Torry asked.

The young woman shouted, "Cheese Doodles!" and proceeded to take a picture.

"Perfect! Now take one of me!" she said, handing me her cell. I glanced over at Torry, who looked just as baffled as I was. Honestly, I didn't know what the hell was going on and simply wanted to start hiking again.

"I'm not sure I understand," I said as I looked down at the pink iPhone she'd just handed me. She stood near the edge of the cliff as Torry grinned suddenly.

"I just need you to take a picture, that's all," she responded impatiently, as if *I* was holding *her* up.

After I took a picture, she approached and asked me for yet another favor.

"I'd like to get a picture of me jumping in the air with that view in the background now. Make sure to get Atlanta in the picture," she said, pointing to the open expanse laid out before us. The Atlanta skyline behind her existed as nothing more than a distant blur and outlines of shapes with no clear definition, due to air pollution. I hardly doubt it would even show within the smeared pixels of her cell-phone camera.

I handed the phone to Torry.

"Here, you wanna take some pictures for a while? I'm gonna head off," I muttered as he nodded and began taking photographs for this young woman who had called herself Hawaii.

I suppose you needed a character of every sort out here.

As we clambered down the mountain, it was not long before we approached a sign on the side of the trail that read: Cross the road for trail magic. Torry had already barreled ahead of me and started helping himself to the food laid out on one of the many tables set up in the parking lot of Woody's Gap.

He had started to practically gorge himself, from what I could see. Ryan went ahead too, while I waited impatiently on Woodstock and CookIN to share the good news, as if they wouldn't see it their self upon arrival.

Indiana Jones, a teacher and a former thru-section hiker[8] of the entire AT, had set up a stand at that very road crossing that morning and was passing out food for this year's class of thru-hikers. I had never been so loving of pimento-cheese sandwiches with orange and banana slices before in my life.

She also had peanut-butter-and-jelly sandwiches with chips and Vienna sausages.

"This is incredible, isn't it?" Torry asked, with a mouthful of canned meat. He was laughing, and shaking his head with disbelief. I only smiled and took a bite of cheese spread smeared thick on the white bread.

---

[8] Thru-Section Hiker: A term given to an individual who has completed the entirety of the Appalachian Trail, via section hikes throughout different periods in their life.

It was a thousand times better than noodles, rice, or oatmeal again.

After thanking her for her kindness, we hiked on. I wondered in that moment if I would have fond memories of hiking this trail someday. So much so that I'd come back and do some trail magic of my own as well.

If only to pay it forward.

As Torry and I entered Blood Mountain forest, we mocked the name by using deep dramatic voices. I made ominous music sounds as Torry bellowed out, "And they were never heard from again, as they entered..." He paused as I added in a *da da dummmm*!

"Blood Mountain Forest!" he yelled, with an evil laugh skirting maniacally behind it.

"So I got a question for ya. How do you think this place got its name?" I asked, following behind Torry as he slid his trek poles into either sides of his pack to let them hang freely. Contemplation painted his face briefly before he glanced back at me.

"Something to do with a battle between Creek and Cherokee Indians in the area supposedly, I think. They said you could see the mountaintop tinged with blood for miles and miles away," he explained as I looked around the forest. I was looking for these eerie signs of *blood* he had mentioned, or markings that had been made in blood. Really, just anything *to do* with blood.

Of course I found nothing.

We made a mad scramble for Lance Creek, where we (along with pretty much *everyone* else hiking the Appalachian Trail that year) set up camp for the evening. This is because we had all learned that up ahead, past Jarrard Gap, you were not allowed to camp anywhere between there and Neels Gap without a two-pound bear canister[9] in tow.

At first I didn't even know what a bear canister *was*.

When I asked Lindsey later that day if she knew what one was, she explained to me that it was basically a can to hold your food in to keep bears from getting at it. Suddenly I wondered why I even *needed* a canister and couldn't just hang my food bag, via the bear cables that had been at every other campsite or shelter along the way.

"I think it has something to do with how aggressive the bears in the area are," she explained, regarding the distinction between the two. Frankly, in either case, if the bear wanted the canister or the food via bear cables

---

[9] Bear Canister: Generally accepted as an alternative to bear cables or hanging your food from tree branches, bear canisters are hardened containers often manufactured with materials such as carbon fiber or polycarbonate to withstand both the strength and intelligence of wildlife. Many of these canisters are installed with rubber gaskets to prevent the scent of food from escaping the container as well.

that badly, the bear could have it. I wasn't going to fist-fight the creature for it.

When we set up, it was only two in the afternoon and a general disgust followed Torry and I because of how quickly we had ended our hike for the day.

To be fair though, Blood Mountain had quite a reputation for being "one big sonofabitch." As it was, we had been told that there was no camping allowed beyond the summit or even sleeping within the shelter that had been built on top without those pesky canisters. So we decided on saving it for the next day instead of pushing out sixteen miles that evening.

I was clueless about what areas I needed to have a permit to camp in, or which areas I needed certain equipment or rules to follow. I had a mind-set that told me, *If I need to know it, somebody will tell me.*

Let me tell you, there was no shortage of people on the trail that had either section-hiked large portions of the AT or were second- or third-time thru-hikers.

That didn't give me (or anybody) an excuse to *not* look up this readily available information on my own beforehand, and I probably should have.

Still, had these people not been around to inform me of these things, I was possibly looking at a fine of some kind, as well as having my gear confiscated, all while I was escorted out of the woods like a bad school kid of some sort by law enforcement. I knew it was pertinent to pay closer attention to the regulations of these areas that the AT took me through.

After setting up my hammock on two pine trees along the track of road called Lance Creek, I sat on a stump overlooking the nearby water source and watched the steady flow of hikers falling in. CookIN and Woodstock seemed to have been carrying the same pace as Torry and I the last few days, and they quickly secured two tent pads for themselves not too far up from where we had established ours.

I found this resting site rather odd, if only because it appeared to have been made on an old forest or logging road of some kind. If you followed it south, it appeared that at least a decade before (through still existing ruts) it had curved up around a nearby smaller bluff.

Because of the age of the trees in the area, I wondered if it had in fact, been a logging zone in the recent past.

There was no privy here, and so this was my first learning adventure with "land mines." Torry was puffing on a cigarette as he glanced over at me.

"So you finally shit yet?" he asked rather crassly and intrusively.

"Yeah, yesterday. Wanna know what color it was?" I replied sarcastically as I glanced up from my phone screen. I thought I had a wandering signal on it, which flashed if only momentarily, to check for messages, but it was mostly nonexistent. I threw the phone into my hammock and walked over to Torry, sitting beside him.

"Not a bad day, huh?" he asked as I bummed a cigarette from him, lit it up, and took a slow drag.

"Not bad at all. How crowded do you think it'll get here tonight?" I asked him as we watched five more hikers slowly walk through the middle of our camp looking for spots to set themselves up for the end of the day.

"Well, you look at it like this. Neels Gap is around seven or eight miles from here, and it's already three in the afternoon, so it'll be dark in around three or four more hours. There's no camping allowed between Jarrard Gap, which is a few miles north of here, and Neels Gap without a bear canister, so I figure that we'll be getting quite a bit of people here that just wanna hurry and set up and relax. Maybe around twenty-five or thirty, I'd estimate," he said, lying back into the bed of fallen oak leaves carpeting the earth. "I was thinking, by the way—"

"About how cold it was last night and how these ThermaRest pads are absolute pieces of garbage in our hammocks?" I spouted off bitterly, despite the fact it had nothing to do with what we were talking about. I could be a bit ADHD at times.

He paused momentarily and then shifted the conversation to what I was complaining about.

"Well, I thought about that too." He sat up and reached into his hammock, which was adjacently hanging above us. He removed his silk sleeping bag liner.

I looked at him strangely.

"We should cuddle?" I asked.

He just laughed. "Exactly! And I can stab you to death afterward," he replied, shaking his head.

I smirked at his response.

"But what I was thinking was, I could stuff this bag full of leaves and lay on top of it like a barrier. All of the little pockets of air caught in between each leaf will act as pockets of heat," he explained.

"Oh yeah? Sounds good. And when the brown recluse or black widow spider bites you in the middle of the night, tell me how that worked out for you," I responded sarcastically as I took another drag from my cigarette. I only said that because I had remembered my evening back in the Uwharrie Mountains when I had fallen from out of my hammock and then arose, to use the restroom in the middle of the night. I had seen thousands of spiders perched atop the leaves, looking out into the darkness as they hunted for their prey.

It made me shiver in disgust to think someone could be making a bed with those things in it.

"Eh, I'll be fine," he said, snuffing his cigarette butt out and putting it into his carry-along trash bag. I did the same and stood slowly.

"Well, time to take my official second dump while on the trail. Wish me luck," I called out to him as I made my way to my backpack and removed my toilet paper.

"Watch out for the landmines," he called after me, though I was still unsure of what he had meant by that vague statement.

I passed Lindsey and Jenna and quickly tucked the toilet paper beneath my arm out of shame. I huddled over, feeling rather embarrassed should they find out that I was on my way into the deep thicket to use the restroom.

"Hey, how are you?" Lindsey asked, smiling at me.

"Good" was all I replied, short and curt, as I passed by. It was all I had wanted to say. I tried to move on as quickly as possible until she stopped, turned, and engaged me in conversation.

"Are there any places left to set up here?" she asked, looking past me and standing on her tiptoes to get a better view of the surrounding area.

Great. Now she was going to start asking me questions?

"I uh…I think so. You know my buddy Tor—well, as you know him…uh…Stupid? He could probably help you find a spot," I said.

"I'm sure I can find one myself. I was just hoping there were some more pads so we weren't sleeping in people's way or blocking the trail." She then smiled, which brought attention to some rather cute dimples that formed on her cheeks.

I won't lie, I found her attractive.

"Well then...good...luck" was all I could think of to reply. My bowels grumbled, and I prayed to God she hadn't heard them. The three of us stood there awkwardly for a moment before Jenna spoke up. "I think I'm gonna go find a place to pee."

She threw her backpack off suddenly and started rummaging around for toilet paper in the front zipper pocket.

As I watched her briefly, and was caught off guard when I accidentally dropped my own roll of toilet paper, Lindsey broke in. "Oh, I'm sorry. Were you on your way to use the bathroom too?" she asked.

I smiled, as my face turned blood red for some incomprehensible reason. Mostly because this complete stranger could probably discern that I was about to poop in the woods, and despite the fact that it was completely *normal* under these conditions for me to do so, I was still rather ashamed of making my restroom habits public. I hadn't been in the hiking culture long enough for it to become a normal, accepted practice, I suppose, to walk unabashedly and shout out to complete strangers, "Time to drop the kids off at the pool!"

"I uh…actually, I have to go," I coughed, feeling my words stuttering within my own mouth. "I have to… uh…pee too." I lied, not even thinking about what I had just said.

Lindsey bit her bottom lip uncomfortably as she looked at the toilet paper clasped within my writhing hands and then to me again. I wondered briefly how stupid I had just sounded and immediately became aware of how much more awkward I'd made the situation. With an odd laugh and a nervous good-bye wave, I quickly shuffled off into the woods.

Remember that "learning experience" I told you about regarding land mines? I approached a flat, densely forested section of earth and saw random twigs sticking out of the ground like a little graveyard of some sort. I wasn't quite sure what had been buried there, so I slowly removed one of the little sticks poking up from the earth. At the end was a clump of smelly yellowish-brown gunk clinging to the end of it.

"Yep. That's shit," I uttered, so greatly horrified I almost felt like vomiting immediately. I dropped the twig and backed away slowly, with a twisted look of disgust on my retching face. If at that moment it was available, I'd have gladly dropped my entire arm into a vat of sulfuric acid.

I suppose the best way to learn something can sometimes be the hardest way. Sure, I could have inquired about these land mines Torry had spoken of, but as he hadn't elaborated, I didn't think to ask.

Now I knew.

In the future, every twig sticking oddly out of the ground was a buried mound of somebody's feces to me... regardless of whether that was in fact true.

At around one I awoke feeling as if I was freezing to death and was never able to get back to sleep.

It had dropped down to twenty-three degrees, and as I searched the tag on my bedroll restlessly again, just as I had the night prior, I knew I was only prolonging my anger by reminding myself that my sleeping bag had been rated down to seventeen degrees.

I was beginning to hate my hammock though, as well, as I grouchily rolled from side to side and jerked wildly at the separating Velcro entrance that had been installed with this specific model. It had started to wear completely.

"What a piece of junk!" I snarled angrily.

This stupid hammock with its asymmetrical rain-fly—and no included stakes—had sent me over the edge. Deep down though, I was truly angry at myself. I had tried to be frugal in my final weeks before leaving home. Sure, I could've bought my own brand new hammock, but I had been convinced that this decade-old piece of garbage I'd borrowed from my father would work out just fine.

Boy had I been wrong.

At around three, it began sleeting for a while before turning into hard snow, and with the wind blowing me around within its hurricane gusts, I felt like I was sway-ing about like a morbidly obese wind chime of some kind.

But more than anything else, I was getting disgrun-tled with my ThermaRest pad, which had all but been pushed out from beneath me and wrapped around my legs unintentionally as I shifted restlessly from side to side throughout the night. I was doing or trying *anything* to remain comfortably warm.

"Damned thing!" I growled between clenched teeth in as much of an anger-contained hush as I could pos-sibly give in this moment of my rage.

I ripped at the corners violently until the Velcro seal-ing on my hammock gave way beneath my weight and I fell out into the newly sticking snow on the ground.

In the process I had managed to jar my spine on my own backpack that I had laid beneath my hammock tent. I cried out in pain and bit down on my bottom lip to keep from waking the entire camp. But Lord knew they wouldn't have heard me much in those gale-force winds anyhow.

The sun that was our alarm clock came so slowly the morning after it was painful. For eight hours I had lain there within my hanging tent trying to get the same sleep everybody else had been getting and of course failing miserably at it.

I could finally no longer take it. I kept peeking out from beneath my rainfly in Torry's direction. His hammock hadn't stirred a bit.

The hell with it! He can catch up with me later, I thought to myself as I climbed out of my haggard home and began packing.

CookIN and Woodstock were already up and smiled over at me.

"Snow. Can you believe it?" Woodstock called up to me, laughing, with a handful of the white fluff falling from between his fingers.

I smiled, muttering back, "*Why* did I decide to come out here again?"

"I'm sorry?" he called out to me.

But I only put on my best, fakest smile and replied, "Nothing, my friend. I love snow and being cold." I knew I sounded sarcastic, but my irritability was so high it was hard to function without letting off a little bit of steam.

"Yo!" I heard behind me suddenly. I turned to find Torry looking out at me from his hammock with a fully rested face and slightly rosy cheeks.

"You OK?" he asked from the comfort of his warm bed.

"Great. Not a wink of sleep. I hate this damned ThermaRest," I said, ripping it out of my tent and slamming it on the ground. I kicked it a few times as well for good measure.

I regained my composure after I saw a few other hikers, who were headed out, look up in my general direction. I smiled, nicely waving my hand at them as they passed back cautious looks.

"Told you, buddy. These leaves worked out *great*," Torry said, almost rubbing it in my face. He had begun stretching just before slipping his hands behind his head comfortably.

"Oh yeah? Well that's nice. Hey, you got anything *important* to say otherwise, asshole? Or can we get ready to go?" I replied bitterly, not willing to acknowledge his working idea out of spite.

"Hey, hey! Whoa! Calm down, buddy. You're in the presence of a fine young woman. No need to get all worked up," he replied smugly. I started to call him another childish insult when suddenly I saw somebody standing in tennis shoes before me as I looked up from my crumpled ThermaRest that I'd left abandoned on the snowy earth.

Lindsey, who had seen my outburst, the bags under my eyes, and the look of maniacal rage behind them approached me slowly.

"I don't mean to bother you while you're packing and all, but do you have any details about the cabins in Neels Gap?" she asked a little reluctantly.

Truth was, none of us were even sure what to expect out of Neels Gap. To Torry and I, it had been called anything from an outfitters, a hiker hostel, a taxi service into town, and a cabin resort of some kind.

It had also been labeled as a "last bastion of hope to all that chose to abandon ship."

Last night, before we had all vanished to our tents for the evening, Torry, Woodstock, CookIN, and I had stood around a fire and talked about our future projections and places we'd planned to stay along the way as we headed north. It was in this time we talked about possibly splitting the cost of a cabin there at Neels Gap, which we had been told from other hikers hovered at around sixty bucks a night.

Split up four ways that was only fifteen dollars a person.

Itineraries seemed pointless out here in the grand scheme of things, if only because plans could change on a *dime* the *very second* bad weather came about. But we were all still new out here, and everything was a learning experience. Hell, it had only taken Torry and I a *day* to realize that the fifteen-to-eighteen-mile markers we had originally laid out for ourselves were never going to work.

We'd given up *that* idea the second we scaled Amicalola Falls and fell sweating and panting for air on the grass at the top.

As I looked at all the beauty that was Lindsey standing before me, I was reminded of how little I actually had to offer her.

She had shared a tent with the limited space offered at Lance Creek with a tall, lanky, blond-headed fellow she had called Wales. He got his name, I suppose, because he had gone to a private school in England growing up. Even at twenty-two, he spoke as if quite a bit of both the dialect and accent had rubbed off on him. He was very proper with his complete pronunciations of words, and every last syllable he spoke had a rather shy, introverted, and reserved personality all its own.

We'd heard laughter erupt from within his tent several times between him and the other two girls as CookIN, Torry, Woodstock, and I stood around the fire nearby.

"Lucky bum," I had said, envious as Torry and Woodstock both laughed.

They could have all been laughing over jokes for all I knew, or playing Tickle Bunny. Regardless, I was jealous.

Now here Lindsey was, standing before us the morning after, asking me about cabins, and all I could think was how I paled in comparison to Wales.

"You really know as much as I do about them," I said as she smiled and nodded.

"All right, well thanks anyway," she said.

Torry then spoke up.

"Hey, if you're looking to split a room at a cabin, so are we," Torry interjected. I looked over at him. He smiled at me approvingly and gave me a thumbs-up.

While she appreciated the offer, her friends Jenna, Wales, and an older gentleman who called himself Gray Loon had been talking about snagging a cabin of their own and she had only wanted information on them.

When she went back to pack her things, I looked over at him.

"Whatta ya mean *we have room*?" I asked.

"What? As it stands, it's gonna be a sausage fest in that cabin. I just thought it'd be nice to see some split tail in there is all," he said, fishing a cigarette out of his trail-worn pack.

"You have a girlfriend, let me remind you. Remember? You got on me yesterday," I informed him, as if he was never aware of that himself.

"I have an open relationship right now, actually. I texted Pam last night. We only just met each other before I came out here. We haven't made *any* commitments yet," he assured me.

I thought about Melody in that moment. The sad look on her face when I told her that I loved her had forewarned of our future. A future that hadn't appeared very bright in that empty parking lot back in Greensboro.

I wasn't out here to find a woman. I was out here to live my life, and I had every intention of being dedicated *only* to her. But as it stood, she never wanted me to go and left me open to the presumption she was *never* going to love me again, let alone text me or even see how I was doing.

I looked away slowly, with distant eyes, and then went back to my things.

I was too cold for breakfast, and truthfully, I was too cold to gather water either.

It was ten when we finally headed out. As we traversed some of the smaller summits leading up to Blood Mountain, I began to realize how dangerous this trek was starting to be without the proper gear. I had thought I was going to be fine without gloves, but as the wind tore into us that day, I found I could no longer warm them with my breath, or even by placing them in my pockets beneath the thin material of my quick-dry synthetic pants. Big puffs of lightly falling snow swirled about within the huge wind gusts.

Sometimes sections of snow that had gathered on tree branches above blew down on us and fell into the backs of our shirts. This left icy, melting trails dripping down our spines.

Several times as we pushed uphill through the snow, Torry would stop to remind me that the tips of my ears were beginning to look dangerously "waxy." He was concerned with the possibility of frostbite, so I finally retrieved my toboggan from my backpack and threw it on. It did little to protect much of anything though.

We had a moment of reprieve from the incessant wind once we reached Slaughter Creek, which sat at a trail crossroads. As we stood there, it didn't take long for the sweat on our backs to begin chilling us again.

So once more without rest, we were off, if for no other reason than to combat this.

Breathing the thin, frozen air had been torture, and over the course of a few hours, it began to make our throats and lungs feel raw.

I was rather numb and unaccustomed to winter hiking of any kind. Hiking too slow only made me colder and the onslaught of the wind more torturous. Hiking too fast made me sweat, making standing still to rest for a moment a life-threatening act because of hypothermia. I began to furiously open and close my hands to get blood circulating, as I could no longer feel anything from the tips of my fingers to my elbows. I literally pumped my hands open and closed for two hours without end, to no avail. In a short time, the wind had frozen the bottles of water on the sides of our packs to slush. When I tried to take a sip from my camelback, I realized that the hose line had completely frozen inside and out as well.

Torry's had suffered the same fate.

Ascending Blood Mountain, we caught up with CookIN and passed him. He looked just as beat up and miserable in the cold as we did, but he was still trucking along all the same. We promised him we would reserve the cabin for both him and Woodstock should we arrive at Neels Gap before they did. Not soon after, we passed Woodstock too and relayed the same information to him.

I began to feel stronger, even though my feet were on fire with pain. My nose and eyes were waterfalls, and I could no longer feel my face as we climbed boulders about the size of tote-boxes or clothes dressers on our way up. The large stones were coated in thick sheets of ice.

Hikers that had pushed out earlier than us had left established, careful footprints behind where they had cautiously chiseled or stamped out paths up these dangerous places. And we were stepping into those very same footprints whenever it became applicable.

Though my left knee was rotten with pain, as it had never seen the length of workout or strenuous activity as it had within the last few days, I had come to find I was able to get through by popping ibuprofen like candy and zoning out.

Early on, the trip had truly been purely mental for me. Down the road it could have been physical, but at that very moment, my brain was telling me: *You could be at home with your girlfriend right now* or *You could still fix this. Go back home and get your job back. Nobody would fault you.*

Yet deep down, I knew that would never be the case. I would go back to those drunken lonely nights passed out on a bathroom floor in my own vomit. I'd continue to sit at stoplight intersections and gaze into oblivion as I dreamed of my past and everything I'd lost and given up.

Worse was the fact that I wouldn't be able to live, haunted by my own failure in never completing the journey. I wanted to make my father proud. I wanted him to have *something* he could describe to people that would make them stop and say, "Wow, your son *really* did that?"

I'd managed to give him *nothing* like that so far.

When Torry and I reached the Blood Mountain shelter, I was in awe. It was like a giant nest of carefully placed stones, mortar, and wooden planks that overlooked any- and everything as far as the eye could see. Upon reach- ing the summit of one of the most difficult mountains on the trail early on, I experienced a natural high that I unfortunately will never be able to convey into words. The awe and the beauty erased, if only for a second, any thoughts of fear or doubt within, and it was in that moment that I found I was most alive—existing within some extraterrestrial plane where nothing mattered but the view.

Still, our appreciation of the scenery lasted a whole fifteen seconds before Torry and I quickly ducked inside the cabin as the wind pounded mercilessly upon the al- most-hundred-year-old structure.

"Christ, I'm about to freeze to death, dude!" I stut- tered, dropping my backpack and throwing my DriDown jacket on. It did little to stop the cold, and my back was still soaked from sweat and melted snow that had fallen off of the branches above us.

"We need to get a fire going, but it looks like the chimneys have been sealed up. And I can barely move my fingers," Torry said, shaking them and pumping his fists much like I had been doing for the past three hours.

"Maybe we should just get the hell out of here?" I offered.

He slowly shook his head. "No, we need to get something warm inside us to help thaw out." He dug around in his backpack.

He removed our denatured-alcohol cook kit and began to assemble it. Upon striking matches or trying to light the liquid with our lighters, we realized it was simply too cold to catch.

"Let's try some Everclear," I suggested, only that would end up failing too. It wasn't too long after that when Woodstock arrived.

"Forget it," Torry said and poured out the Everclear onto the stone floor. Sadly, the shelter didn't even have doors on the windows to block out the wind.

"It's miserable out there," Woodstock said, clearly stating the obvious. I hocked a loogie that had built up from my excessive post-nasal drip. It had been dripping like a leaking faucet for hours down the back of my throat. I spit out the window only for the wad to be blown back in at me and land on the sill.

Ten seconds later that spit was frozen solid to the wooden plank.

"What are you guys trying to do?" Woodstock asked as he rubbed his hands together and blew warm breath into them.

"Trying to get a fire going," Torry replied, attempting to light the fluid that had been poured out onto the floor.

"Christ, just give me the lighter so that I can just set my hands on fire and thaw my fingers that way," I growled miserably.

That was when the liquid finally took.

Torry had managed to get a small flame burning from the Everclear he had poured out. The flame slowly built and spread out over the puddle.

"Nice!" I shouted as we all huddled around the flames upon the stone floor, warming our hands. I also managed to heat up some of the slush water in my bottles quickly enough to add to some granola, powdered milk, and freeze-dried raspberries I had prepacked too.

I ate a small serving of the hot cereal, and that helped thaw my insides just a bit much like Torry had said.

It wasn't long after that we pushed on.

Before us deep valleys and wrinkles in the earth made us imagine the lines of an old man's face. Mountain laurel, rhododendrons, and pine trees twisted and gnarled into the air around the rocky outcroppings at random.

Torry eventually pulled ahead of me, and for the first time on the journey, I got to enjoy a little alone time.

It's scary though, when you're walking along and find that there are no white blazes[10] along the trail you're currently traversing.

---

[10] White blaze: the term describes a 2x6 inch white rectangle painted onto trees to mark the direction of the Appalachian Trail. Usually

That was because the snow that had covered everything on that summit, and it made me wonder if I had missed a sign somewhere or taken a wrong turn.

I was about to begrudgingly turn around and head back up to a split in the trail roughly a mile back, until I heard cars and saw a small sliver of road down between the trees.

"Screw it. If this isn't the right way, I'll just hitch a damn ride into Neels Gap," I said to myself out loud as I continued downhill. Luckily I found I had jumped to conclusions too soon, because the outfitter store slowly came into view. As I walked up, Torry was already off in his own world checking out equipment inside the structure, and Woodstock was eating a hotdog outside on the patio.

While it was still chilly out, it was nowhere *near* what we had been subjected to up on the summit. It literally had to be thirty to forty degrees warmer down in the gap. The skies were clear and a lot of people were enjoying the sunny day.

Hikers, bicyclists, and motorcyclists alike were standing around chatting as I dropped my backpack with Woodstock outside, who offered to look after my things while I went inside.

---

placed at eye level, these blazes vary in color based on different trails or paths surrounding the AT.

I spent twenty-three bucks on a frozen cheeseburger, a frozen steak chimichanga, a Powerade, a bag of potato sticks, and some jolly ranchers.

My God, was this place unreasonably pricey. But you aren't very picky when you're starving for something other than ramen noodles.

As I looked around the store, I came across a weight scale. I was curious to see if I'd lost any fat thus far, so I put my purchases down and stepped slowly onto the scale.

According to the thing, I had lost eleven pounds since starting the journey just five days before.

"Can I try?" Lindsey asked, coming up behind me. I smiled and stepped aside.

As she hopped on, she glanced back at me. "No peeking!" she ordered as I held up both hands in surrender and walked slowly backward.

"What! This piece of junk says I've *gained* four pounds," she said, stepping down.

"Piece of junk scale," I concurred, shaking my head slowly.

"Gained weight? From what? All that walking? Pfft, yeah right," she added.

"Yeah! From all that walking, pshhht," I said, playfully parroting her.

After talking to the cashier, I learned that you had your choice of two places to sleep at Neels Gap. You could spend fourteen dollars to stay in the hostel, which did *not* include the price to do laundry (another four dollars), or you could rent a cabin at sixty bucks a night, split it four ways, and your laundry was washed for free. Moreover, they were cleaner than staying in the hostel, which appeared to be filled with a plethora of cats and the thick smell of urine.

It wasn't hard for us to make a decision after checking out the hostel.

For dinner, Woodstock, CookIN, Torry, and I bought Tombstone pizzas for ten bucks each (though usually retailed for $2.99 in your local Walmart), and we each completely devoured an entire pizza to ourselves.

Being in that cold had absolutely starved us.

As evening progressed and we settled into our cabin, which had been filled to the gills with dead, stuffed raccoons perched on overhangs, and hanging from the walls, I decided to get the four of us a treat. I walked from the Blood Mountain cabins back up to the hostel and asked around if I could get a ride from anyone to a nearby gas station.

A man called Pirate offered his services for five dollars in gas.

"Whatta ya need? Smokes? Beer or something?" he asked in a *Slingblade[11]*-type voice. I kinda expected him to randomly spout, "I like mustard on mah biscuits,"

---

[11] Sling Blade: 1996 film starring Billy Bob Thornton, and Dwight Yoakam.

but he never did. I was wondering if he was just messing around with me and I wasn't catching on.

"I was just gonna get some beer for my friends and I," I explained.

"Nectar of the gods. Give me the five, and let's go," he said, holding his hand out.

I plopped the bill into his palm, and we were off five minutes later.

"So what's your story?" he asked as he sped down the mountain on a twisty old highway in a ragged van.

"I'm sorry...story?"

"Yeah, everyone has one. Why'd you come out here?"

"Well, I quit my job...and my girlfriend left me because I wanted to get away for a while. This has kinda been a dream since my father did a portion of the AT up in Virginia and came back with wild stories," I explained.

"You said yer girl left ya?" he asked.

"Something like that," I said somberly as I glanced out the window at the passing trees. I didn't want to think about her again in that moment. I didn't want to feel hurt from the subject anymore, period.

"Bitch," he said suddenly. "Not to offend you or nothin'," he quickly added.

"It's all good," I said, unsure of how else to reply to such a crass response. He gave me some choice words of advice out of nowhere suddenly: "Women are like a city bus. Wait around fifteen minutes and another one's bound to come by."

He glanced over at me without so much as a hint of humor on his face after he had said it.

"Yeah…" was all I replied, not finding the comment all that funny. Instead, I remembered the photograph I had taken of Melody's face in my mind the moment I had kissed her good-bye back in Greensboro.

It takes five days out in the wilderness without a real bath or shower of any kind to make you realize just how much you can truly miss the amenities of a home in the modern world.

That first shower had to have been the highlight of my day, hell, maybe even my whole week!

"Come on, get out!" I was shouted at impatiently by Torry as I scrubbed away what felt like years of grime that had collected on my body. The floor of the bathtub was black with dirt that had come off me.

"*I'm trying to get clean here, got it?*" I shouted back out at him.

When I came out, Woodstock was still contemplating heading out as he had been the night before. Meanwhile Torry, CookIN, and I had already decided on staying another day in the cabins after reports of bad weather rolling in had littered the local news channels.

On the weather channel the following morning, we saw the reports of rain and snow the *next three days,* which was only hours away from starting. Woodstock sighed miserably as he looked from us to his backpack.

"You guys don't mind if I decide to stay an extra day with you all, do you?" he asked us sheepishly.

No!

Of course not!

Take a load off, buddy!

We all affirmed him unanimously.

The Blood Mountain store had a collection of miscellaneous items you could purchase, such as hotel-sized travel shampoos and light camping gear. The store also sold frozen foods and ice cream and had twenty-five-cent cups of coffee. They offered free Wi-Fi, so I used the Internet access to load my journal pages up to the Trail journals website, along with some photos I had taken along the way to my Facebook account.

There were messages and emails, some of encouragement, and others not so much.

There were a few people back at home who had counted on my giving up any day now. Comments like: "Quit kidding yourself, John. Go back home" or "I don't want to sound rude…but I just don't think you have the willpower to go all the way."

As I read over these messages—some of which were from people I had once considered *friends*—I felt my heart sink slowly. Angrily I shut off my phone screen and looked down at my boots.

What do they know? Forget them. If they don't want to believe in you, then they were never truly your friends to begin with.

I suddenly received a notification on my phone out of nowhere. It was a text message from Melody:

Melody: "where are you now?"
John: "still in georgia, haven't made it very far
     yet. How have you been"
Melody: "i miss you so much john"

I looked at that line of text and felt my eyes burning. I guess she hadn't truly been as heartless as I had thought her to be.

I took a slow breath and replied: "i miss you too. you should come out and see me once I reach north carolina"

Melody: "i dont know if i have the time"
John: "make it"
Melody: "well let me know where i can pick you
     up"
John: "i will do some research. i'm probably think-
     ing somewhere in the vicinity of hot springs"
John: "Have you been reading my posts?"
Melody: "no. i dont care about your stupid hike. i
     already told you that. if you want to tell
     me about it, you can call or text me."

I sighed and acknowledged the response.

Out here, a tumultuous back-and-forth relationship can bring your spirits down after a hard day of hiking. It affects your mentality, making you wonder why you're even out here at all. It makes you second-guess yourself and think that maybe you were *wrong* for going out into the world to reset your life.

Maybe I *was* conceited because I wanted a little recognition from Melody? Maybe I was too dependent on signs of encouragement?

I took my time milling about in the hiker box[12] they had inside, just to pass time.

Along the trail and within hostels or motels, town outfitters, and so on, if a hiker has an abundance of items because he or she, those items can be deposited in these hiker boxes.

The same could be said of those who were getting off of the trail altogether. These boxes were essential to any hiker coming along that looked at the item and said "You know what? I could actually *use* this hatchet and pair of winter gloves that somebody just threw away in here!" Sometimes you could find enough food to last you a week.

---

[12] Hiker Box: Usually found in hostels, restaurants or establishments nearby or close to the Appalachian Trail; these containers usually hold items abandoned by the previous owners (hikers) in lieu of needed room within their backpacks, or for the option of less carried weight.

I had found some gloves that fit perfectly and some tent stakes nobody had wanted as well. This was going to help me with my rainfly, which up to that point I had been using sharpened sticks as stakes for.

I then decided to go through *my* things and figure out what I could drop that was simply worthless weight. There wasn't much I felt too confident in giving up as of yet though, but I was able to drop some unneeded para cord, extra shoelaces, and two aluminum plates I had no use for. I put them in the hiker box for anyone else that wanted them.

I then looked at our denatured-alcohol can stove we had tried to use on top of Blood Mountain and shook my head in disdain. This piece of junk hadn't worked at all in the cold, and I was no longer going to rely on it from here out. Besides, Torry had already purchased a compressed gas can powered cook-kit during our stay in Neels Gap. I placed our homemade one in the box and later heard an excited hiker rummaging through the things come across it and say, "I've been looking for one of these! Awesome!"

Well I hoped he would have better luck with it than *we* had.

Early spring in Georgia's Appalachians was beginning to be a rather awkward weather experience. In fact, it would go down in the books as nearly one of coldest years on record since 1895. Had I known this ahead of time, I can't say I would've been so willing to throw myself out there into the elements.

Not only did it pack a punch against your already dwindling willpower, but it was great at making your morale sink as well.

While Torry and I had planned an eleven-mile day up to Rocky Mountain campground, we weren't feeling too confident when we looked at the cold rain coming down outside.

At our current pace we were set to reach the town of Hiawassee, Georgia in four or five days, where we planned to get a ride to the Blueberry Patch Hostel and receive our first mail drop from my father.

I was expecting my water filter, which I had left at home, as well as a resupply of such things as hygienic items, food, and medicines.

Meanwhile, Torry had tired of the size of his hammock and had asked my father to send him a replacement he had stored at my parents' house among the rest of our care packages we had staged there.

As it was, we were outside on the back porch of our rented cabin when I explained to Torry that I was worried about the cost of the trip thus far. I couldn't afford $165 every five days. I would be broke before I hit Pennsylvania at that rate. But he was quick to remind me that our first few days were a "learning experience."

We learned what we needed and what we didn't.

"Besides," he went on, "I've dropped about four hundred since I've gotten here, and I'm not nearly worried about it at all."

"What the hell did you buy?"

"Food and equipment. I bought some Marmot rain gear that cost a hundred and fifty bucks."

"Good God, man! You know they had some plastic ponchos for a dollar ninety-nine, right?" I informed him.

"That crap won't hold up in that rain out there," he replied.

"I bought the things we needed and nothing else, like our new cook kit that we'll be using. We no longer have to rely on that coke can and denatured-alcohol junk anymore. I made no extravagant purchases for gear that I just up and felt like carrying for no reason at all," he explained. "Besides, why would I want the weight of an object I didn't really need?" he added, looking at the screen of his smartphone for any incoming messages. He had been quite consistent with responding to the never-ending flow of text messages he was getting from his new girlfriend.

Personally, I was aware that my rain poncho wasn't the best in the world, but I had supplemented its worth with a plastic emergency rain poncho for a buck…because I wasn't about to drop a hundred and some-odd dollars for a Marmot rain suit like he had.

All the same, my poncho wasn't all too grand either. It was as useful as an oversized garbage bag and just as suffocating.

As I hiked in it, I began to believe it didn't truly matter *what* you did or what you wore. Either way, you were going to get wet both from sweating and from the condensation building up within the poncho itself.

Having put that poncho on, I had decidedly taken it off again once I'd been hiking in it for no more than thirty minutes. That was because my shirt had become so soaked that I couldn't find any real use for it on *or* off.

CookIN and Woodstock were up and had hit the trail long before Torry and I had. As we hiked, I threw on some Chapstick because my lips had been cracking and bleeding from the cold and the relentless wind.

As Torry was turning in our cabin key, I walked up ahead to the store on the hill where the trail continued on. I sat on the picnic tables out back, where a group of thru-hikers were telling stories and trying to impress a female hiker nearby.

"Yeah, we've already thru-hiked before. You have these fags and losers that come out here and have never hiked a day in their life, getting all worried about some stupid mountain between here and the Whites. They haven't seen *anything* till they get up north," a hiker with a bare-shaved head exclaimed. "So it's pretty bad up north, eh?" I asked, interjecting myself into the conversation.

The guy that had been talking gave an annoyed glance in my general direction and then continued on.

"Anyways, we'll always be nearby. So come looking for me if you need information on anything," he went on.

"Thank you. I may actually take you up on that offer!" the female hiker replied rather enthusiastically.

I realized I had just been completely snuffed out of the conversation, but then again maybe it had been rude of me to even bother asking a question at all?

I wouldn't be lying if I said I was actually a little pissed off by the response though.

"Excuse me. What was your name?" I asked, standing and walking over to the group. The rude thru-hiker's buddy had a blond beard with filthy-looking dreadlocks dangling from his head. He laughed and shook his head slowly, almost as if speaking for his friend's disinterest in my presence.

"I didn't give it," he replied.

"Well, I'm Morris the Cat, and I was just wondering if you could describe the Whites," I said, meaning the White Mountains of course.

He gave an irritated eye roll and sighed. "Whatta ya wanna know, kid?" He was clearly bored and annoyed.

Strangely enough, I actually imagined in that moment smiling and replying, *Oh, nothing in particular!* before impaling him in the eye with my trek pole.

But I never did that, as I usually just lived in my mind whenever such anger overtook me.

"Are they hard? What are the elevation changes like?"

"Are they hard…" His buddy with the beard laughed.

"Yeah, that's what I asked," I was angry now.

"If you make it—and that is *if* you make it—it'll probably be the hardest section on the trail," he said, standing up from the picnic table and throwing his backpack on.

"You wanna head out?" he asked the female friend. I never got any of their names and quickly realized how shitty people could be, even while out on the Appalachian Trail.

"Yeah, I do. I just wanna stop by and say good-bye to Pirate before I do."

"Oh, hey, I met Pirate. He's a pretty cool guy," I said, desperately trying to be social.

"Yeah, he is. Good-bye now," she replied as the other two guys just looked at me and laughed.

As they walked off, I heard the skinhead mutter to the two of them. "He won't make it past the NOC. I guarantee you."

I glared but said nothing as I watched them walk off.

So it appeared there was this "hierarchy" class system that I had come across a few times in my short venture out here into the wilds of the Appalachians. I was new to this, and I didn't know a lot of things, things I would learn for myself and things that hopefully other people would be kind enough to teach me. Yet there appeared to be some kind of convoluted "probationary dropout period" everybody had been talking about. As a result, either section-hikers or former thru-hikers sometimes became snippety or pretentious. I wasn't taken seriously in conversations when expressing my determination to hike and my love of the trail.

Because I was still green and "wet behind the ears" in a sense, there seemed to be no point in getting to know me when there was some monumental statistic clicking behind my head that spoke of my ever-looming failure and inevitable departure from the trail. Yet the last time I checked, this hike was *not* a competition. It was a self-made journey.

I always felt that if you'd thru-hiked the trail before, good for you. What's it ultimately mean? You have experience. You have knowledge. That's great. But what it doesn't do is make you better than anyone else.

Had I been a former thru-hiker, I would *gladly* be a wealth of knowledge to new people, and furthermore, I would not only urge others on but proclaim my belief in their ability to make it. Because at the end, the greatest reason for this hike wasn't solely a few mountain summit views but the incredible people you met and the friends you made along the way. I was almost certain of that.

If you happened to exist as one of those egotistical types that had thru-hiked and now "couldn't be bothered" for sharing information or you scoff at what you deem to be ignorant or naive questions, it doesn't make you cool or tough.

It makes you an asshole.

It was raining as we headed out, and I had sought momentary reprieve while waiting for Torry within the store. Already I was missing our warm cabin with the television and the soft beds and the frozen pizzas and the walls littered with dead animals.

Because at least in there, it had been dry.

There were also no views that day as a result of the heavy precipitation.

Fog crept along ridges, masking any and everything thirty to fifty feet in front of us, leaving only the black, ghostly silhouettes of trees in the distance.

It was dreamlike and reverent.

When we reached Low Gap, we had met up with other thru-hikers, who called themselves Noodles and

Knutt. Aussie, G-man, Molly, Obi, Turtle, and a handful of others were there as well. We had never met most of these individuals before, but we were always open to meeting new people all the same.

It was freezing as Torry and I set up our hammock tents beside the shelter. That was because there was no room inside it.

"What we need heerya is a fy-yah," Noodles said, but he was none too quick to offer any help to build one.

I began to get a sense of the type of person Noodles was once I got around him. He enjoyed ordering Knutt around and getting people to do things for him. He wasn't ashamed to break out some weed, only it was never from his own stash. It was whatever he had hocked off of others.

"There any room in there?" I asked him, referring to the shelter. Rain had steadily begun coming down again, and all I had received from anybody was indiscernible replies or grumbles.

Clearly nobody wanted to share the space.

"You gets ah fire goin', yous got yourself a spot, pal. How's 'bout dat?" Noodles asked.

It wasn't too bad of a request. Not for a dry place to sleep so that the following morning I didn't have to pack up a wet hammock.

So I got to work. I used the techniques that Torry had taught me, and he eventually even joined in to help me once he found me struggling to keep a spark.

We spent the next three hours doing *everything* in our power to finally get a fire going in the rain.

We were praised once we had, and everybody started gathering around the warm flames as the precipitation lightened up.

And *that's* when Robert (otherwise known as Candy Cane) showed up. We hadn't seen him since day one, when he split the cost of a taxi with us from the Gainesville train station and hiked up out of Amicalola Falls.

"Hey, I went to take a piss and found this laying under a pile of leaves," Robert said as he shook a prescription bottle of cough medicine in his hand. The label was practically worn away from the weather, but he handed it to Torry, who read off the ingredient.

"Co…co-something. Wait, codeine? This has codeine in it."

"Where? Lemme see that," Robert said, taking it back.

"You're gonna wanna throw that shit away if you're thinking of drinking it, Candy Cane," Turtle said, looking up at him from the fire. Robert only slipped the bottle back into his pocket and broke out his cook kit.

"I think I wanna go by the name Pack Rat now. Somebody gave it to me, and I think it fits me perfectly," he said as he poured water into a pot and set it down on the fire sloppily. After he did, the pot fell over, dousing the flames.

Dude, what are you doin'?

Aww shit, look what you did, dummy.

Well, there goes our three-hour-built fire.

Just get outta here.

Everybody was firing off at the same time as he apologized and grabbed his pot carefully, avoiding the flames. We all began frantically trying to revive the fire, which had almost completely been destroyed as a result of his carelessness.

I sighed and sat down at the picnic table as Robert went on to say, as if nothing had happened, "I bet no one will dare me to drink some of this cough syrup."

"Nobody's asking you to," I replied, annoyed.

"Yeah, go ahead and drink it. See what happens," Torry exclaimed suddenly. I shot him a look of concern.

Torry grinned back at me.

"You should probably finish it off actually," he added.

"He's just kidding. Don't drink it," I said, pushing the bottle down toward the tabletop.

"I's can do...wut I's wants," he responded, pulling his arm back out of reach.

Robert already had the cap off and was sniffing it. "It doesn't *smell* bad," he said, before taking a swig.

"Disgusting," Obi said, shaking her head and looking away.

"You don't know who had that before you or *what* kind of illness they had, and you're just slurping away on it," Aussie said, slapping his knee and laughing.

Clearly at this point the kid was looking for attention and recognition of some kind. It was blatantly obvious he had wanted us to all pay him mind as he acted like this.

He was silent for the next thirty minutes before he started either exaggerating his symptoms feeling he was losing our attention, or because he was actually experiencing them.

"My fingers are melded together," he said, waving his hands before his eyes.

"Yeah, well, you're probably dying," I said, shaking my head in disbelief.

"Maybe you should take another sip to take the edge off," Torry said. I elbowed him.

"You tryin' to kill the kid?" I asked. Torry just laughed.

It wasn't too soon after that Robert stumbled off uphill, exclaiming, "I don't feel so good..."

The bottle of expired codeine-filled cough syrup dropped from his hand along the side of the trail as he stumbled on.

It would be the last time we saw him for quite a few weeks.

We all ate and played cards on the picnic table in front of the shelter with the fire newly restored and roaring again. Noodles toked up and barked out orders to everybody around him with his thick Chicago accent between taking hits off his bowl.

Also, it appeared that there was no room in the shelter (of course) despite the deal we had made, and so Torry and I went back to our hammock tents we had set up for the evening.

When I *again* awoke to a wet sleeping bag in the middle of the night, I fought the urge to scream in rage. This time it soaked completely through all the layers of my bag, thermal shirts, and down jacket. I had hung the tent lower this time and taken forty-five minutes to ensure the rainfly had encompassed it wholly. Yet still I had awakened within this frigid puddle of slush.

Looking at the rainfly, I figured out why. Condensation from my breath had built up inside the fabric while the outer layer continued to be pounded on for hours by precipitation. Eventually it got the rainfly to sag low enough that it was rubbing back and forth against the bug net on the hammock tent itself.

This in turn caused the rainwater to leak through in a steady stream at my feet and pool up around my butt during the night.

The wind tore through the trees like a freight train all around us. I knew the evening had called for precipitation but this was just insane. There would be 60 percent chance for rain hourly throughout the day, without stop, until the following evening, when it was supposed to turn into snow by the early morning.

Our hike wasn't going to work out for us that well with wet gear and clothes.

So we waited around while everyone cleared the shelter and headed out on their own way the following morning.

"By da way, gentlemen, I likes how yous got dat fire goin' down dere, and I wanted to offer you twos a job. I put t'gether auto shows in Vegas, and I need tah hire 'round t'irty or forty people. Yous interested?" Noodles asked us. I wasn't really interested, because he got on my nerves, but Torry seemed to have bought into the guy's shtick.

"Sure, sounds fun," Torry replied, falling amicably into Noodles' routine as he gave the guy his phone number.

When the shelter was clear, Torry and I went about taking out our things and drying them as best as we could in cold, rainy weather.

Torry, it had appeared, hadn't escaped dry from the downpour either. Only *his* ordeal came about because he had used some crappy tent stakes we both found in the hiker box at Neels Gap, and one had come loose during the wind and rain, flapping about wildly in the night.

"I woke, staring straight up at the sky as the rain was pissing all over me, soaking my down sleeping bag completely along with everything else," he explained to me that morning with a battered, sleep-exhausted look.

So one day out from Neels Gap, after a two-day hiatus, we were already going to take *another* zero day[13] inside the Low Gap shelter.

Even better, it was supposed to snow later that night.

I had never lived a very successful life. Granted, I was able to make it out into the world on my own and live a comfortable existence, but still, I was never very successful in relative terms.

Most of the time, we judge our success on our monetary income, while others who could never achieve that to a complete end tend to live in a surreal world where they base their success on lifetime ventures achieved through travel or family, friends, and other relationships or dedication to a career, no matter how mentally or physically crippling it might be.

---

[13] Zero day: A term used to describe the mileage made by a hiker, who took a day off to rest, resupply or attend to time devouring chores instead of hiking.

I didn't pretend to know myself or what I wanted and at nearly thirty years of age, I sometimes found fear in that fact.

I didn't know what I wanted to achieve. I only knew that whatever the outcome, I did not want to end up regretting my choices.

Out here, in the trees, within the rain and sunshine, I found a peace I had never known before, despite the hardships I had faced.

The wind spoke to me (when not gusting wildly).

The leaves fell delicately from the trees (when not accompanied by falling branches), brushing lightly against my face (when not smashing into my skull), and I felt solace in not knowing what to expect at times (life or death).

It was not a truly comfortable life out on the trail, but nobody ever said it would be.

But when you had nothing in your life before to hold you back, there was symbolism in the feelings that welled up within. Suddenly my fearful thoughts, my status both financial and social, and the things as a civilization that at one time had meant so much to me no longer mattered.

Bills? No.

Insurance premium increases? No thanks.

The next American Idol? Who the hell *cared*?

I might have disliked being cold and walking in the rain, but if I was to concentrate on nothing but the negatives, those warm, sunny days to come would never reach me soon enough. Because it was on those sunny days that I could reflect on that frozen, rainy night and find comfort in the fact that I had gone on.

All the same, our second night at the Low Gap shelter was insanely bitter.

There had been a few more hikers inbound that evening that took up residence in the mostly emptied shelter. Only difference was tonight they were sharing it with Torry and I.

As the lot of us gathered for bed around eight, the wind picked up with gale force, just as it did almost every evening.

It rocked the trees back and forth, creaking and cracking, some even splitting in the icy wind. The shelter rumbled, and thin cracks in the walls were like pressurized gas hoses shooting air through the gaps and against our bodies and faces.

Earlier in the day I had spent four hours trying to maintain a fire in the rain with wet wood and was surprisingly successful. Meanwhile Torry took the day to sleep in his wet down bag inside the shelter to attempt to dry it with his own body heat. Turtle, who had decided on staying another day as well, helped me, and together we were able to stoke the flames high enough for us to cook as much moisture out of our gear as possible. So the day, in a simplistic sense, could have counted as rather productive.

During the night, I awoke to snowflakes blowing into the shelter and melting against my face. The temperatures dropped to the teens there in the gap. I had layered up with every piece of clothing I had brought with me on my journey, which included two pairs of synthetic clothes, a thermal top and bottom, and two pairs of wool socks each on my hands and feet. Yet *still* I was shivering within my seventeen-degree-rated sleeping bag.

As I closed my eyes, quaking, I was able to drift off for about an hour. The wind was incessant, but I somehow was able to imagine it as a large fan lulling me to sleep. It was quiet, if only for a moment, and then the mice staged their assault.

March 28, 2013—Morris the Cat at the
North Carolina/Georgia border.

CHAPTER 5

Learning Curve

⁓

ONE LITTLE GRAY MOUSE RAN up along my body from the tip of my feet. I was constricted inside my mummy sleeping bag, but I was able to buck him off into the wall. As I did, one dashed by my head and another crawled up from my feet again.

I struggled with my crappy zipper, trying to roll back and forth as the rodent clutched on tightly. I bucked my hips hard and sent the mouse hurtling into the guy sleeping beside me. It scurried up his sleeping body, past his shoulders, and then ran toward Torry on the other side of him. They were both fast asleep as this happened. I wanted to call out, "Hey, there's a mouse running on top of you!" but to wake the entire shelter up would've probably made me look like a jerk.

I tugged maniacally at my zipper, unable to get it to budge, and finally thought, *To hell with it*. I jammed one arm up and out of the opening for my head.

Now there I was, one arm locked straight above me, attempting to fight off a vermin assault without waking anybody up. It was ridiculous!

Believe it or not, I was so cold and tired that after the little bastards had all scurried away, I curled my extended arm beneath my head and fell asleep for a couple of minutes.

Well, that was until I felt a curious nip on my right index finger.

This time, I was flipping out. I began bucking back and forth and ramming the guy sleeping next to me as I wildly swung my crazy arm, pinned in the upward position above my head. I was trying to smash the mouse at this point but had lost sight of the creature rather quickly.

I finally pried both arms out and was able to unzip my bag from the outside.

I sat up slowly and inspected my finger for an abrasion but found nothing. I had heard of the diseases these shelter mice possibly carried. Luckily I was fine, and I saw no cut or break in the skin that could have led to infection.

The mice were gone again, at least temporarily, but I was still wild and awake with adrenaline.

As I stared out into the night, illuminated only with a ghostly, waning, silvery light cast by the moon, I felt at peace with the utter silence that started to overtake my senses.

Some way and somehow, I had tuned out the snoring of the other hikers within the shelter and stared out into the silhouettes of the trees, sure something was out there on the edges of the obsidian night.

As I watched, I saw a woman with long, black, flowing hair that might've been nothing more than a shadow cast by branches. I was rather exhausted, after all.

All the same, I felt almost certain that the woman I was imagining was Melody. She appeared from behind one of those trunks with a mysterious smile dancing upon her face, just as she turned to face me. I imagined myself in third person, not just walking out to her but almost being *pulled* by her telepathically as the tips of my toes lightly dragged across the snowy earth. I thought of taking her into my arms as I pressed her lightly against that tree, that black void. The portal from whence she had come.

Kissing her as snowflakes lightly danced along either of our rosy cheeks.

And most important, I imagined her loving me again, all before she vanished back into nothing once more.

As I lay back down, I wondered over conversations and fights we'd had in the past.

How trivial they could be and how much wasted time we had spent on arguing. Only now, I wished I had taken blame for all of them so they could have been better memories.

When I was able to fall back to sleep, it was only after remaining alert for a good hour, still awaiting another mouse attack at any moment.

But I wasn't bothered for the rest of the evening.

When I awoke in the morning, there was an inch of snow on the ground, and I was shivering again. In fact, the very reason I had awakened was *because* my teeth had been chattering. I lay there, with a bursting bladder, looking out at the fresh coat of snow on the base of my sleeping bag. When I could no longer stand it, I sprinted out from my bag and ran out of the shelter barefoot. I skidded quickly through the fallen snow, lost my balance, but managed to regain it quite ungracefully.

As I rounded the rear of the shelter, I stubbed my toe on a rock and fell forward—almost in slow motion—just before I reasserted myself.

I did a quick look to make sure no one was in sight and then jerked open my pants and tore down the zipper.

As I stood behind the shelter relieving myself, I groaned at the pain ricocheting through my big toe and looked down to see a bright-red stream of blood contrasting against the pure white snow.

I had bent the toenail back completely and ripped it out of the corner of the cuticle.

Everybody in the shelter was up and packing, including Torry, and it wouldn't be too much longer before he was heading out ahead with the rest of the group as well.

After I had wrapped my recent injury, our destination was Unicoi Gap, and I was lagging behind that morning mostly because of my newly busted toe.

We hiked uphill to the Blue Mountain shelter through four inches of snow as the wind cut through us once more, numbing our bodies to the core.

Ice had started to form on the beard I had been growing up to that point, as well as on Torry's face beneath his running nose.

Huge gusts of wind kept blanketing us with carpets of snow collected on the branches above us as we stomped through drifts as deep as eight inches in some areas.

With more precipitation and lower temperatures for the night reported, Torry called the Budget Inn down in the little town of Hiawassee, which we had heard ran shuttles from Unicoi Gap.

The only problem was that they were full for the evening.

"Look at the radar," Torry said, handing me his cell.

I brushed aside flakes of snow that were resting on the screen to see that large accumulations of clouds were shifting our way, according to the weather graphic playing out on his phone. In fact, the snow had already started to fall around us tenfold.

Every other hiker had taken up residence inside hotels down in Hiawassee and/or made plans to leave the trail in search of something or somewhere decent to sleep in town.

"You're gonna wanna find a place real quick though 'cause all dey talkin' 'bout on the television is Winter Storm Virgil this and Winter Storm Virgil that. Sooner den' lata all da motels 'round hee'ya gon' be filled up with you people," the man from the Budget Inn had explained over the phone in a thick country accent.

When he referred to me as *you people,* I assumed he meant all of us hikers. It was only a little bit insulting, for some reason, as if we were vagabonds or inconveniences of some sort.

The gentleman over the phone then proceeded to tell us to call a place named Mulls Inn.

We thanked him for the information and hung up.

Torry looked around at the skies momentarily before glancing back at me.

"Whatta ya say?" he asked.

"Is it even a question? I say we go the hell into town. I don't wanna stay out here in this crap." I kicked the snow out from beneath my feet to emphasize the point.

So we continued on down the trail after Torry had called Mulls Inn.

He'd managed to reach a woman over the phone who had explained she only had one room left that she couldn't hold for us very long. She had been used to hikers changing their minds at the last minute and as a result, lost other potential business.

We huffed it down the mountain, slipping on boulders covered in snow and ice or along muddy descents.

At some points I actually almost stepped *off* of the mountain completely. Thank God for my trek poles, which had been there to rescue me. It was hard to see basketball-sized boulders on the trail when so much snow had fallen that everything on the trail had looked flat.

I was surprised we didn't break our ankles, despite rolling them a few times.

Once we had reached Unicoi Gap, there was a white tent in the parking lot and a woman and man waving us over.

Highway 17/75 was rife with traffic from manic drivers hurrying to get home and prepare for what might have very well been a weather lockdown over the next few days.

As we crossed the road, Torry held his nose up in the air.

"Somebody is grilling something," he remarked as his eyes instantly turned ravenous.

Sure enough, it appeared that a local ministry group had set up some trail magic consisting of grilled burgers, hot dogs, and chips in the Unicoi Gap parking lot. They had soda and granola bars and fresh fruit as well.

"This is like *heaven*!" I exclaimed as I ran wildly through the slush of mud and snow in the parking lot with my arms waving like an excited child.

Torry had already reached it before me and was downing a hot cup of coffee with shaking hands. "Oh man, you don't know how good this is right now," he said, holding the steaming black liquid up to me between quaking hands.

I took a quick drink and reveled in the warmth running down my throat.

"Look, they even have hamburgers!" he said excitedly.

"Yes, we have hot dogs too." The group distributing the food laughed at our reactions. We were kids in a candy store, ravenous for sugary sustenance.

"I was thinking to myself that this was just like heaven. Coming down off of that horrible, cold mountain and seeing all of this."

"Well, this isn't heaven, but I can show you how to get there," one of the guys cooking burgers explained, and he handed me a miniature bible and a pamphlet from his church.

I stopped chewing the hamburger I had snagged mid-bite and looked down with confusion as my jaw sort of slacked. I glanced between him the handful of papers he had just given me.

I felt like asking, "Uh, what did you want me to do with this?" but thought that it might sound a bit too rude. Instead, I smiled and held it up appreciatively. When he wasn't looking, I set it back down among the other bibles and pamphlets he had been handing out.

After filling our guts, thanking them immensely and taking their picture for memories of their kindness, Torry and I walked to the edge of the road.

"Think that was a scumbag thing of us to do?" I asked him as he finished the last of the hot dog he had gorged down.

"Whaff?" he asked, with a full mouth of food, completely unaware of anything going on around him except what was tumbling down into his stomach.

"We just stuffed our faces and didn't give a second glance at their religious stuff," I said, feeling just a tad guilty about it.

Torry only shrugged and swallowed the rest of his food before responding. "I don't think they expect every hiker in the world to be religious. They're just doing a good gesture."

"I guess…" I replied with uncertainty.

"Ever hitched before?" he asked me, changing the subject rather suddenly. I only shook my head no in response as he stepped up to the shoulder and threw a thumb out into the frigid air.

When the first passing truck stopped, I looked at him in awe as a confident grin passed over his face and he began jogging toward it.

"No way…" I started to say.

He shouted out to me in mid-jog. "I don't know about you, but I'm headed to Hiawassee for a shower and a clean bed. You comin' or not?" He called back.

"Wait for me!" I shouted, holding onto my backpack straps tightly as I jogged after him.

Our hitch had dropped us off 11.8 miles north in the little Georgian town of Hiawassee.

The name originated from Cherokee dialect as a corruption of the term *meadow* or *savannah* and had been built upon ancient Cherokee trails.

Preserved at one time in isolation, remnants of old English terms and pronunciations were still used by today's generations, passed down by locals and their ancestors. It definitely had an interesting history.

As the driver we'd hitched a ride with dropped us off, he glanced with squinted eyes out at the dilapidated structure rotting away before us, covered in thick blankets of snow. The lot was empty and the second-floor balcony appeared to be sagging slightly.

"Uh, not to be rude, but are you sure *this* is where you guys wanted to stay?" the driver asked us both.

I looked out the window past him and withdrew in disgust just a little. Truthfully I didn't want to stay anywhere *near* that crumbling building. But it was all we could afford and apparently all that was left available in town.

"It's…cheap, I guess," I muttered sadly, as if that was a positive connotation of some sort. I slowly opened the door and got out of the truck.

After thanking the driver for the ride, we each threw our backpacks over one shoulder and trudged through the snow coming down into the office.

Inside, it smelled like cat urine and fifty years of cigarette residue built up on the walls.

"That lady said over the phone that there was only *one room* left," I whispered to Torry.

"It was a trick. She's really going to put us in a dungeon and gas us to death and then stuff our bodies and use us as mannequins," he whispered back.

I smacked his arm in disbelief.

"What?" he asked.

"Do you have to be that morbid? Jesus…"

On a television in the office, the weather channel was going on and on about the temperatures dropping even lower than they had the night before—and suddenly our decision to come into town hadn't looked so bad or self-defeating after all.

That was until we got to enjoy the *awesomeness* that was Mulls Inn.

"*How I Caught Hepatitis on the Appalachian Trail.* Yeah, if I ever write a book, that's probably how I should title it," I said after we had shoulder-rammed the warped door to our room open. Our bed, if you could call it that, was shaped like a *U*, with decades of use apparent in its shape.

"So…how much did we pay for this room again?" I asked.

"Sixty damn dollars. Not including tax," Torry spat bitterly as he threw his backpack to the floor.

"Why does it smell so bad in here?" he asked. I thought momentarily that it was probably us, only I knew we weren't rotting and decaying away either.

"Pretty sure somebody died in here recently. Gross, look. Somebody has been spitting loogies on the wall!" I said, pointing to a corner with dried saliva and mucus drip marks running down the 1970s paneling.

"I really do hope that's only snot," he said with a disgusted look.

The bathroom was overrun with wood ants, and there was black mold on the ceiling and growing onto the shower curtain as well. The bathtub floor was stained and appeared as if it hadn't been cleaned in who knew *how* many years. Unfortunately I didn't find that out until I had taken my first shower and looked down to find my feet swimming in a bathtub of curly black pubic hairs.

"Christ, I gotta get outta here," I said to Torry, who was untying his boots.

"And I thought we asked for *two* beds?"

"Well we got one, and we have to share it. Get over it," he said bluntly.

While I was convinced the bed was probably teeming with lice and bedbugs, I stretched out my sleeping bag atop it all the same and lay down on the cardboard blankets.

"I dare you..." I said to Torry.

"Dare me to what?" he asked.

"Take off that pillowcase and see how long it's been since they've washed the pillow itself," I challenged.

He gave me a stern look and then went back to removing his boots.

"Scared?" I asked.

"I know that if I look beneath that pillowcase and see all those stains on it that I am *sure* are probably there, I'm not going to want to use it. Then at some point I'll probably even end up sleeping on the floor. And I didn't pay sixty bucks to sleep on *that*," he stated, pointing toward the warped flooring and the sticky carpeting that appeared matted with every kind of human excrement and discharge possible, over the decades.

"*How I Spent Sixty Dollars Catching Hepatitis on the Appalachian Trail*," I said as a new title to our book, laughing out loud as Torry joined in.

While in town, Torry and I happened to come across Woodstock and CookIN, who were staying in the exact same motel as we were.

While exploring Hiawassee on foot, we also managed to stumble upon Ryan and Bubblegum again as well. They had all decided to avoid the winter storm headed our way and had snagged rooms in various places throughout the town.

Everything there was packed, and it was funny to see a line of hikers trekking back and forth down the street or hitching a ride everywhere and anywhere they could.

I felt like I had fallen out of normal civilization and had some way, somehow found myself in this traveling band of gypsy walkers.

Woodstock, CookIN, Ryan, Torry, and I went to an all-you-can-eat buffet one evening on what would become our second day in town as we all waited out the storm. It had your run-of-the-mill iceberg-lettuce salad bar and then southern food favorites such as fried giz-zards, fried chicken, and creamed corn.

There was mashed potatoes with biscuits and sausage gravy. They had rolls, cornbread, and collard greens with pinto beans and sliced beets to boot.

I was drooling as I scarfed down the food, barely tasting it. Craving anything other than *more* prepack-aged, dehydrated meals.

Torry and I also saw Stephanie and some of the Warrior Hikers here, and with each passing moment, I realized this was becoming more and more the social trip and less the rugged, somber wilderness I had originally thought it was going to be. And while I had initially wanted to escape civilization, there were times you missed gatherings such as this among new friends, new faces, and new people.

Hell even Wales, Lindsey, and Jenna were there in Hiawassee!

"Can I get you anything else?" our waitress asked after bringing our table the checks. Torry looked up at her with dreamy eyes, practically batting his lashes at her with one of the cheesiest smiles upon his face I had ever seen.

It had to be one of the corniest expressions in exis-tence, and initially I thought he was purposefully doing it to be humorous.

"I think we're good. Thank you," he said, using a smoother voice than I had ever heard him use before in the four years I had known him. I immediately burst into laughter as she walked off.

He looked over at me slowly after checking out her "assets."

"What?" he asked.

"What the hell was *that*?" I inquired, trying to hold back more laughter.

"You wouldn't know anything about it," he said, almost completely dismissing me.

"No really, what was that? Tell me. Were you trying to flirt with her or what?"

"It's all about the *bang-me* eyes, dude. You have to draw them in. That's how you pick up a woman."

"Right. She's not going to think you're flirting. She thinks you're having a stroke." I said as our whole table erupted with laughter. And while Torry proceeded to claim that the only reason it hadn't worked was because I had *ruined his mojo,* I felt I knew otherwise.

Despite our setbacks thus far in the weather, it was starting to become one of the more enjoyable moments of my life, being out there. These people were strangers, but there was some weird connection that passed between us all like we'd been friends our whole lives. We helped each other, hiked together, gave information to each other, and sometimes even shared our resources with each other. We bitched about the trail or reminisced about the beautiful moments or wildlife we'd seen thus far.

Can you imagine?

Becoming friends with people you didn't even know after a week and would more than likely never see again. I was happy for the first time in a long time.

"I only want you to see what I've been up to, Melody," I pleaded into the phone receiver to her.

"John, why do we have to keep going over this? I don't *care* about your stupid hike. If I had it my way, you'd be back home with me, and we would be going on about our lives. Living together and taking care of our dog, Otis," she shouted into the phone.

I pulled the receiver away from my ear as Torry glanced over at me after hearing her yelling from the speaker, clear across the room.

"Really? She hasn't talked to you in a week, and the first thing she decided to do is yell?" he asked. I held my hand up to him and stood, walking outside with the phone pinched back down between my shoulder and ear.

I'd gotten no sleep. It's strange sleeping in a bed when you've gotten used to the cold, hard floorboards of a shelter or a wet hammock for so many days. And I won't even begin to explain how weird it was to share a bed with another man. I'd kept fearing that at some point he was going to imagine I was Pam and place a sleepy, half-conscious kiss upon my neck during the night.

Thank God *that* had never happened.

As I opened the door to our roach motel, I was greeted with a blast of icy wind, snowflakes, and a freshly white-carpeted earth. I sat outside in one of the plastic lawn chairs Mull's had set up on the balcony.

"John, if you want to tell me about your walk, then you can just tell me over the phone," Melody said more calmly.

"I guess I just don't understand what's so wrong with reading the things I wrote. I just want you to know I'm OK and what I've been through," I replied sadly. It was clear that out in the middle of nowhere, I wasn't always going to have phone service with which to engage in long conversations with her. Sometimes there existed just a blip of a signal that gave me time enough to hit Post on a web page when there had been no Internet connection the three seconds prior to posting my blog.

When I tried to explain this to her, she replied, "Well, it will make our conversations that much longer and interesting the next time you call me then."

"OK," I replied, surrendering. There was an awkward silence between us.

"How do you think it makes *me* feel, John?" she asked, her voice cracking slightly. I could almost see the tears in her eyes from hundreds of miles away.

"I don't know…"

"You have all these people on your Facebook page telling you to 'Go on!' or 'You can do it! Don't give up!' and I hate them! I hate each and every one of them! And I am starting to believe that the only reason you're still out there is for *them*."

"But you'd be wrong."

"I don't think I am. I think you're out there because you have a bunch of people saying 'You're gonna make it!' and other inspirational crap, and you're just trying to make them happy."

"Would you believe I'm having the time of my life out here?" I tried to interject, but she completely shut it down, stubborn and unrelenting.

"You *think* you're having a good time. Oh, what, so you're saying that you enjoy it out *there* more than being with the woman you *supposedly* love?"

I sighed, feeling that it was such an immature question that I didn't even want to respond to it.

"I'm gonna go, Melody. If you want to come visit me, you're more than welcome to at any time. But I'm not quitting."

"Fine. Fuck off and go hike!" she shouted into the receiver before hanging up on me.

I glared angrily at the phone for a few minutes and then tried to divert the stress headache coming by smoking a cigarette.

"Everything cool, man?" Torry asked as he came out of the room minutes later.

"Yeah, great. Melody hates me again. Whatta ya know? It only took a week this time," I replied glumly.

"Well hell, who doesn't hate you? You're a complete piece of shit," he said, lighting his own cigarette and taking a slow drag. I looked up at him, expressionless.

"I'm just kidding, buddy," he assured me, laughing and patting my shoulder.

"Don't worry. What is she mad about anyways? That you're still out here?" he asked me.

"She feels I abandoned her. I don't know...do you think this was selfish of me?"

He took a seat in the empty lawn chair beside me as he contemplated what I had just asked him.

"I think you could look at what we did and call it selfish, yes. Because we all have somebody out there, back at home that generally loves us and cares for our well-being. Say for example you had never met Melody. Who's to say that your mother doesn't miss you...which clearly after calling your parents, you see she does."

"So what are we supposed to do? Sit around our whole lives and placate *others* while never living out our dreams?" I asked.

"When you have a family, a wife and kids, then yes. Your whole world is about shaping *their* lives. Giving *them* the best that you can offer, even if it's at the sacrifice of your own happiness. But you don't have a wife, and you don't have any kids. Sad to say, but Otis is a dog, and as much as you and Melody mutually love him, *he's a dog,*" Torry said, letting out a stream of smoke that was indistinguishable from the fog in the frigid air.

"All I wanted to do was escape everything I knew to be 'life' at that moment in time. I was tired of drinking myself stupid and feeling depressed and alone, and I hated my job. We worked with some amazing people—don't get me wrong—but I felt like I was living in a radioactive cement tomb," I tried to emphasize to him.

But I didn't need to try because he had worked there too. Although almost three years shy of me, he had been there long enough to feel the exact same way I had.

"A wise man I once knew asked the question, 'Do you want to die wondering what if you could have done something? Or do you want to die saying *'I remember when I did…'*?" He quoted me with a grin.

"Yeah well, that guy sounds like an idiot," I replied cynically. He laughed.

"She'll come around, John. If she loves you like she proclaimed so wholeheartedly while you two were together, believe me, she'll come around."

The day that we had wanted to leave for the trail, Mother Nature held no reserve in showing us she was rather bitter, cold, and unreasonable. We found a room at the Budget Inn for $50.95 a night as a result of her sporadic behavior.

Not only was it fifteen dollars cheaper than Mulls had been, but it was actually a lot cleaner as well. Better than that, they offered a shuttle back to Unicoi Gap where we had left off.

As we were hikers and we had no car, we began the half-mile hike up the main strip until we reached the motel. It was packed with desperate hikers looking to buy or split rooms with somebody. These were people who had *just* come down off of the mountain.

Weary, envious hiker eyes fell upon Torry and I as word had already spread of *some hiker that had called and reserved a room.*

"You looking to split a room with any of them, you can only take in two, and it'll be an additional ten dollars per person," the manager explained to us.

I looked outside at the twenty or more people eyeing Torry and I as they stood with their packs by their feet.

And though they were clearly hoping we would come out from the office and say *All right, who wants to share a room?* I knew none of them and had no desire to ask such a question.

I looked at Torry. "Do you wanna split a room with any of those guys?"

"Not really. If it was Woodstock or CookIN out there, I'd say sure. But I don't know those people, and I don't want to have to worry about leaving my things and someone stealing from me and then jumping back on the trail. We'd never catch them."

I liked Torry, if only because we had the same thought process almost 70 percent of the time.

As we stepped outside, I was already getting offers of people wanting to stay with us.

"I mean I'd be happy to give you an extra ten dollars. I just need a place to keep my things. Ya know?" I was asked immediately.

I smiled nervously, nodding my head as I tried to push in between the clusterfuck of people.

"Hey, forget him. I'll give you twenty bucks, my friend," another guy said, tugging at my pack. I gently brushed him away though.

Eventually they drifted aside as the manager came out from the office and informed them all that they had better find a room somewhere else before everything was closed up in town for the night.

On our way to our room, we bumped into Lindsey, Jenna, and Wales again, who had hiked on to Dicks Creek the day before and had then taken a shuttle back to this very same Budget Inn. They were seventeen miles ahead of us now along the AT.

Meanwhile, Woodstock and CookIN, who had headed back out to the trail that same morning, would be seventeen miles ahead of us after tonight themselves.

As evening rolled in, Torry and I decided to eat at Georgia Mountain Buffet, under the recommendation of our buddy Bubblegum. And boy, what a mistake that had been.

For $10.53, these were your choices—let me repeat—these were *all* your choices:

* biscuits
* cornbread
* fried chicken livers
* fried hamburger steak
* fried squash
* straight-from-the-can pie filling with crust on top
* instant mashed potatoes (I know the difference after being on the trail and eating it every day!)
* gravy from a can
* oven-baked, bland chicken, not fully cooked

To top it all off, there was your run-of-the-mill iceberg-lettuce salad bar.

That's it. There was your buffet. Never had I wanted to see a Golden Corral more before in my life.

"Do you think the chef in there even *cares*? There's no seasoning on this chicken at all. They didn't put garlic, pepper, salt...*nothing*. They took frozen chicken breasts, put them on a pan, and baked them," I said, peeling off horrifying globs of fat and gristle from the Grade D piece of meat.

"You see, they've got it down to a science. They make the chicken bland and disgusting so that you won't go back up for more," Torry said. I doubled over in laughter. A few of the passing waitresses and other customers looked our way before going back to minding their own business.

"When they were hiring, they asked the chef, 'Do you know how to cook?' and the guy replied 'Duh...I know how to throw eggs at the wall,'" I replied.

"You're hired!" Torry said. We both burst out into cackles again, as if we were the only ones in the restaurant.

When we paid the cashier, she asked us how we had enjoyed our dinner.

Torry replied in a dull tone, "It was food. I guess."

I tried to hold back laughter and felt tears welling up in my eyes. I wasn't even sure why I had thought the whole experience had been as funny as it was.

We left, limping down the sidewalk with strange stomach cramps and loosening bowels from what we had ingested, in desperation to get back to our room for the evening.

Torry and I stood in the laundry room at the Budget Inn as Lindsey brought in her clothes to wash. He passed me a glance before letting his eyes quickly fall back down to his phone, which, like most people these days, he seemed to live on. Still, his expression had said it all with nothing more than that mischievous glance he had given me in the blink of an eye.

She was cute; there was no denying that. The look Torry had given me as she placed her things in the washer spoke volumes without him ever uttering a single vowel. A pair of her panties fell on the floor in front of him, and he cast an unabashed look at her as she snatched it quickly, blushing quite a deep shade of red.

Torry was in a unique sort of place when it came to the binds of a relationship. Fresh out of a marriage, he was energetic and eager to hop back out into the world of dating again as if the act of "moving on" (with all of those "benefits" in tow) was the only thing to live for anymore. It appeared some life-draining curse of age and fatigue had been lifted from him. And while he and I had both traded words over the past week about how cute we mutually found Lindsey to be, deep down we both were never truly interested.

She was too young for Torry, who was in his midforties, and I was still too heartbroken over Melody to seriously pursue some random woman hiking the Appalachian Trail.

Regardless, there seemed to be this primal, competitive male nature arising within us both.

"Not without a fight," my expression said to Torry, challenging him in some imaginary male-libido-driven contest that had been subconsciously raging beneath our calm demeanors.

There was no reason to do this. If anything, I only felt confident because I didn't fear failing at the prospect of interesting this young woman with the emerald-green eyes anyhow. And out here I felt free in the sense that I could do or be or act however I wanted because this had become *my time*. As long as I wasn't hurting anybody in the process.

"Weather says we're looking at a few days of sunshine not too far off from today," Torry said, practically kissing the screen of his Droid with his eyes. Lindsey looked back at the sudden conversation starter with a momentary hurried and unsure response.

"Oh? Well I'd say it's about time," she replied, pouring an individual load of detergent powder into the washer.

"Torry really likes to try to look like a tough guy, walking around with that dorky knife hanging off his side," I said, despite the fact it had nothing to do with his conversation starter whatsoever. She passed me a confused look and then burst out in laughter.

"Uh…OK," she said, unsure whether I was serious or not. I left my smirk on my face all the same, and Torry's skin turned beet red as he laughed it off.

"Yeah, but it's a pretty lime-green color," she said, deflecting if only a little in his defense as she pointed to the half-filet knife, half-spark igniter hooked to Torry's belt loop.

I wanted to go on to say, "Seems like a sign of insecurity to me," but I knew that saying such a thing would appear too aggressive too soon.

"I would have gotten it in a tactical black, but if I had dropped it in the forest, I didn't want to lose it," Torry went on.

"Oh, that's a good idea," Lindsey added.

I rolled my eyes.

"See, what Morris the Cat doesn't understand is, if we come to a situation or a complication where we need to use my knife, he can't just *eat* the problem away," Torry replied, gesturing toward my stomach as I bit my bottom lip and nodded my head slowly.

"That so? That's what I do, huh?" I asked, smiling between gritted teeth.

"Yeah, it is," he assured me, turning his back to me rather dismissively and joining Lindsey in a laughter session on my behalf.

"By the way, did Torry ever tell you he was geriatric?" I asked Lindsey, who was already chuckling.

"Hey, Gramps, how old are you getting to be now, ya' raggedy piece of sh—"

"Hey! No bad language in front of the nice lady," he said, gesturing to Lindsey. "I tell you, kids these days. They just have no respect for their elders…or…well, their own bodies." He indicated my gut again.

There was another round of laughter on *my behalf* and when Torry winked at me, I nodded with a shameful smile and a momentary concession of defeat. I stepped outside and made my way back toward our room to grab some quarters for our laundry. We would need the change to dry our clothes. I stole a quick look at the television we had left on the Weather Channel, which was talking about the dismal days we had ahead of us. *Is this crap* ever *gonna clear up?* I thought, turning the television off.

Just as I was about to head back out the door, Torry stepped through rather abruptly.

"Let me get those quarters. I can finish our laundry," he exclaimed as he held out his hand in front of me like a beggar.

I smiled passively and sat down slowly on my bed. I jingled the change in my palm tauntingly.

"Your *fuck-me* eyes are gonna do nothing but creep her out, old man. Didn't work on the waitress. Won't work on her," I said.

"Come on, dude. The only reason it didn't work was because *you* screwed it up by laughing at me."

I mocked him by batting my eyelashes cartoonishly. "Hi, I'm Torry. Wanna have sex with me? I'm a creepy old man with a pocket full of Viagra," I said in an equally cartoonish voice.

"You …" he trailed off, annoyed as he walked out the door. There was a hint of irritation and anger in his eyes, if only briefly.

I walked back to the laundry room behind him to find Lindsey had gone.

"Where'd she go?" I asked, closing the door behind us.

"She's calling the police because you're clearly the stalker type," he said sardonically. I rolled my eyes.

It wasn't too long after Lindsey had gone that Torry and I were talking about the trail ahead and the town of Hot Springs.

I informed him that Melody and I had been conversing throughout the day once again, despite the argument we'd had the night before, and she had expressed possible interest in visiting me once we had reached that area. I was looking to take a couple of days off and possibly reignite the flame that had been waning between her and me.

This was perfect for Torry as well though because it left opportunity for him and his own girlfriend, Pam, to take a few days off for themselves. He had explained this *overwhelming attraction* he had for this woman, but still I had yet to see what she had looked like or know anything about her.

"I just hope things work out between Melody and me. It bothers me that she doesn't seem to care much at all about this hike. It's literally maddening," I complained, searching for any sort of comforting string of words from him.

"If she is willing to drive out here to visit you, John, there's gotta be a reason. If she's talking about ten hours round trip, maybe there *is* something there after all," he said, face buried in his smartphone.

Little did I know at the time that Torry was going to use that bit of information as ammunition in the moments to come.

"Do you think I should shave my beard for her? She doesn't like it much. Says it's *gross* and *icky* and that she thinks it'll scratch her face."

Torry was barely in the real world as he watched a YouTube video playing on his Droid.

"I'm also worried about ticks," I added, just as Lindsey walked back into the laundry room.

"Ticks in your beard? No, they like places like the backs of your legs, your head, or your armpits," Torry replied.

Lindsey added, "I thought you said *tits* when I walked in. I wasn't sure what the hell you guys were talking about." We all laughed.

"Damn, girl, I don't know what you're talking about, but I like it," I said in a pestering voice.

"Hey, guys, I'm worried about *tits in my beard*," Torry said in a lisping accent, mocking me now by flipping his hand in a feminine gesture as they both had a good little laugh. I angrily joined in at my own expense.

Lindsey proceeded to proclaim, like others had in the past, that she didn't feel comfortable calling Torry by his trail name, Stupid. She went on to say, "Besides, Torry is a great name."

I was losing this battle quick.

I informed her pugnaciously that he was some kind of weird, verbal sadomasochist and that he got off every time somebody called him by that name.

Torry responded, "So Morris, what were you saying again about Melody coming to meet you in Hot Springs?" His eyes flashed *check and mate,* coupled with a taunting smile.

I gritted my teeth as I tried to think of what to say.

"I, uh…yeah…she'll be coming…and we'll be… uh…spending a couple days together," I replied, clearing my voice and trailing off.

Lindsey looked closely at us both, back and forth.

Tory: 1, John: 0.

"I would've won. I should've brought up Pam," I said, reminiscing.

"You wouldn't have gotten her number. You're not quick enough, kid." Torry said, scruffing my hair as we hopped into the shuttle leaving the Budget Inn behind.

It was nine in the morning, and we were in a large van packed with twelve other hikers. Most of them were people we didn't know who had caught up to us in the recent string of days we had taken off.

The old vehicle struggled going uphill in route to our destination but surprisingly made it there all the same. There were only four hikers going to Unicoi Gap: me, Torry, and a couple with their dog. The rest were headed on to Dicks Creek.

I was surprised at how many people were skipping this section for whatever reason. They expressed no interest in the next seventeen miles of trail whatsoever.

"But I thought they called themselves purists?" I asked out loud.

The woman with the dog and boyfriend gave me a leering look. "God, you're not one of *those* types are you?" she asked me, as if I knew exactly what she was talking about.

"Uh, one of what types?"

"Dude, we're talking about over two thousand miles. Besides, what do *you* care if they skip a few here or there?"

she asked me angrily. Her boyfriend, noticing the tone change in his girlfriend's voice, glanced over at me.

"I *don't* care. I'm just asking. They said they were purists, and...you know what? Never mind." I stopped trying to defend myself, not even knowing *why* I had started to begin with. I hadn't said the comment to be rude. I was simply inquiring as to why people who had been so dedicated days before about walking every inch of the trail suddenly didn't give a damn about what sections they decided to skip. I wasn't chastising them. Frankly I couldn't care less *what* they did.

The girl just shook her head, and the rest of the ride was fairly silent from there on out.

When the four of us were dropped off, I watched the couple plow on ahead of us, clearly in a rush to leave us in the dust.

"Lindsey and Wales are two days ahead of us. I'm guessing CookIN and Woodstock probably are day ahead as well," I said, watching as the couple and their dog climbed the first ridge of the day.

Torry nodded his head slowly. "How many miles you wanna do?" There was a positive tone in his voice.

I shrugged sheepishly. He knew *my* answer. Even if I never gave him a distinct number, he knew it would always be low. "I don't care. How many miles do you feel like doing?" I asked him.

So on his decision, which eventually turned mutual once I'd given in, we had decided to attempt seventeen miles straight through to Dicks Creek.

He took off ahead of me as I looked down at my phone and saw a text message I had received from Melody.

"where r u?" it asked.

"middle of nowhere," I replied. The text was followed up by an automated message stating that my dialogue had not been sent through because of signal loss. I shut off my phone and began my first ascent.

Halfway up the first mountain I realized I had forgotten my phone charger and extra battery in the outlet behind the dresser back at the Budget Inn in Hiawassee. Unfortunately, while it was a good idea to retrace my steps and make sure I had packed everything prior to leaving a place, I found I was usually always only doing this once I had hit the trail again.

Once I reached the first summit out of the gap, I called the Budget Inn and told the manager my predicament. "Well, as I sees it...ya gotch' ya'self two options. Donate it to tha other hikers, or I's can ship it to ya."

"You'd ship it to me for free?" I asked incredulously. It wasn't until after I had hung up that I realized how naive I must've sounded to the manager.

"Well, not to some post office, no. But I can have it shipped to the Budget Inn in Franklin or the Three Eagles Outfitters there for free. Our owner, Ron, deals between the businesses."

I wasn't sure how far away Franklin was from where I currently stood, and I sure as hell didn't know who the heck Ron was, but I accepted the offer all the same. After I thanked him and hung up, I received another text from Melody:

"Ignoring me won't make me read your stupid journals."

I sighed, irritated with her and technology both at once. I found it unreasonable and insane how I could have a conversation with someone over the phone, but now standing in the exact same spot minutes later, I couldn't even send a text message out for some reason.

Throughout the day, I walked up and down ice-covered slopes with muddy descents that left me wishing I had protective wet gear to put on. I couldn't count on two hands how many times I had slipped and fallen into cold, muddy slush.

At times, some of the descents were scary because the trail literally looked as if a herd of five thousand buffalo had walked it in the rain. The mud was at least four inches deep in some places, completely swallowing my feet.

For every three steps we took, we were sliding a step back on inclines, which began to get rather taxing by midday.

The sun was bright and shining all the same for the first time in over a week. Snow *was* melting and things were thawing out for the time being, until night draped across the landscape later that evening. The clear, blue skies welcomed us with opened arms despite the cold wind snaps that blasted us around every corner.

I arrived an hour after Torry had already gotten to the gap.

The sun was setting, and it was just before dusk as eighteen-wheelers blared down Highway 76.

I looked around for a privy, but nothing was available.

"Do we even have water here?" I asked somberly. My back was aching, and my feet felt like they had been smashed with sledgehammers.

"Yeah, the ditch down there," Torry said, pointing to a small bathtub-sized collection of trash-filled gray water. McDonald's cups and bloated garbage bags sat half-submerged beneath the gelatinous liquid. My stomach rolled, until he laughed at me.

"I'm kidding. The stream's right next to us, moron." He pointed toward a gushing creek coming down off of the mountain. I had been so weary from the seventeen-mile *death march*, I felt a slight bit delirious. I hadn't even noticed it upon arrival.

After hydrating, I ate a quick dinner with leftover bread CookIN had given me back as far as Gooch Gap. I made two pepperoni-Jimmy-Dean-garlic-summer-sausage-and-cheddar-cheese sandwiches.

To somebody starving after a full day of hiking, they were amazing.

"Who's that guy?" I asked Torry, pointing toward a tent just a few feet away from where we sat on the picnic tables.

"Strider, I think he said his name was," he replied, taking a hit from his cigarette while playing some game on his smartphone.

"He hiking the whole thing?" I asked. Torry was in another world and simply nodded his head in response, though I found it doubtful he had ever even heard my question at all.

As it was dark, I quickly set up my hammock tent on the hill. After looking again for a privy and finding there was none available, as a second choice I followed trails of uncovered toilet paper pieces out of the gap just a bit, to a high embankment maybe thirty feet from the highway.

Signs that this had been bulldozed many years ago were still prevalent, most notably by the ruts still frozen in the earth. But trees had started to retake this parcel of land, and five-to-seven-year-old pines had already started growing.

As cars drove by, I tried to confidently *do my business,* asking myself if those drivers knew that just a few feet away there was some guy using the restroom on the side of the road.

Afterwards, I stripped my clothes and took a "hiker bath" comprised of disposable Wet Ones wipes. I then hid the evidence by burying them with my droppings, and then sticking a twig out of the mound in the earth, thus marking the land mine for the safety of future hikers. When I reached camp again, Torry had already retired to his hammock, and I was left alone with the pimpled ass cheeks of a stranger waving his crack back and forth from the door of his ground tent.

"How, um…are you?" I called out, averting my eyes slowly.

The heavyset guy turned around, exposing a patchy-bearded face with horn-rimmed glasses.

"Oh, I'm fine," he replied in a nasally voice before turning back to whatever it was he was doing inside his tent. He tugged roughly at what I assume was his sleeping bag and then crawled back inside.

"That's nice. I'm good too," I muttered quietly to myself as he zipped up his tent and vanished inside.

Guess he wasn't much for conversation.

It was too bad we didn't have phone service here, if only because the Blueberry Patch Hostel was right down the road about eight miles or so according to my AT guide book. They took donations in exchange for stay, which included their staple breakfast of blueberry pancakes.

After our seventeen-mile day, my knees were screaming with pain, and a hot shower would've done me good. And though I had just eaten, I had a hankering for some blueberry pancakes dripping with maple syrup as well and a glass of cold milk.

I swallowed a handful of ibuprofen and attempted to go to sleep, though the aching wouldn't let me.

As we were set up beside a highway, the sleep was easier said than done. Every time a semi went by, I sat up wide awake as it gunned the gas going uphill.

It made for quite the miserable night.

"Ugh, go away..." I groaned at the sun, pulling my sleeping bag up over my head. It was March 28, and thick orange rays had started cutting through the trees just above the ridgeline and zeroed in directly on my face.

When I eventually crawled out of my hammock, I swung my legs out of the Velcro opening and stood slowly, only to realize I had forgotten I had set up my hammock on a downward slope of a hill.

I quickly slid on the loose, thick layer of pine straw and landed hard on my ass, coasting twenty feet down to the bottom on both butt cheeks.

"Today's *going to be great!*" I shouted, with blatant sarcasm.

That morning, my feet felt like I had been stepping on broken glass the last seventeen miles of the day prior. I had no idea how I was going to manage hiking again at all.

All the same, I collected myself and began packing my things.

The Blueberry Patch Hostel, which had been in operation since 1991, had shuttled people off at nine thirty that very morning.

When the owner of the hostel showed up again a little later, Torry and I found ourselves crossing paths with Woodstock and CookIN as they were getting dropped off onto the AT. They were as surprised (as much as I was) that we had both busted out seventeen miles just the day prior.

"Let's be honest, it's not all *that* grand," I said, trying to sound humble, though inside my mind it felt good to have my ego stroked just a little bit.

While Woodstock and CookIN were hitting the trail that very morning, Torry and I still had to receive our first mail drop sent from my father.

"It's too bad you didn't get to stay there. They had incredible pancakes," Woodstock said.

He saw the saddened, hungry expression on my face and quickly restated, "But I've uh…I've had…better…I mean…"

I smiled at him and his attempt to comfort me.

"We'll catch up to you guys later," I said, patting him on the shoulder. After we wished each other well, they were gone.

Torry and I hopped into the hostel owner's Jeep Cherokee and asked for a ride before we'd given him a chance to say no. Upon arrival, there was little to say this was a hostel of any kind, at least from the look on the outside. It simply appeared to be a house with a garage on the side of the road and expansive farmland extending beyond that. Had we decided to try and find it on our own without Internet signal or maps, we'd have simply thought it was somebody's house and kept on walking by.

We slowly opened the door to the garage as the owner said, "I'll just be inside. When you both are ready to go, let me know."

As I looked about the garage-turned-bunk-room-and-kitchen, *I didn't want to leave*. The heat was on high, and I was already feeling sleepy just standing there.

There was a rules notice on the wall. This was a Christian place, and therefore alcohol, smoking, and cursing were not allowed. "The hell if I'm staying somewhere I can't have a cigarette," Torry said as he looked around the room.

I gave him an annoyed look for his crass comment.

"How about showing a little respect, asshole?" I whispered hoarsely at him. He proceeded to grab my chin and turn my face towards the sign hanging upon the wall.

"No cursing, *asshole*," he said with a chuckle as I jerked my face free from his grip, and shoved him away.

We retrieved our drop box from a stack of *many* others and slowly and excitedly went through it, as if we didn't already know the contents inside.

I looked depressingly upon some garlic, grits, and squid jerky I had vacuum-sealed together. Don't even ask me what I had been thinking at the time I'd thrown it all together. It was cheap, it had carbs and protein, and that was all I knew. I figured if I was truly hungry, I would have thrown it down without complaint.

But as Torry and I eyed it warily, we decided to toss it into the hiker's box.

"Dude, check this thing out. Somebody is about to get one hell of a present," Torry exclaimed as he removed his hammock tent from his backpack and tossed it into the hiker box as well.

"What the hell are you doing!" I asked, looking at him like he was a complete madman.

"Remember? I had your parents ship me *this* hammock instead," he said as he removed another Hennessy

Hammock from the bottom of the prepackaged box. "The other one was way too small." he said, spinning the new hammock in his hand.

Torry, upon originally purchasing his tent, had received a complimentary "cub hammock," which was made for children with the purchase. His plan had been to extend the wear and tear on his new hammock by utilizing both. But what became obvious in time was that he was too tall for the cub hammock. I had forgotten that Torry had asked my parents to ship it, and as a result he was now tossing the cub hammock into the hiker's box for anybody else that would've wanted it.

"Don't you want to ship it home? Have it for later?" I asked.

He only shook his head. "If somebody else can get some use out of it, let 'em."

As we packed our food bags, we somberly realized how heavy the contents were. It was weird because initially you seem to think you're going to be starving out in the wilderness, but your first few weeks out on the trail, you learn it can be quite easy to lose your appetite out there. At the end of a day, sometimes you're just so tired and in so much pain you want nothing else but sleep, despite the fact that you *know* you should be eating something. Then when morning comes, sometimes after slipping out from beneath a comfortable sleeping bag, you find yourself too cold to sit in one place or go through the hassle to make and eat something warm for breakfast.

I still had more than enough food from starting out back at day one to make it five more days north without needing a resupply. Even then, that was only if I was eating every two hours. We didn't really need the food but took most of it anyway. What we couldn't pack out, we placed in the hiker box for anyone else that could use it.

Doing that made me immediately think of Robert—previously known as Candy Cane, now known as Pack Rat—who we had initially met at the start of our journey. He had spoken of how he had lived out of hiker boxes most of the time and the food that had been left behind in them.

When I saw the mixture of garlic powder, grits, and squid jerky we'd left behind, I felt my stomach roll.

I found a better place for them.

In the trash. Nobody, no matter how desperate, should have to suffer through such a disgusting meal.

As the weight of our packs increased to almost another third of our overall weight, we came to the realization that one, you don't need nearly as much food as you think you will; and two, it costs way too much to ship things through the US Postal Service.

Reading the drop-box receipt plastered to the outside of the box, we'd found that it had cost my parents twenty-one dollars to send that package out to us.

Part of the reason Torry had left his old hammock tent in the hiker box was *because* of the shipping price. I left behind the protein powder and candy bars that were far too heavy to carry as well. I left packets of condiments such as mustard, mayo, ketchup, and honey too.

As we were headed back out with our spines already aching, a young girl that couldn't have been older than twenty-two or twenty-three walked in. I had to look twice because she appeared to be a taller version of my ex-fiancée, Wendy. She was walking about barefoot, and her feet appeared to be absolutely mangled, as if a bear had chewed on them for a couple of hours and then she'd decided to walk through mud.

"Christ, what the hell happened to you?" I asked, hunching down and getting a closer look at her badly bandaged feet.

"Just blisters and a few cuts is all," she said.

"My God, do your boots have nails jutting out inside of them or what?" I asked as Torry just raised his eyebrows, inspecting just as closely as I was.

"Well, I'm trying to hike barefoot. I'm just waiting for my feet to adjust," she explained.

Was this lady insane?

Her name was Wrong Way, and it just so happened that she was originally from Durham, North Carolina, which was no more than a forty-five-minute drive from where I used to live. She had been going to the North Carolina School of Math and Science and was taking a few months off to hike the AT. Because of bad blisters, she was going to take another zero day there at the hostel before hitting the trail once more. But from the look of her feet and the damage done to them, I was pretty sure she was going to need a lot more time than that.

"You know it's been snowing, right?" I asked, still in awe and disbelief that she would do this to herself.

"I know…and I'm prepared for those days…"

"And what about hookworms or stepping in people's shit or—" Torry began.

"Probably all things I could just as easily find in the water we drink and don't purify," she said.

Well, aside from a few times where the water was coming directly out of the earth or the side of a rock wall, I had *always* purified my water with Aqua Mira, iodine tablets, or by boiling it, as had Torry.

"You sure you don't wanna stay here a night?" I asked Torry suddenly, who only shook his head, as if he was dealing with a thirty-year-old man-baby. "Did we come out here to hike? Or bounce from hotel to hostel to inn to motel room?"

"I guess you're right," I muttered, shame-faced. I'd wanted to hear more of Wrong Way's story, but I guess I'd just have to hope I met her again someday.

"You guys take care out there," the girl with the bad feet said as we headed out. I stopped and slowly turned back to her.

"How did you get your name?" I asked.

"I woke up one morning and found I was hiking south, in the wrong direction. Somebody had to remind me which way I was supposed to be going," she said with an embarrassed laugh.

.

April 3, 2013—Wales, 2.3 miles south of
the NOC in North Carolina.

CHAPTER 6

Into the Cold

WE GOT A RIDE BACK up to Dicks Creek from the Blueberry Patch Hostel owner, and I gave him a ten-dollar tip. Initially he shied away, saying he didn't need the money, until I insisted. In return, he asked if he could pray for either of us before setting out.

Torry and I were not outwardly religious, but we had no objection to prayer unless it had in some way, shape, or form become suffocating or mandatory to us. We had a mutual feeling toward religion. As long as you weren't *forcing* your ideologies or opinions or theocracies down our throats, we would get along with you just fine.

We stood outside in the parking lot by the busy highway as cars flew by, holding each other's hands in a circle. I felt just a little bit awkward only because I hadn't done anything like this since I was a child.

"Lord, I ask that you be with Morris the Cat and his friend…Stup—" he began but stopped.

Deep down I'd really wanted to hear him call Torry by his trail name, Stupid, in the middle of his prayer. Only the hostel owner quickly changed the sentence.

"God, I ask you to look out for both of these gentlemen on their journey along the Appalachian Trail."

I looked up at Torry, who was holding back a chuckle, which in turn was starting to make me chuckle.

"We ask that you keep them safe within your arms as they seek the answers to the questions they have and the problems they yearn to solve. In Jesus's name."

"Amen," we all said at once.

We started off our day strong, but while Torry appeared to have gotten his trail legs and blazed ahead, my knee was screaming angrily at me, *Not yet, bro!*

Torry almost regularly hiked ahead, while I was always a mile or so behind him.

He was definitely moving, especially despite the trail being so brutal. While we had wanted to go further than nine miles, it was all we could see to knock out for the day. We had randomly been looking at the guide off and on, but only for water sources or for shelters toward the end of a day to see where we would be setting up for the evening.

When we passed the Georgia–North Carolina border, we were actually rather surprised. We came around the corner to a tent city—and low and behold, there was CookIN.

"Hey! How ya doin', guy?" I asked as we walked over to him. It was good to see a familiar face as we shook hands. "Where's Woodstock?" I asked, looking around.

"He wasn't ready to stop. He went on ahead to the next campsite," CookIN replied as he scratched his Santa-like beard.

"He went on to Bly Gap?" I asked, but CookIN shook his head.

"*This* is Bly Gap. I'm not sure if he was pushing past Standing Indian Mountain today or not."

I nodded my head slowly, as Torry had already vanished to search for a place to set up for the evening.

The water source here was little more than a trickling mud stream, which you had to cross en route to the campsite. Lots of hikers had carelessly stomped through it on their way to camp, muddying it up and making for quite the debris-filled drink. And while I now had a purifier, as I looked upon the filthy stream that people had cleaned their plates and bowls out carelessly in, I found I would've rather grabbed some snow for water rather than drink from *that*.

Though it was cold outside, I used what I assumed to be the cleanest part of my sweat-soaked synthetic shirt to filter some of the debris from the snow water that I was trying to purify. No point in clogging a thirty-dollar filter so soon.

The following morning started like most do, with Torry and I stumbling from our hammock tents long after most of the other, more determined hikers had already left.

"Lookin' to be a miserable day," a hiker that went by the name Captain Dan called out to me, with a purposeful smirk. The skies were dark gray.

"You gettin' a room in Franklin?" he asked me as I rolled my sleeping pad into a ball and stuffed it into a compression sack.

"I don't know, maybe. Why?"

"Your friend…Shithead, no, I mean…Dumbass, er *whatever* his name was, said something about it," he replied, throwing some leftover trash into a Ziploc baggy and then pushing it into a side pocket.

"You mean *Stupid*?" I asked.

"Yeah, Stupid. I'll never understand why the hell he'd call himself that," Captain Dan said wonderingly. "Anyways, if you're looking for a good place to stay, see me when you get to Franklin and I'll hook you up with a reduced price at the Holiday Inn. I happen to know somebody there."

I nodded my head and thanked him. The idea was nice, but I was still mulling over the last text message I had received from Melody the night before.

She had been angry that it had taken me so long to get back to her. When I explained that I didn't always have a phone signal to have long text-message conversations with her, she had replied, "It sounds like you're no longer trying. Maybe I really should give up on us."

"All right, Cat, we'll be seein' ya," Captain Dan said, saluting me before throwing his backpack on and heading up the foggy path north.

He had a rather interesting story, Captain Dan.

He had spent ten years in a maximum-security prison for smuggling marijuana into the United States when he had been a yacht-boat captain. He had no reservations about telling us he had hocked away quite a bit of loot from those days where he had funneled his money into offshore accounts so that when he got out of prison he had the freedom to take adventures like hiking the AT or whatever else he had wanted to do with the rest of his life.

Like I said, *all* walks of life hiked the Appalachian Trail.

It would be an hour later when Torry and I left. While today would be marred by an additional six miles than we had done the day before, the terrain would be a hell of a lot easier.

Climbing higher in elevation had us crunching along iced-over snow that had melted and refrozen during the night. Our paths followed the footprints of hikers far more committed than Torry and I were, having set out hours before *we* had. Soft snow drifts ran up along the minute banks of the trails and melted just feet down along the ridgelines from whence we traipsed. Our worlds were centered through the tunnels of rhododendrons, which aside from moss existed as the only radiant color outwardly noticeable in a forest of dried and dead browns.

It was six when we reached Carters Gap, and I sat down to inspect my boots, which appeared to have already started to fall apart.

"Unbelievable..." I muttered, tugging at the Keen Targhee IIs I had been told to purchase from an REI sales associate long before I'd left ever home. The soles on the bottoms had started to peel away from the rest of the boot.

I dropped my foot and looked up, searching for Torry.

He had blasted ahead of me, eager to hurry and get into the next town because he and Pam were in the process of arranging to possibly meet in Franklin.

Meanwhile, my time would be spent alone.

A common hiker occurrence I've come across out here is our mucus production.

At times it seems everyone coughs like life-long smokers, even if they've never smoked a day in their lives. During the night our sinuses drain into our lungs because of the cold weather or after heating up too much from hiking. At times you can actually follow fat globs of snot on the trails like bread crumbs.

It was no longer unreasonable to watch a woman in her fifties hock a loogie or snot-rocket a load of boogers onto the trunk of a passing tree.

We had absolutely become animals out here in the seclusion of the wilds.

Torry and I followed the trail of one such one woman, in her late forties, who was coughing out chunks of phlegm, having recently been stricken with an upper-respiratory infection. Her face was miserable and pale aside from her bright-red nose and bloodshot eyes.

She stopped about fifty feet in front of us and looked at the shelter and then at the way ahead.

Shrugging, she decided to pass up staying.

When Torry and I had reached the campsite for the evening, however, we allowed our tired feet to guide us to the structure.

The local weather reports had called for more rain as we had headed out the following morning, but instead it had been sunny and beautiful throughout the day.

We hustled and bustled up vertical climbs with our packs on, literally hand over hand across boulders going *straight up*.

As we stopped for a second to rest, I propped my back against a tree. I looked back down at Torry, who was panting just as heavily as I was twenty-five feet below me.

The Appalachian Trail hugged a wall of rock that had become slick with thin ice layers only now melting beneath the beating sun above. Little more than two feet wide in some sections, the trail had places you could look down at the thousand-foot drop beneath you, if you felt like being dealt a blow of vertigo.

Along the side of the trail, we eventually and quite occasionally saw a dirt road that seemed to mirror the trail we were on. The forest road was flat and ran up along the cliffside while the trail actually went *along* the wall of the cliff itself.

I looked longingly at Torry, but his face remained stern and devoid of weakness.

"Maybe it'll—"

"We're staying on the trail. We're hiking the AT, not some nameless forest road," he said almost immediately.

I looked up at the climb to the summit of Mount Albert with renewed determination.

Ten minutes later: "You think that *road* is still over there?" Torry asked me, panting for air as he leaned over onto a boulder for support.

"Hey, look! We're here!" I shouted excitedly back down to him. As I pulled myself up over a stone boulder and grappled the root of a small tree, I was able to scramble up yet another ledge among the many we had passed over before.

"Thank God," Torry muttered into his hands appreciatively.

Then I sighed and looked back down at him. "False summit."

His face dropped sadly, and we continued on.

After we reached the peak, we came upon a group of hikers we had met intermittently along the trail. Torry talked to a German couple (Runner Up and Pacemaker), who were in America on a six-month visa, about the places he had been in their homeland when he was in the army. Woodstock was there as well.

"You guys seen CookIN anywhere?" he asked us. "Nah, thought he was hiking with you!" I answered. I had hoped that some great calamity hadn't befallen him, and had an odd sense of worry for some reason.

As everyone left and started to trickle away, Torry asked me, "You comin'?"

"Go on ahead. I'll catch up." I sat on a cliff behind a fence guard that looked out over the Little Tennessee River Valley.

I then looked at all the graffiti and names that had been scrawled into the paint of the towers legs or on the sign they had up there giving information on the site and the area's purpose.

The furthest date back I saw was "Mike Luvs Jessie Numan 4ever—'88."

I had been five years old in 1988. Five years old when somebody had carved that message into that wooden sign. I wondered where Mike and Jessie Numan were now. Where their love had gone? Had it

ever flourished or had it simply been a childhood lesson once they split ways?

Maybe they were no longer even alive.

Deep down though, I liked to imagine that their relationship still flourished. And if it had ever been special to
anybody, I was content with going on through life accepting
their memory. A memory they had wanted the entire world
to know about. I put my pack back on and huffed it another
six miles down the trail not too shortly after.

My, was it beautiful.

The twelve-mile section between Carters Gap and Rock
Creek Gap was absolutely astounding.

There were camping spots all along the trail *and* on
top of Mount Albert, with a view overlooking a few farms
and a distant small collection of buildings.

Natural water sources were everywhere as well. Hell,
you even walked right through the middle and down
through streams as part of the Appalachian Trail at
times. Up to that point, I hadn't used my water filter
but only a handful of times since receiving it back at the
Blueberry Patch Hostel. Most of the time I simply relied
on common sense.

I didn't drink from stagnant pools of water, and when
I collected it, I made sure it was always from the middle

of a stream, not the top, due to floating debris, and never the bottom, for sludge to leak in.

Rock Creek Gap had been a beautiful place to walk to, but I was in turn dead tired. As I settled down for the evening, I had no real interest in being social with the others but eventually caved in as I watched Torry talking to the other hikers and occasionally pointing over at me.

I sort of wondered what he was telling them and quickly decided I didn't care. I was too exhausted to care about anything.

Later in the evening, Woodstock managed to show up eventually as well, and I asked him the same question I'd asked atop Mount Albert.

"Have you seen CookIN?"

He explained he had seen him a while back but didn't think he had planned on making it to us today because of foot blisters.

That was unfortunate because I now considered him a part of our group, though I had only really just met him.

Someone in the group of hikers at that specific shelter had packed in two cases of boxed wine and went about sharing the alcohol with the lot of us. As the wine flowed, I met several different hikers whose names would later escape me.

Mountain Goat, Peanut, Monk, and Jolly, as well as many others.

We passed around different experiences we'd all had after standing around a fire for a little bit and getting tipsy on cheap alcohol.

Drunk and unbalanced, I stumbled back to my hammock tent as the party started to die down after the sun set. My eyelids felt heavy, and I couldn't remember the last time I had felt this inebriated over a little wine.

I sat on my hammock, with my vision blurred and the distant fire embers appearing as nothing more than bright streaks and lines.

I felt my phone buzz lightly and used what little strength I had left to dig it out of my back pocket.

It was a text message from Melody.

"i wont be coming to see you in franklin, or hot springs. i realized today that I just have to get over you… and i know this hurts both of us. but i have to move on."

I laughed, unsure of whether to be confused, happy, sad, angry, or everything all at once.

I threw my phone at the earth, where it bounced somewhere beneath the hammock. Part of me knew that it not only had pictures on it but my whole journal up to that point. But I was too angry and intoxicated to care anymore.

My hands started shaking, and it made zipping my sleeping bag up rather tough.

As soon as I lay back, the rain began falling and became a soothing rhythmic hum within the forest that was already lulling me to sleep. Still, I continued to shake.

And though my phone was somewhere out there in the thick of the downpour, I didn't care. I didn't care about *anything* anymore.

All I wanted to do was sleep.

The weather the day before had struck us with intermittent snow flurries. The same tiring actions began to become chore-like. By that I mean that it became a pain in the ass to start off hiking cold, stopping to strip clothes because of sweating, and then putting them back on when we stopped *again* for a break later down the trail. It was relentless out there with the change in temperature by nothing more than a few thousand feet. Sometimes summits were a toss-up in either heat from direct burning sunlight or freezing cold because of a constant onslaught of icy wind gusts.

Regardless, if anything I felt good knowing that I was back home in North Carolina.

The trails here were laden with gentle switchbacks, which were noticeably different compared to the straight-up-and-downs we had experienced in Georgia.

But the rain seemed to be just about the same *everywhere* we went.

I woke during the night to the sounds of voltage-warning notifications bleeping incessantly on my phone. I searched wildly for it within my tent before noticing its blinking red light barely visible from beneath a pile of wet leaves outside my hammock.

"Shit!" I almost shouted. That phone had *everything* I'd written on it, the notes I had taken, as well as pictures I had never backed up on any other storage device!

How the hell had it gotten out there? I asked myself, ransacking my mind for answers. I unzipped my hammock and reached down, grabbing the rather soaked device. The battery was all but drained and water had gotten into the charging port causing the voltage warning notifications. I quickly turned it off and disassembled it, only to notice that there was rainwater in the battery compartment as well.

I would need to look for a new battery once I reached Franklin because this one appeared to have become swollen overnight with the addition of water within the compartment. I carefully placed it in a holding pouch above my head but became wary of its bulging sides.

"Christ, if that explodes battery acid in my eyes..." I said to myself out loud, knowing *none* of the mechanics or workings of a lithium-ion battery. *Did* they even explode? Was there acid inside them? I didn't know, but I didn't want to find out the hard way either.

I carefully set the battery on the ground outside my hammock and covered it with what few dry leaves were beneath my rainfly.

"Franklin is just in sight. Don't worry, John," I said to myself, and then suddenly I had in fact remembered why I'd thrown my phone outside to begin with.

Melody was no longer going to meet me there. I stared in Torry's direction but could see nothing in the darkness and heavy downpour of rain surrounding me.

My watch told me it was 1:22 a.m., only it felt a lot later than that.

"Yeah, dude, he headed out late last night and told me to let you know he went on ahead to Franklin," one of the guys who had managed a sleeping spot within the shelter explained to me.

"Wait, what time did he leave?" I asked, confused.

"Uh…what was it, Jeff?" he asked his friend. Clearly the use of trail names had gone out the window at this point.

"I think it was like two or three in the morning?" he replied, packing his sleeping bag into the base pouch of his Gregory 65-liter pack.

I was confused as to why Torry wouldn't just come over and wake me up himself to let me know he was pushing on in the middle of the night. What if these people had left before I'd ever even awakened? I'd have never known what the hell had happened to him. Torry had the cook kit and I had the water purifier, so in a sense we were sort of tied to each other.

But this seemed reckless to me and only made me angry as I set out that morning alone.

The night prior, Woodstock and I had talked about splitting the cost of a room once we reached Franklin since Torry was expecting a visit from his online girlfriend, and I no longer had anybody coming to meet *me*.

Unfortunately, I was going to need a room to dry off because despite two rainflies and a rain poncho thrown over the top of my hammock tent, I had managed to wake up in yet another pool of water. Furthermore, my backpack—*despite* the waterproof covering and Duck's Back[14] it had been covered with—had still managed to soak through. *None* of my gear seemed to be working at all anymore.

It was as if each individual piece of equipment I owned had decided all at once to quit on me.

---

[14] Duck's Back: is an REI brand name cover, made for keeping rainwater out of backpacks. Typically coated in polyurethane, the cover is made to encompass the entirety of the pack, is cinched with a toggle spring stop and keeps water from soaking through your pack while hiking in the rain.

When I reached Winding Stair Gap, I looked down the road and wondered where or how Torry had gotten into Franklin.

Part of me felt crippled in a sense because he had been the one to hitch our ride for us back at Unicoi Gap. I didn't know how to get into town, what I was supposed to do, or even which way to go. And part of me found that disgusting about myself. I had become so dependent, I didn't know how to think or act or feel without somebody telling or guiding me.

As I sat on the side of the road, I thumbed through my Appalachian Trail guidebook looking for phone numbers and shuttle services. Without this thing I would've been absolutely clueless as to what I was supposed to do next other than walking blindly in some random direction.

As I sat there, a couple of other hikers were getting dropped off by a woman in a gray Toyota Camry. She popped the rear trunk for them and came out of the front driver's side of the car, leaving the engine running.

"Thanks so much for the ride."

"We really appreciate it," two guys climbing out of the rear passenger seats said to the driver.

A third hiker, a short blonde who appeared to be hiking with the two men, hugged the woman, who was a bit thrown off by it but hugged back all the same.

"It was no problem. I hope you guys are safe out there…and remember what I told you about the guy with the red truck. Be careful, OK?" she added.

Suddenly *I* wanted to know about this "guy with a red truck" she had mentioned. Nobody could simply hear that collection of words and say they weren't slightly curious.

"Oh, by the way. Here you go," she said, opening a cooler that had been shoved as far back as it could go into the rear of her trunk. Inside was half a cooler of melted ice, which she had the two male hikers heft out for her and then tip over. Clear water and pieces of ice washed over the black asphalt.

"Thanks, I needed to get that drained before it spilled all over the back some day. Take these with you," she said handing the gentlemen and the girl some beers and cans of sodas from out of the cooler, much to their excitement.

When the woman drove off, the female hiker stated bluntly, "I couldn't believe she kept her hand on the .357 the whole time."

"Hey, we could've been rapists for all she knew. I'm just glad we didn't get mugged," one of the male hikers said as he hefted his pack onto his back.

"I feel bad for anybody that happens to hitch a ride in that red truck she talked about that has been picking hikers up," the other male hiker said.

My curiosity at this point was too much to take.

I quickly walked over to them before they had started to head out.

"I, uh…excuse me…" I called out to them as the taller man with the red bandanna tied around his curly blond hair turned to face me first.

"I wasn't trying to be rude or nosy or anything, but what were you saying about a red truck? Or something like that?"

"Oh, yeah. You a thru-hiker or something?" he asked.

"Yeah, I am. I'm about to hitch into Franklin right now actually."

"That lady that dropped us off told us that there is a guy in a red truck going around and picking up hikers at these gaps like this one right here, or at road crossings, and taking them into the woods and mugging them," the girl said.

Suddenly I thought about Torry.

I thanked them for the brief information as the trio crossed the highway and walked into the forest across the way.

Looking in the guide again, I found that the Budget Inn down in Franklin offered shuttle services to hikers. Maybe *that* was how Torry had reached Franklin? Then again, maybe he'd been picked up by the dreaded *guy in the red truck* or whatever. I would never know if I didn't find him soon.

I put my disassembled phone back together and prayed that the swollen battery would work so that I could possibly call him.

As soon as I turned it on, it stated it had 15 percent battery life left.

"Better make this quick," I said, holding my cell phone in the air and hoping it would pick up a signal.

My phone then started to vibrate and notify me of both its low battery which I was already aware of, and then the voltage warning as well. When I checked the screen in frustration, the whole thing died on me.

So for the next three to five minutes, I screamed obscenities at my phone and mocked smashing it on the ground or stomping out my frustrations on it. If I was going to hitch into Franklin, I wasn't even sure which way I was supposed to start heading.

That's when a shuttle bus pulled up.

There was a heavy man behind the wheel, with steely eyes and short black hair. He had a dark-brown mustache as well. "Where ya headed, son?" he asked with a strong southern accent. "Franklin," I began, before I heard, "Hey! It's Morris the Cat." I turned and saw Woodstock sitting in the very front seat of the bus.

"Oh thank God, there's *someone* I know," I said, hopping on board.

On the ride down, Ron Haven, the driver, didn't mind explaining that he was somewhat of a town celebrity. He was a commissioner, he had been a professional wrestler, and he ran two Budget Inn motels as well.

"What'ya do for a livin'?" he asked me, looking at me in the rearview mirror.

"Nothing now. Quit my job…and sold everything I owned to hike this trail," I replied proudly. I expected it to be a symbol of my ultimate freedom. Only, Ron's face slightly soured.

"So you're unemployed?" he asked, reconfirming with a hint of disdain.

I replied, "Yes…" and then endured awkward silence from him for the rest of the ride into town.

We were driven to the Budget Inn in Franklin, where the crotchety old woman manning the check-in counter collected our information with impatience. A line had built up, and it was clear that we wouldn't be the *only* hikers staying there that evening. As more and more thru-hikers stripped their backpacks and started to shovel into the tight office area, the old woman pinched her fingers across her nose and shouted angrily at everybody, "I can't stand your smells! Only one at a time! One at a time!"

A few hikers scoffed bitterly and muttered curse words under their breath as they stood outside in the cold rain that was beginning to fall down.

When it was our turn to go in, Woodstock turned to me slowly and said, "Just wait out here. I don't wanna hear her bitching. I'll pay for the room now and you can spot me your half later."

"Well, I've gotta get my spare cell-phone battery and charger that was shipped from Hiawassee to here," I replied. He looked back at the bitter woman behind the counter and sighed as we pushed the door open and walked in together.

"Seems like if these things meant so much to hikers, they wouldn't just be leaving them lying around left and right," she said, dropping the battery and charger onto the counter quite rudely. I felt a surge of anger rise to the surface but quickly took a deep breath.

I had wanted to blurt out sarcastically to her, "You know, you are just so beautiful and perfect," but instead, I kept the remark to myself.

"She's right," I said, shrugging as I glanced over at Woodstock. "I'm a complete idiot. Sometimes I don't know why I just don't punch myself in the face spontaneously." I nodded my head and forcefully laughed while Woodstock gave me a confused expression. The woman looked at me oddly before handing us our keys.

"Get out," she muttered as we grabbed our packs and happily left her presence.

We unlocked the door to our room and began unpacking our things and stripping off our clothes. It certainly hadn't taken long for the small space to begin to smell like hot garbage.

After the rain let up outside, I took some time to walk around town and get a sense of my surroundings.

I met Hawaii and Noodles at the Sapphire Motel.

Noodles was quick to inform me that I had really missed out on quite the hiker bash.

"Dere was weed *everywhere*. And ya had dese li'l sluts takin' dere tops off'n shit," he said crudely.

He had said two sentences and already I was bothered by him. He slowly put his arm around my shoulders and whispered into my ear as he pointed a stubby finger at Hawaii. "I got dat one last night." He raised his eyebrows up and down. Of course I didn't believe for a second that she had done anything with the guy whatsoever. But who was I to say "you're a rotten liar, you short, bald-headed freak" in defense of the girl?

I was actually glad I hadn't made it to the festivities. That's not the lifestyle I had come out there to find. I wasn't looking to get high, and the couple of times that Torry had already engaged himself in those kind of activities, both at Hawk Mountain shelter, and Low Gap, I had looked down on it from atop my high horse.

Part of my reasoning for disliking Noodles was because of this. I wasn't trying to come off as a prude, but I didn't want Torry to become disillusioned on why he had come out to the trail.

His plan hadn't been to come out and blow his money on alcohol and weed; it was to hike the Appalachian Trail from beginning to end.

And suddenly I felt like I was trying to be his protector, of sorts.

I said my good-byes as quickly as possible before Noodles could start asking me for some money and walked across the street to grab one of the new Jim Beam half-pound burgers from Hardee's and some curly fries that were being advertised. As I was eating, a woman working behind the counter approached me and said, "You look hungry enough to eat three or four of these meals. Take these on the house."

She handed me a free serving of onion rings! I wasn't aware I had looked so helpless. Maybe they were throwaways or from a wrong order? Maybe they'd even been dropped on the floor and some Good Samaritan in the back was like, "I'm sure that hideous homeless man in the corner out in our dining room would eat them."

I didn't care because either way they were good.

When I was done eating, I walked down the cracked sidewalks of an empty town and looked at the hilly and rather crumbling facade of Franklin. The sky was already darkening for what was going to be yet *another* downpour overnight.

I turned in for the evening.

It had always been funny to Torry and me to categorize people we had met along the trail.

You had some guys that were a bit hard up and had latched on to a female hiking alone or with a friend. They normally got overprotective and on most occasions gave you the stink eye just because you may happen upon a conversation with what they had possessively decided was "their woman." This was usually unbeknown to the woman hiker herself, of course, who chose blind naivety because she enjoyed the attention.

Which leads me to our next category, Trail Lizards. Now and again you would come along these types who hopped on and off and back and forth on the trails just looking to get laid, party, get drunk, and then find someone else in the herd to move along with further north or south, really wherever their next interest was headed. This often made me think of their hygiene, but more than that, it made me shiver in disgust at that thought as well. Sometimes a good bathing stream was four days away, and at times a hotel room with a proper shower was as much as a week.

I can't honestly say I'd want to hop into the sack with someone who smelled as filthy (or worse) as I did after three or four days.

Then there were the Trail Rats who would slink in, leech off your or others' food and cigarettes, never giving anything, even so much as decent conversation, and then leave, somehow ruining your equipment and gear by accident in the process. When you thought you'd lost them, sometimes they would mysteriously show back up later to beg for more food or to use your portable battery charger for their phone and then "accidentally misplace it." They were always asking for handouts and had usually perfected the art of looking helpless.

You had the Party Hard guys or girls, who didn't give a damn about anything other than getting drunk and high. And a hiker was always the easiest person to befriend. That's due to the fact that as humans we're social creatures and we have an urgency to communicate often with each other. It's no wonder Twitter and Facebook have exploded into such out-of-this-world entities.

When you're out here in the middle of nowhere, it's a little comforting to complain in unison about the last SOB of a mountain you had to scale to get where you were or to share stories regarding different life-threatening scenarios you'd both experienced. It also helped to alleviate the shock of almost seriously injuring yourself by talking about it. The Party Hard type listened or at least pretended to listen but in all honestly couldn't give a damn past the next time they thought they were smoking up or getting trashed in town.

These people pretty much *never* made it all the way to Katahdin, normally expending all of their monetary resources sometimes as quickly as a quarter of the way up the AT.

Of course, being the asshole I knew I was, I never looked at myself or Torry as completely without flaws. I knew I was naïve, and that wasn't purposeful. I was well aware I was dependent, and I knew that I was also reckless and quite immature more often than not.

I hadn't come to face all of my flaws as of that specific moment in time yet, but I knew the day was coming.

The day when the fingers of judgement I pointed at others, would turn back on me.

When I awoke, the room was hot, and the music on my phone had stopped playing because the battery had died.

I slowly removed my earbuds and heard Woodstock snoring away just as loudly as he had been back at Hawk Mountain shelter just our second day on the trail.

I stepped outside into the cold and sat on the shoddy lawn furniture staged outside my motel door. Torry was sitting outside too, dressed only in a pair of shorts, with his face illuminated by the light of his smartphone.

"How ya doin', buddy?" he asked as he smiled up at me from his seat. He looked well rested, fully at peace and content, with a glow about him.

"So what the hell happened to you?" I asked, pulling out a cigarette and sparking it to life. I offered him one, and he took it.

"Woke up on the ground in the middle of that rainstorm back at Rock Creek Gap or whatever it was called, and I'd had it with that hammock. You can use it from here on out if you want," he said as I took a drag and looked up at the waning moon.

"You don't want it anymore?" I asked.

"I'm going to get a ground tent, something better at keeping the rain out. I'm tired of either falling out of trees or waking up wet because the rainfly came loose no matter what I do," he said as he turned the screen to his phone off and looked at me.

"So how'd you get to Franklin?" I asked.

"Called Pam in the middle of the night and asked if she wanted to come visit me. She'd just gotten off of work and drove all the way there to get me. I sat in that rain for six hours just outside Indian Campground or whatever it was called."

"Six hours?" I asked disbelievingly.

He nodded his head and laughed.

"So what about the two miles between Winding Stair Gap and that Indian campground...or whatever," I asked.

"I'll go back and do it...maybe. But then again, who cares? It's only two miles, so..."

I had wondered to myself many times while hiking if I had truly planned on walking *every last inch* of the AT. More and more I was getting tired of "rules" and the thought that I'd have to pass every last white blaze to be a purist.

I had come to escape rules and procedures and sought out only freedom. Freedom to walk where I wanted to walk and do what I wanted to do.

Maybe being a purist wasn't the way I needed to go? But for the time being, I was sticking to it.

"She asleep?" I asked him, in reference to Pam.

He shook his head. "She's texting her daughter. You know she's been reading your journals, right?" he asked.

"R…really? Why?"

"Well, she noticed I don't post a lot of things for people to read, and besides, she likes your writing style."

I was flattered by the comment and didn't know how to respond, until I thought of Melody. "Complete strangers read my journals every day, and I can't get my own pretend girlfriend to read *one*." I took a deep drag from my cigarette and felt a heavy stone drop in my stomach.

My throat clicked as I swallowed.

"You're still calling her your *girlfriend*?" he asked, as if privy to some information that I wasn't.

I didn't seek to pursue it though because his question was fair. What *was* she to me as of that moment?

The sky was black, and stars were impossible to see in the cloud-clogged world above us.

Word had traveled the day prior from a few hikers about some trail magic headed our way later that morning from a local church.

Apparently at seven in the morning, a church shuttle would be picking us up for an all-you-can-eat breakfast buffet at their ministry. My stomach growled as I thought about platefuls of greasy, sopping bacon and eggs.

"This was the best thing we could have ever done, you know," Torry said, breaking me out of my dream world.

"The Budget Inn? Sorry to say, but I'm sure we could've found better…"

"No dude, being out here. *Doing this,*" he clarified.

I looked back up at the starless sky. "Do you think we'll make it all the way?"

"Oh yeah, without a doubt, brother. Look at what we gave up to be out here. We've done so many things to show that it's not the end of the world if you quit your job and leave your comfortable niche behind."

"Easy to say that with a woman to mentally and emotionally support you waiting in a room only ten feet away," I added glumly.

There was momentary silence before Torry smiled. "You want a kiss, baby?"

"What!" I responded as he touched my arm.

"You need some emotional support, sexy?" he asked playfully.

"Get the hell outta here," I said as I stood and flicked the last of my cigarette away. "Have a good night, dude." I nodded toward his bedroom window.

"Oh, I'll handle mine. You take care of Woodstock in there, all right?" He laughed as I shook my head and walked inside my rented room for the evening.

Breakfast came without a hitch but the want for our salvation was absolutely critical to the members of the church serving us our food. There was a bit of a hiccup in that to attend the breakfast buffet, it was mandatory that you allowed the members to not only take your picture but for you to be present during their morning prayer.

When challenged by those of either atheist backgrounds or of completely different religions, they were told, "Nobody is *making* you attend the buffet. If you feel uncomfortable you can wait outside of the church by the vans."

I found this response to be particularly cold and uninviting. Moreover I didn't like it when supposed kindness was handed out with a catch of some kind.

I had started learning how to find comfort in so little, and that was not meant to be a negative observation. I had become simple.

Less complicated by worldly possessions.

Less regulated by complex social environments.

My feet hurt when I walked, sure, but I was renewed. I was bruised in various places from trips and falls, but as a result I had in turn learned. I was lined from head to toe with cuts and scratches, scabbed over in dirt, but I was alive.

I look at my marred reflection in the windows of abandoned or closed shops and noticed that the shell of what I used to be had been overgrown by "life" in its purest form.

I walked along broken sidewalks with my hands in my pockets and read the signs of the past fading on building walls. Old stores and advertisements from over a hundred years ago, now faded and worn with time.

I was transparent in these moments as I passed through people, rather than by them, and felt a part of every conversation that had anything and nothing to do with me.

In fact, that very day I had sat on a street curb with an apple, enjoying the brief moment of sunshine as it washed over my body, warming me and reminding me that sunny days were still to come. It was a miracle of beauty if only for a second before the clouds carried it away for some other soul to cherish further down the trail.

I ate my fruit and watched a couple laughing in the Dollar General parking lot before kissing each other and getting into their car.

They looked so happy, and it had felt as if it had been so long since I had something similar to what they felt in that moment together.

A group of teenagers drove by, blaring their horn at me. I only watched them as they passed. It clearly wasn't the response they were searching for by the estranged looks on their faces when I did nothing but smile and wave a friendly hello back at them.

Later in the day, I ate a simple lunch alone in a cafe just south of a flea market.

I got a few looks of uneasiness as I sat down and ordered my meal while dressed in the dirty rags I called clothing. I guess I didn't look all that great with a beard and a ratty haircut to boot.

The waitress at the cafe was an incredibly nice older woman in her seventies. She had perfected the art of smiling in her years of service and loosely engaged me in conversation about my trip while not looking down or keeping me at distance with a gaze as everybody else had been doing in town.

She had made me feel as if she actually cared for my safety. The safety of a complete stranger. And well, maybe she did? Who the hell was *I* to say different?

I gave her a hearty ten-dollar tip for an eight-dollar meal just for making me feel warm with her earnest interest in my life. "Was everything OK?" she asked, sliding my card in the reader.

"You made it perfect," I replied.

She hadn't heard me. "And you have a nice day…Mr. Morris," she said, looking at the card.

I thanked her and left with a smile and a full stomach.

I walked to a nearby outfitters that claimed they would be able to exchange my recently broken boots for a new pair since the store would be credited by taking in mine. Upon running this through the store manager though, he was quick to explain that he didn't do that anymore.

"Richard, you did it the other day for that woman," the store employee whispered over the phone. Either the frequency had been perfect or I had lucked out at pivoting my ear in the exact location it took to hear Richard's response over the receiver. "That was different. I knew her. Tell the guy he's outta Luck."

Then there was a click, and the store employee looked at the phone's speaker in anger. I continued to eye local merchandise with an oblivious look on my face as the sales employee put his "disappointed" look on and set the phone back down on the hook.

"I'm sorry, but—"

"It's fine. You did everything you could. What was this place called again?" I asked.

"This is Outdoors Seventy-Six," he said. I nodded, looking around, and thanked him again before leaving.

On my way out, I spied some tents they had for sale that were grossly overpriced. Curious if for no other reason than future interest, I checked some of them out.

I had decided to keep Torry's hammock-tent setup, despite his switching to a ground tent. I had no intention of paying $200 to $400 for a new one-person ultralight ground tent like he had.

And while I realized that I may still get wet and cold, warmer days were sure to come, and I had already decided I would rather have money in my pockets to complete this trip. I had convinced myself that suffering through the hardships now would only help me appreciate the small things in life down the road.

I would be a better man for that.

Regardless of my newfound frugality, I had spent $140 total during my two days in Franklin, getting gear, a few supplies for the trail, and some trail food. Not to mention the cost to stay in a room for the night.

It was April 2, 2013, and seven o'clock had come about way too early that morning. Woodstock and I had purchased a discounted room at the Budget Inn, which Ron charged ten dollars a night for. It was nothing more than a hallway, a kitchen, and a clogged bathroom with an almost worthless shower.

So much calcium and rust had built up over the years that the shower head only spritzed drops of water, and it was clear that the thing hadn't been cleaned in ages by the amount of pubic and body hair clogging the drain like a miniature Afro.

I felt sick standing in the grayish-white backwash coming up from the sewer drain and even dirtier than I had going in after using it.

And while I was well aware this was nothing more than a cheap place to stay geared toward frugal, less picky hikers, I felt Ron should have really hired some more efficient cleaners or at least paid them better to have managed the place.

There were no beds, so Woodstock, another hiker, and I rolled our sleeping bags out onto the kitchenette's floor and slept there side by side for the evening.

I couldn't complain too much because at least it was warm and I could charge my electronics with the outlets provided. Meanwhile Torry had been enjoying a real room and the arms of his woman. There was a hint of jealousy within me, but I quickly got over it. All the same I still envied him but not the $120 price tag he'd run up staying in that motel room for three days.

As I looked about the sagging, warped structure we were calling a home, the other hiker staying in the room with Woodstock and I was making plans to leave the trail over his cell phone.

"Daughter's picking me up," he said to me, cupping his hand over the receiver.

"You OK?" I asked. He stood slowly and turned, lifting his shirt and exposing a baseball-sized black-and-blue knot on the lower lumbar region of his spine.

"I fell back at Mount Albert where the trail had you scrambling up hand over hand over all of those boulders. Fell ten, maybe even fifteen feet and landed directly on my spine and now I can barely walk. I'm pretty sure I fractured something," he said as he dropped his shirt.

I began to ask him details of the incident when he suddenly held up his hand and returned to the conversation over his cell phone.

"Yeah, I'm here, baby. You bringin' my granddaughter to come see me too?" he asked the woman over the phone. The tone in his voice made it sound as if the thought of having to quit wasn't even a letdown to him.

I left the room to give him his privacy, feeling rather bad for him. But maybe in a sense it was a good thing? Now he got to be reunited with his daughter and grandchild. Sure, maybe part of him felt bad that he hadn't been able to finish his thru-hike, but then again maybe he was *ready* to be done. I knew that if the roles had been reversed, I would have been *devastated*. I didn't want a one-time injury to end my adventure. I couldn't even

imagine that without becoming if only a little bit worried by it.

"Hey! You wanna clean up that Mohawk of yours?"
Torry asked, with Pam sitting in his lap.

I had unknowingly crossed the parking lot while in
my thoughts and was now looking down at CookIN, Pam,
Torry, and Woodstock in the rear of the motel. It brought
me out of my world of mental reflection as I looked over
their smiling faces. Morning had come, and I would be
setting out today. Torry meanwhile had convinced Pam to
stay an extra day, and she would be dropping him off at
Indian Campground, where he had left off.

Despite the fact that Torry had the cook kit, I had
planned to charge on ahead without him, using either
hand-built fires or eating foods that didn't require cooking.

"What about water? You'll need my purifier," I said,
not being completely serious about it either. He grinned
all the same, with a cigarette hanging from the corner of
his mouth.

"The water in those running streams *are* pure,
my friend. You and I haven't used that filter almost at
all, and we haven't died yet," he replied confidently. I
frowned, thinking that wasn't a very safe assumption
though.

As I made my way down into the rear of the Budget
Inn parking lot, he slapped Pam's thighs to convey that he
needed to stand. As she got up from his lap, Torry went

into his rented room and retrieved a towel. Meanwhile CookIN and Woodstock were talking only feet away with grave expressions on their faces.

"Come on, sit down, pal," Torry said happily, tapping the back of the chair. So I followed directions and sat down on the raggedy lawn furniture the motel kept outside each room as Torry draped the towel around my neck.

"Hey, this cloth better be clean," I warned, looking back and forth between Pam and him.

"Don't worry. We used the other towels for *that*," he said, chuckling.

"Torry! That's none of his business!" Pam shouted with a shocked expression.

Torry simply chuckled.

He had a portable set of battery-powered clippers he had used to shave his head and face when the hair got too long out on the trail. Now he was using them on me, to clean up my Mohawk, which had started to fade in with the rest of the hair growing on my scalp.

So there we were, Torry, Woodstock, Pam, CookIN, and I, sitting outside in a Budget Inn parking lot with beers in our hands, some of us smoking cigarettes, and Torry cutting my hair with clippers.

"I don't know why, but this is just funny," Woodstock said as he took a swig from a can of Yuengling that Torry had given him.

"Nice, it looks good," Pam said as she brushed some hair from my shoulder.

"Morris, I'm not sure if you heard or not, but I'm headed home." CookIN broke in suddenly, and I looked over at him.

"Wait, what?" I asked. Suddenly I understood the grave look that had been on Woodstock's face.

"My feet have been bothering me…and hell, you know I haven't really hiked a day in my life before I came out here."

I looked down at his feet, which were absolutely slaughtered with blisters and sores, some of which appeared infected. During his days off in Franklin, CookIN had visited a doctor to retrieve some antibiotics for the infections in his feet and the open wounds.

I never for a second thought it was going to take him off the trail though.

"I hate to do it," he said.

"There's nothing you can do? Maybe you just need a new pair of boots and another day off or something?" I tried to explain, but he smiled gently and shook his head slowly.

"It's beautiful out here, and it's been fun hiking with you all, but I think I'm ready to go back home. I think my wife will appreciate my return as well," he said.

I sighed as Torry finished my hair and dusted off my scalp with the towel.

"You're done," he said as he flicked the butt of his cigarette across the parking lot.

I looked up at him, and then to Woodstock and back at CookIN.

"You know why I'm glad I got to meet you and Woodstock, CookIN? Because I trust you guys. It was nice to know I could share a place with a complete stranger and not have to worry about my things being stolen. Or that I could leave money out on the stand and not have to count it the next morning. I'm gonna miss you, buddy," I said, extending my hand to him.

"I hate to go, but…" He shook my hand, and I felt he didn't have to finish his sentence. I had understood it completely.

I never *wanted* to see him go, but I understood that when the trail was no longer fun, there was no reason to extend the journey.

I liked Ron, I really did. Up to that point on the trail, he was the most hiker-friendly person I'd ever met. But I started to tire of his offhanded jokes about Mexicans coming into our country illegally and "stealing our fat, ugly white women" and his impersonations of Asian people speaking broken English. Especially while saying these things amongst the Asian hikers we had on board the shuttle, who took offense to the comments. Normally I would've ignored that kind of stuff, but I had tired of hearing him degrade the fact that I was unemployed as well, just because I chose to walk the trail.

"Looks like my taxes will be supporting you now too," he'd said snidely on the bus ride back up to Winding Stair Gap. Though I didn't reply, I thought to myself, *No, Ron. I'll get a job when I get home. You won't have to pay for jack shit.*

He was late picking us up that morning at the Budget Inn, which in the end meant that we couldn't hike that far for the day. As we awaited his arrival, a group of outbound hikers gathered in the parking lot, talking about all the things we'd heard Ron did in his life.

"I just heard he used to be a pro wrestler," one guy said.

"He also used to drive trucks," someone else piped up.

"And now he's just a *slumlord,*" Woodstock whispered to me, referring to the ten-dollar room we had stayed in the night before. While it had in fact been a filthy room, I had to be fair by reiterating that it was only ten dollars, so you couldn't rightly fault Ron on the quality of the room.

It was a warm roof over your head at least.

Ron had been a staple in hikers' lives and their adventures in the area. It was pertinent to remember everything that he had done to help everyone out, and from what I'd gathered, he was generally a pretty decent guy.

It was important to understand, that everybody had their individual quirks. I was no better myself, but I was honest with my hypocrisy at the times I'd noticed it. Sometimes these things just needed to be said to complete the story and to give detail to a person's character.

I appreciated Ron and what he did to help the local hiker community.

That's the most important description of the man I have to give.

When we arrived back at Winding Stair Gap, I watched as Woodstock walked over to the exact spot he had gotten onto the bus two days prior. He was counting his footsteps back toward the trail.

"Are you accounting for *every* last step?" I asked.

Woodstock nodded his head.

"Dude, it's one thing to be a purest but another thing to be anal," I joked with him.

He smiled and replied, "Hike your own hike, fat ass."

I laughed and continued on north behind him.

I wasn't aware of how far I was going or *where* I was going either. Part of me had wanted to wait on Torry for the day I knew I'd get ahead of him, but I also wanted to knock out some mileage. I would go on to bust out eleven miles that day, quite excited to get on down the trail.

Along the way, I crossed Siler Bald, where there were a group of hikers soaking up the sunshine and laying out in the field as I walked by. Two of the individuals I had remembered seeing back at Bly Gap. "Willow...and... Rainbow Brite?" I asked as I pointed to them. They glanced up with no response.

I nodded, feeling awkward for trying to be social with either of them and simply walked on down the trail, content with no response.

Further on I came across another bald. I was curious as to how these had been created or why they even existed. I didn't understand why somebody would climb all the way to the top of a mountain to clear land and plant a field, which would seem to be more detrimental on the crops than down in the valley. There was in fact some debate as to how these were created though.

Supposedly, Native Americans claimed the balds were there before they were.

But settlers had passed down that the balds were fields created by the Native Americans themselves. There were also claims that they were used as signaling between tribes to warn of attacks or to communicate by smoke.

Regardless, I found them to be quite uplifting and a treat that offered grand views and spacious grassland for one to lay out and soak up the sun.

Along the way, on one of the unmarked sections of trail, I got lost on an old logging road while not paying attention and decided to cut back up through the woods to reassert myself navigationally. Sure enough, it was the hardest hike of my life, pushing through briar fields uphill with a fifty-pound pack on. The ground was rather loose as well, which made for a consistent ritual of falling face first into the thorns. When I got back up to the top of some random North Carolina bald summit, I realized I was at a cell-phone or radio tower of some sort.

What the hell is this? Where am I? I thought miserably to myself as I looked down at my bleeding forearms. They were absolutely shredded and stung with the sweat dripping into the cuts.

I looked behind me and saw the trail winding like a scar through the trees about a tenth of a mile off into the distance.

I brushed the blood off on either sides of my pants and sighed as I clambered back down into the briars, tripping and falling even more on the way back. It was then I realized that I had suddenly become the "anal purist" I had joked to Woodstock about being.

The trail curved evenly along the dark faces of treetops hidden beneath cloudy afternoon skies. It didn't take long for me to realize I was walking through a completely dead forest.

Every now and again, I would pass by a monolithic-looking tree that was no longer living and neither were its sproutlings, which surrounded the infertile earth around it.

Entire halves of huge trees had been rotted away from the inside out as if some plague had swept through there decades ago, leaving only the hollowed out carcasses of what once was.

I didn't understand why so many trees had died within this two-mile section, but it was like traversing through a graveyard.

As it was getting dark, I began to pick up pace. This was no place to have to set up camp for a night. Not with so many *widow-makers*[15] around. It would've literally taken one strong breeze to bring a five-hundred-year-old rotted tree down on top of me in the middle of the night. I wasn't looking to camp anywhere near there.

Moss hung like clumps of corpse hair from the rotted branches, brushing my face as I passed by or underneath.

It was maybe two hours later when I finally turned a corner after climbing a couple hundred feet in elevation and found the road split between Wayah Bald and the Wayah Lookout Tower.

---

[15] Widow-makers: is generally a term used to describe dead standing trees, and the unpredictability of their sturdiness during storms. Quite often they could snap in half, or lose rotted branches that could crush and injure you at any point, possibly even killing you if you took to camping in the area they existed.

A wave of nostalgic memories came flooding back from my youth, when I had seen this place as a teenager. I had come here on a field trip nine years earlier when I had attended the Job Corp campus, which wasn't too far away.

"And then I was like, 'Hey, asshole, ah'm walkin' ova here!' but he wasn't listenin'," a voice said from the distance. I sighed and realized immediately that Noodles was up around here somewhere, and there was a pang of regret already stirring in my stomach. I just didn't feel like being around the guy.

As I had presumed I would, I saw Noodles among three other people I had never met before at the viewing area.

"Hey, Cat-shitter! What's goin' on, boss?" Noodles asked as he clubbed me in the shoulder with a playful jab.

"Not much. Just looking to get to the next shelter before it fills up," I replied, rubbing my shoulder where he had hit me.

"Don'tcha worry, 'cause I'll saves ya a place inside," he promised, much like he had before.

I looked at his company and waved my hand, saying hello. "Morris the Cat. Nice to meet you guys," I said, offering my hand.

"Mountain Man, Nomad, and Piper," Noodles stated, introducing them to me one after the other.

I took a picture of the view, posted it on my Facebook page, and began smoking once I caught Piper and Mountain Man doing the same.

"Don't know why yous guys smoke that shit when I have the *real* weed here," Noodles said, waving a baggie of marijuana.

Here we go again...

"Hey, Cat, or whateva ya name was, lemme get one of your cigarettes. I need the paper," he said, holding his hand out, as if by asking I was immediately going to say, "Sure, why not?"

"Can't spare any. I'm running low."

"Hey, kid, stick with me and you'll *nevah* be low. Yous gets what ahm sayin'?" he asked, waving a bag of 'shrooms he had pulled out from his other pocket. He then burst into a laughing fit that nobody else joined in on.

I shook my head slowly. "I'm good, thanks. Take care," I said, turning my back to him as I walked over toward the summit view.

"This guy," I muttered to Mountain Man and Nomad while gesturing in Noodles's direction. They both chuckled lightly and shook their heads from side to side in understanding.

"So you going all the way?" I asked Piper, who was staring off into the middle of nowhere.

He glanced back at me from the boulder he was sitting on. "Yeah, I am. You?"

"That's the plan. What'd you do before you came out here?"

"I'm looking to get into forest management now, or something in that field. Before I just went to college for music. I love it out here, man. I did music theory before this."

"Never too old to live, never too young to die," I said as I gave him a relaxed salute and kept on to the Wayah Tower.

"What the hells *that* supposed to mean?" he asked.

I just shrugged. "I've always wanted to leave a conversation with a quote," I called back. He smiled and waved good-bye.

The last time I had been here was in 2004. Nine years later, the old tower had been rebuilt and the land looked a lot different than how I remembered it. Some of the original shrubbery had been cleared off at some point.

There was a moment of remembrance as I thought of the girl my heart had once chased after here, when I was a teenager.

I looked for the names she and I had once scrawled into the wood in regard to our youthful love for each other. Too bad it had all been paved over with new mortar and new rocks.

I immediately began to think about Mount Albert, where I had seen the text "Mike Luvs Jessie Numan 4ever—'88" knifed into an old sign that had fallen over. I had wondered at the time if they lived happily ever after. I like to think they did.

The only reason I wondered was because the relationship I'd made at Job Corp had been a complete five-year travesty and a waste of time. I had carved our initials, "JRM & SCS 4ever," into the wood with misguided naivety. At such a young age, my ignorance was laughable. I'd truly believed that the tragedy of what had befallen our puppy love was all I was ever going to get for the rest of my life.

And in our youth, it always feels that way, doesn't it?

I had thought, *If I already told this girl I'd love her forever, then what will that make every other woman I ever meet should we break up?*

As rain clouds were rolling in, I pushed on to the Wayah Bald shelter. Unfortunately it was full. Noodles had assured me he was going to save a spot for me until a couple of women came along. This would make the *second* time he had lied to me.

"Nah! Nobody's sleeping here. Come on in next to me, ladies. I don't bite. Unless of course you *want* me to," Noodles said to the two women, laughing in his creepy old man's voice.

I looked on and shook my head sadly…and opted not to say anything.

After I found I no longer had a spot to sleep inside the shelter, I began to get just a little more excited about trying out Torry's hammock that he'd given to me in light of his new ground tent.

I laid back in the hammock after setting it up, which had been a million times easier in Torry's than the ten-year-old tent I'd taken from my father. It also felt a hell of a lot more secure.

As I lay there, I listened to random conversations within the shelter. The topics of jock itch and yeast infections while on the trail were in hot debate as to which was worse.

I turned on my phone to check my messages and found I had received two. One from Melody and another from Torry informing me that CookIN was officially gone.

I sighed and thought of the days the four of us—Woodstock, Torry, CookIN, and I—could've had together down the road, once we'd all reached the summit of Katahdin.

Those were days none of us would ever see together. At least not the way I had dreamed they would unfold. But still, I felt happy for CookIN because he had tried. He had gotten a hell of a lot farther than others had who had quit back as early as Neels Gap.

I looked at the next text message from Melody.

"youre all i think about john. im ready to talk" the message read. I took a deep breath and felt a large weight within my chest rise. I closed my eyes momentarily, wishing I had a decent enough signal to call her right then and there and profess my undying love to her.

But with the in-and-out service I was getting, it would've proved useless.

Instead I closed my eyes and imagined falling into her arms as she cradled me and kissed me, telling me everything was going to be just fine.

I missed her lips and how perfectly they had always kissed mine. I missed the smell of her perfume and her well-kept fingernails she would always lightly rake across my skin when touching me.

I missed her soft breathing against my chest during the night, when we held on to each other like new lovers always did.

More than anything, I simply missed *her*.

April 4, 2013—Snow continued to fall late into the year of 2013.

CHAPTER 7

Close to Death

BAD WEATHER WARNINGS AND A new threat of winter storms were the only good news we'd been told by both hikers and our weather apps on our smartphones. I looked dismally at the predictions on my screen and sighed.

"It never goes away, does it?" Fast Track asked as he tossed me the bottom half of his Slim Jim. I tossed him a cigarette in return, and our hiker trade was complete.

"Kinda sick of it, dude. I really am. But you know, I've always had this kind of curse on me my entire life where *whenever* I go out on vacation, the bad weather always comes along with me. I mean, there are people who can *testify* to this being a fact. I don't know why that is."

Fast Track laughed.

"You should definitely stay the hell away from me then, and either get your ass up the trail or wait for all of us to pass you by," he replied.

I smiled. Lindsey came walking by at that moment with her friend, Jenna.

"Whoa! Look who it is!" I said.

She smiled and waved. "You guys seen Wales anywhere out here?" she asked. I shook my head, as did Fast Track.

"I've been looking for Woodstock myself. Kinda got ahead of him, I guess, and I'm not sure if he passed me or what. How've you been?" I asked.

She gave a sad smile in response.

"That bad?" I asked as I saw her slowly reaching down to her right ankle.

"Sprained it pretty bad. It hurts a bit, but I'm trying to get over it," she responded, more toward her ankle than to me.

"Here, let me take a look at it," Fast Track offered as he dropped his backpack and squatted down. He gently picked her foot up and began to remove her boot.

"Whoa, what are you doing?" she asked, stumbling and almost losing her balance.

"Here, sit down a second and trust me," he said, politely directing her to the fallen log on the side of the trail that I was sitting on. Lindsey sat beside me as Jenna commented quietly in her reserved voice that she was going to be up ahead. She took off with a strange expression on her face that was reflective of what was going on.

"So what I'm doing is known as a—"

"Pervert move. What you're doing is a pervert move, you sicko," I said as Lindsey burst into laughter.

"Actually, I'm applying pressure to the damaged tissue, which—"

"Which is just an excuse to touch some lady's stinky ol' feet," I interjected.

"Hey! My feet aren't stinky!" Lindsey said, playfully slapping my shoulder. I reached down slowly and grabbed her boot, waving it in her face then.

"Yeah? That smell like roses to you? Cause it stinks from right here!" I said as she laughed and cringed away.

"Guys, this isn't gonna work when you're squirming around," Fast Track stated, mocking annoyance in his tone. I complied, zipping my mouth shut, and Lindsey giggled. I peeked childishly over her shoulder and looked down at this hiker-turned-physical-therapist kneading his thumb into the sides of her foot.

"That's where it hurts, right?" he asked as Lindsey bit her bottom lip and nodded. "How's this feel?" he asked as she smiled a painful smile.

"You're killing her. That's how it feels," I answered for her. He just rolled his eyes.

"Outta the way! Watch a pro," I said as I made a maniacal face and devilishly began rubbing my hands together and licking my lips. I gruffly grabbed her foot.

"Gross! Get outta here!" Lindsey said, playfully pushing me back onto my ass.

"See? Healed!" I said as I stood up and dusted my butt off. As she began to put her boot back on, Fast Track wiped his hands off onto my shirt.

"There ya go. Don't ever say I never gave you anything."

"Thanks buddy," I said sarcastically.

The day was a blur because I was moving as fast as humanly possible to arrive at the NOC[16]. I had been there only a couple of months before on part of a preparation hike prior to coming out to the Appalachian Trail. I was eager to find a bunk room for the evening at only nineteen dollars a night.

Along the way, I downed one thousand milligrams of ibuprofen, as my knees and ankles screamed in protest from the work I so carelessly put on them.

I could no longer even feel either of my big toes, they had become so calloused. But the pain from the weight tugging at those callouses underneath still ate away at my impatience with hiking.

When I approached the Wesser Bald tower and climbed to the top, I was brought to my knees by the beauty of the view. Maybe I was a little overdramatic, but I held my hands up to the sky and beamed a smile right back up at the sun. Light breaking through the clouds

---

[16] NOC: Nantahala Outdoors Center located in Bryson City, North Carolina. The Appalachian Trail goes through this area. The center and surrounding buildings, hostel and restaurants caters to hikers. An equipment shop with maps of the local area is also available by the river.

illuminated whole sections of mountains in the distance and changed directionally based on the wind. I lay down on the wide-open wooden platform with my arms and legs splayed out and soaked in the vitamin D for a few moments.

Part of me felt like sleeping because of how temperate and quiet it was.

"What's going on?" I heard suddenly as I brought my hands up to my forehead and tried to shield my eyes from the sun.

"How're you, Wales?" I asked as he sat down on one of the benches on the platform across from me.

"Good, just enjoying the sights. Have you seen Lindsey lately?" he asked.

I closed my eyes and placed my hands behind my head slowly. "Maybe I did," I responded mysteriously.

He didn't say anything for some time, and then stammered, "W…well, what…does *that* mean?"

"Well, she might've been looking for you earlier. I think she has the hots for you," I said, peeking one eye open at him.

He was smiling. "Where did you last see her?"

"What's the deal, dude? Don't lie to me. You two got a thing goin' on?" I asked.

He immediately began to blush. "I'm not sure I understand what you mean," he said, almost purposefully alluding to something more.

I smirked. "Mm hmm…sure."

"I'm not interested in her like that," he tried to assure me.

"That's good. Because Torry has a thing for her too. Only he has a knife, and he doesn't like you that much," I said with a serious tone.

Wales's once-smiling face turned to one of concern. "A…are you serious?"

"He doesn't play around. Once watched him gut a man for takin' a swig offa his hooch."

"Is…is he m…mad at me?" Wales stammered.

I smiled slowly, feeling rather bad at how gullible this giant called Wales, truly was. I'd barely been able to keep a straight face the entire time I'd been lying.

"I'm just kidding," I said, slowly standing up.

"Oh," Wales said rather doltishly.

"Let's go to the NOC," I said as I began walking down the tower stairs.

"You never answered me. Did you see Lindsey?" he called down after me.

"Yeah, but she's *miles* ahead of us by now!" I called back up.

When Wales and I arrived at the NOC later in the afternoon, I took over and showed him around, as if I was the self-proclaimed guide of the area.

First we went to secure a bunk bed at $19.38 each, which included use of the communal kitchen and the shower room. The showers were laden with empty travel-sized shampoo and body-wash bottles scattered about the tile floors. Sandals people had left behind, along with an occasional moldy sock or two, sat in dusty, cobweb-filled corners. Meanwhile, the kitchen was a mess work of dirty pots and pans that lazy hikers had used and then left to rot as if some imaginary maid was going to come along and clean the mess up for them.

The two of us, clean and donning fresh clothes, then headed down to the River Side restaurant before they closed. It was there that we met Ultra Violet and her boyfriend, who were also thru-hikers. Their dog, Macy, was up in the room they had rented for the night. This was the couple I hadn't seen since the shuttle ride out of Hiawassee. The girl still gave me a disconcerted look, as if I'd done something morally wrong to her in the past. I wasn't sure I understood why.

All I had done was ask why self-proclaimed "purist thru-hikers" had been skipping sections of the trail. She had taken it as an insult, almost as if I was alluding to being judgmental of their hike, when that couldn't have been further from the truth.

All the same, I brushed it off and tapped Wales on the shoulder.

"I'm starving. You wanna go eat?"

We ordered a sixteen-inch cheese pizza each and a dessert to go. We made small talk as we waited at one of the riverside tables overlooking the Nanthahala River outside. We talked about my former job and why I had decided to leave it, as Wales and I had never truly conversed much before. Only, as I talked to him, it appeared to be a subject Wales was pretty nubile at hearing. It appeared as though he had lived a sheltered life, as all he wanted to talk about in return was video games. All the same, we drank tons of root beer, which we commiserated over how much we loved, if we couldn't agree on much else.

Once our food arrived, we finally made our way across the bridge over the Nanthahala River and sat at a seasonally closed diner called Slow Joe's, where we ate our pizzas.

But boy were we disappointed. It had to have been the worse pizza either of us ever had before in our lives. I'd had frozen dollar pizzas that tasted better than this. I burst into laughter as Wales, who had seemed so introverted in personality, suddenly shouted, "I can't believe I wasted forty-five dollars, and I've only been here an hour!"

Our rooms were comfortable at least.

As I walked outside to enjoy the dusk rolling in, I found I finally had a phone signal.

I decided to call Melody.

"Listen, John. You *know* that I love you. You don't need me to read your stupid journals to know that. I'm refusing to read them not because I don't care about you but because I have to protest in *some way*. Everyone is going on about how proud they are of you while not giving a *shit* that you left me behind to *rot*."

"Melody, that's not fair. You're angry because I haven't been able to *call* you. I've been trying to tell you that my signal is spotty at best, and it gives me just enough time to post my blogs but not enough time to talk over the phone," I returned.

She sighed into the receiver, and I could already tell she had *the look* on her face that I had seen so many times before in our arguments in the past. I didn't have to be there in person to know she was stern faced and possibly clenching her teeth in anger. Angry dimples that were both ironically adorable but also the prelude to her rage were probably already appearing on her cheeks at that very moment.

"So as I was saying," she began, exuding in tone just how hard it was for her to be calm, "just tell me what's been happening to *you*."

Part of me wanted to reply once again like I had before, to *just read it,* but I didn't.

"Well a lot. Lindsey sprained her ankle, and a guy named Fast Track was trying to massage it for her—"

"Who the hell is *Lindsey?*" she asked in an irritated tone.

I stopped. This was where I wanted to tell her, "This is why you follow along in my journals. So you sort of know the people I'm hiking with!"

"She's also a thru-hiker—" I began patiently before she sharply cut me off.

"I didn't call you to hear about other people...or some girl. I called to hear about you."

"Well this journey isn't *just* about *me*. Torry met his girlfriend, Pam, finally, and she turned out to be really cool," I began again.

"Yeah, we'll see how long *that* lasts before he breaks up with her too. Didn't he just leave his wife of fifteen years? How the hell could you move on so quickly after that?"

"I don't know the details of their relationship. It's none of my business. Maybe it was a cold relationship? Maybe he felt it was over years before this thing ever happened? I don't know."

"I told you; he's going to screw you over in the end, John. You just wait and see."

As I closed my eyes, I partly wondered at times what I saw in her. It was a hard thing to think about, but it occasionally came up in my thoughts.

"As I was saying—" I started.

"I don't want to hear about them. Once again, since you aren't listening, I called to talk about *you*."

I gritted my teeth, feeling the urge to simply hang up in her ear.

That was our evening conversation.

Somewhere and somehow, we had made our way through the verbal obstacles to agree that she would meet me that weekend, fourteen miles north at the Stecoah Gap road crossing just outside of Robbinsville, North Carolina. She made sure to let me know how enraged it made her to feel *guilt-tripped* into making a five-hour drive to see me two weeks after I had just left.

I took the comments in stride. I missed her for some odd reason probably attributed to loneliness. I had found that in some strange, emotionally destitute sort of way, I was willing to put up with a little ear beating just to hold her again.

Seven thirty the following morning, Wales and I awoke to heavy rain pounding on the roof of our flimsy rented bunk room. I lazily pulled back the curtain and grimaced at how miserable it looked outside. The rain was coming down literally in droves, and I knew that I had to make distance if I was going to see Melody in time. I had one day to make the fourteen-mile hike to the road crossing…only this weather was not going to cooperate with me whatsoever.

I imagined slipping on slick boulders and hurting myself long before I ever even started.

It didn't do much for spurring any early-morning determination.

Wales's cell-phone alarm went off minutes after I'd already been awake, but he promptly silenced it and went back to sleep, as did I. There was this thought process that if need be I would hike through the night just to fall into Melody's arms the day after at the road crossing. What was fourteen miles when I had done a sixteen-mile day before over what was supposed to have been even worse terrain than what I had to look forward to?

When I awoke half an hour later to Wales getting ready to leave, I began to contemplate my decision. I didn't even know where Torry was. All I knew was that he was behind me along the trail somewhere. I wasn't even sure he had received my text message that I was planning on meeting Melody in Robbinsville.

But as I stared out into the wet, miserable, gray world waiting to greet me, Wales was still trying to decide himself whether he really wanted to head out or not.

"I think the decision is easy when you're meeting somebody just fourteen miles away," he said to me.

"I could always just have her pick me up here though," I responded.

"True. It all comes down to how willing you are to stick out the mess going on outside," he said, looking back out at the bleak world on the other side of our window pane.

Hell, we're getting a room together for two days. I'll have plenty of time to dry off. Maybe I could even hitch into Robbinsville this very evening and wait for her in town in a hotel room under my name, I thought. The prospect of ending a fourteen-mile day in a warm, dry hotel room after a hot shower and resting in clean clothes on a clean bed sounded like heaven to me.

I looked outside down toward the river, which ran through the center of the NOC. It was flooded over with the heavy rainfall that had lasted through the night. It's rushing gray water wreaked havoc on the soggy shoreline.

I thought of Melody and her soft, brown eyes looking lovingly up into my face as she draped her arms around my neck. I had only been gone two and a half weeks and had already made up my mind that our separation was intolerable. Time seemed so much longer out here than it did in the real world if only because so much was happening day in and day out.

Just two weeks out here had already felt like two months to me.

The first shelter was at Sassafras Gap. It would be 6.9 miles of uphill climbing with a gradual three-thousand-foot ascent. "Not too bad," I tried to reassure myself. In the grand scheme of things, three thousand feet may not have seemed like a lot, but when the climbs are almost always straight up *instead* of gradual, they can burden you greatly.

I would come to find that AWOL's guidebook down-played the ascent quite a bit.

When I stood, it hurt to move from the mileage I had practically *run* the day before. I took six hundred milligrams of ibuprofen with two-day-old untreated stream water and *made* myself move.

I got words of "good luck" and "please be careful" from anyone and everyone who was surprised I was pushing on in the rain. It seemed the majority of the other hikers had decided *against* moving. They had words and information in their eyes they hadn't had the inclination to share.

"Do you have anything like rain gear, or something?" Wales asked as I groaned under the weight of the backpack I'd just thrown on.

"I've got this," I said, holding up a clear $1.99 plastic poncho. When he only shook his head sadly, it was slightly disturbing to me.

"Be careful," he said, pulling it over my head. My goal was to wrap it around both my backpack *and* my body, and lucky for me the poncho was just large enough to do it.

I set out uphill with thoughts racing through my mind of nothing other than the woman I tried to convince myself I loved to drive me on.

The trail was empty for the most part, with only one fellow hiker I played leapfrog once or twice with before he tired of the game and took off ahead of me.

One would think logically that with climbing in height you were sure to get colder, and while I was well aware of this, I was almost certain that my poncho was going to keep me dry and warm. My frugality was tied in to my naivety.

It didn't work that way. After a mere thirty minutes of hiking, I was soaked from wearing the suffocating bag around my upper torso from just sweat alone. That wasn't to say that the plastic had completely worked at being waterproof either. *Then again in this heavy rain, how could* anything *be waterproof?* I thought dismally. Parts of the poncho that hadn't been brushing against my body accumulated fog patches, which, after consistent buildup of moist air, had turned into drops of condensation within the material.

I was absolutely dripping in my shirt from the start. While I was grateful that I had a dry pair of clothes and thermals in a waterproof compression sack within my backpack, it was only a passing comfortable thought. Mostly because it would be doing me absolutely no good until I stopped later that evening to change.

Each step in elevation had the once warm valley air turning more frigid.

Only I hadn't been ready for it to get *this* cold.

As the wind began picking up, I took shelter beneath an overhang of rhododendrons. My teeth were chattering, and I took a look at my watch. It was 10:00 a.m. when I broke out my guidebook, only to find I'd hardly done any real distance. The onslaught of rain had worsened into heavy, sharper, and fatter drops the higher up I went. Some stung against my bare arms as they struck, and others just made huge splashes.

Coupled with the high winds, I heard more branches cracking around me in these gusts than I was comfortable with. The skies were bulging above me and random growls of thunder bellowed, sounding much closer at this height than I wanted to believe I was hearing.

Warm hotel, remember? Soft clean bed and fresh clothes. Your woman lying beside you in your arms, and real town food to boot. You have everything waiting for you, under eleven miles away now. So get there. I tried to comfort myself.

The rain turned to sleet, which pelted me with BB-sized ice droplets as I continued to climb in elevation.

Only the weather couldn't seem to make up its mind, because minutes later it had turned back into freezing rain in short intervals. I wanted to stop and see the views to get a better idea of where I was at on the map or identify landmarks, but they were mainly obscured by heavy fog rising up from the valley and the low-hanging clouds coming down to greet them.

I began to slip into the first stages of hypothermia as my feet crunched through the ice already forming on the trails. The wind blasted with such ferocity that I began to wonder what I had done to incur nature's wrath so severely. I could no longer feel my fingers, or easily close them, and my feet were numb. The rain had stopped at this point and now only an icy wet slurry somewhere between water and ice began to coat the branches as well as me. I was in awe at how quickly it had begun to develop on the trees around me as I shoved the sagging limbs out of my path. Sometimes they hung so low your only way forward was by crashing through them like glass chandeliers.

Occasionally I stopped under the shades of rhododendron trees to cup my mouth beneath the worthless plastic rain poncho and breathe warmth into my fingers. I was angry and tore at the garbage bag wildly as it wrapped tight around my chest so restrictively that I felt it halting my breaths.

Tired and breathing heavy, I dropped my backpack. At this point the water droplets that had once been wet on either of my arms had now solidified in the wind gusts over the last two miles. I tried to brush them away, but they were frozen to the hair follicles and I couldn't knock them off.

Ice falling from branches above crashed down around me as I felt my mind beginning to get fuzzy. I had impractical reasoning behind the things that I thought I should be doing. For instance, I began to think that if I removed my clothes right then and there and threw on my dry ones that I would be fine. I would warm up and everything would be OK.

But in truth that would have solved nothing, as the onslaught of heavy rain and sleet mixture would've had me soaked again within minutes. At that point I'd have been out of a dry set of clothes altogether and would have completely screwed myself in the long run.

I then began to tell myself that heating up a warm cup of water and downing it would help thaw me from the inside as it had back at Blood Mountain, only I didn't have a cook kit with which to do that. Torry had it, and everything around me to start a fire was absolutely drenched from over twelve hours of constant rainfall. There was no way I would've been able to get a fire started.

I was convinced I was no longer in control of my surroundings, my environment, or my outcome.

My breaths no longer warmed my hands, which were painfully numb completely through. They had puffed, making them look like swollen mitts, and turned a ghastly pale pallor.

I began slowing down and noticed that I was stumbling a lot more often as I walked.

My feet were no longer there as I trudged on, dragging them and not even knowing what they were landing on anymore. My eyes stayed fixated on passing trees as I eyed each white blaze still visible beneath the sagging or broken limbs of the forest.

A fresh coat of ice glazed over the white rectangular shape.

I tried wriggling my toes and looked down at the slush mixture squeezing out from the shoelace holes and gaps in the boots' tongues.

My core temperature was in severe danger at this point, as my breathing began to slow against my will and I started panicking. I was now terrified, and I began yelling out to anybody that could possibly hear me.

As I shouted, my teeth were chattering so badly I was sure my words came out as little more than a garbled collection of sounds that were carried away by the large gusts of gale-force winds hitting me.

My mind began to turn on itself. *What were you thinking, coming out here? You're a failure at everything you've ever done. Now even this. Should've just listened to everybody back at home who told you that you were never going to make it.*

My arms and legs had begun to stiffen, and I slipped not once but twice as I used every last bit of strength left in me to push on and stand back up. The hypothermia had begun to set in an unrelenting fatigue that made me feel as if I had just run twenty marathons.

I was aware of why my arms, fingers, and muscles were painfully twitching and shivering violently.

As the body loses temperature, it's a self-induced defense mechanism to heat you up. I had no mirror to check the color of my lips, so I wasn't sure if they were blue yet. But my flesh was almost ghostly as the veins in my arms had contracted to divert blood and warmth to my vital organs.

If my inner temperature dropped any more, I would have no way to warm myself in this freezing rain.

I briefly scanned the wood line I was walking for anything remotely flat enough and open in which to set up my hammock tent. Ultimately it proved useless if for no other reason than because as I looked down at my backpack, I found it was soaked through.

But foggy visions running through my mind had picturesque images of falling into a dry hammock to weather out the storm.

These foggy moments were always met with rationale that told me that setting up the hammock would prove pointless because it would have been just as wet as my thermals by the time it was hanging, and I had gotten inside.

Walking was once hard and only now impossible. Condensation and snot from my nose had frozen onto my beard, and my clothes were icing over now as the temperature of the elevation change and the onslaught of the wind battering me began to bring the chill factor below freezing. Everything was becoming stiff where it had once only been wet. Though there was no feeling on the outer layer of my skin at this point, I still knew that if I sped up I might be able to warm myself enough to reignite the heat rapidly vanishing inside my body.

Of course this said nothing of the frozen pants I was wearing. The leggings had stiffened into thin, iced-over sheets frozen in time against the matted hairs on my calves and thighs.

I had done little to quench the moisture leaving my body throughout the day, as I had poured with sweat even out of the initial rain in the valley of the NOC. I was more than dehydrated the day before from the sixteen miles I had done, and now here I was, even worse off.

Dehydration can lead to hypothermia in even the least brutal environments at times.

I reached a point when I could no longer make my legs move purposefully, as if I'd lost all control of my motor skills. My heart was racing, and if I wasn't so scared, I felt I could've broken down into tears. I screamed louder now, almost feeling my vocal cords strain as I pushed on relentlessly.

My legs had stopped responding to my commands, and it actually felt like I was trying to tug on a frozen rubber band whenever I attempted to walk. The cold had dulled the outer layers of my flesh, and now only my bones and joints hurt with each step.

Suddenly, there was a loud snap above me, and a thick branch fell under the weight of the ice and smashed onto the ground ten feet in front of me in a brilliant explosion of wood particles and glass ice. I quickly shouted at myself, feeling tears burning through the glaze and fogged hopelessness I had once called my mind.

"*Mooooove!*" I yelled, only at the time it sounded like little more than a groan. Terrifying images flashed through my consciousness as I pulled myself under a large rhododendron tree with my trek poles. My fall was awkward and stiff though, which caused me to smash shoulder first against the trunk of the tree I had chosen to protect me. The brunt force jogged me out of my haze for a moment as I began to shake uncontrollably, lying on my side.

This unyielding brain fog was unlike anything I'd ever experienced before in my life. It was like swimming and striving to stay afloat in a whirlpool that was constantly pulling you down into brain death. You were well aware of what was happening, but at times you weren't, and you only awakened from the haze when your head dipped down beneath the surface of the water, if only to show you that immortality was not real.

You could, in fact, die out there.

The wind picked up, and suddenly it was raining broken branches and sticks around me. I jammed my hand desperately into my frozen pocket to retrieve what I thought was my phone. Instead I only managed to withdraw a frozen red lighter. I cried out in frustration as my thumbs and fingers would no longer work. I couldn't strike a spark, let alone a flame of any kind to get any sort of warmth. The lighter was far too wet anyhow.

A thick branch crashed into the tree just behind me and tore through a few of its branches. It had fallen just on the other side of the very rhododendron I was propped up against, but I was undeterred.

I had wrapped my poncho around my head and upper chest and began inhaling and exhaling rapidly, still finding it impossible to breathe normally in my panic. I wasn't trying to asphyxiate myself or hyperventilate. My thought was that I could recycle my own warmed breath just enough to heat my insides.

I tore into my other pocket at this point and retrieved my phone, only my fingers would no longer move. I had no warmth beneath my arms or behind my knees with which to heat up my hands. As a last resort, I sucked on my index, middle, and ring fingers long enough to feel a minute's hope of warmth reach down to the bones. When I removed them from my mouth, shaking violently, I tried pushing the power button on the phone to bring up the screen.

I begged for even the faintest of signals.

When my fingers wouldn't do the job, I pushed the power button by jamming it against the tree trunk to turn it on. It surprisingly lit up, despite being wet, and the touchscreen glazed over with a paper-thin sheet of ice.

But I had no signal.

"Fuck!" I shouted, exasperated and exhausted.

Images of my family and friends finding out about my death began to run through my mind. Most important, I began to wonder what Melody would think when I was no longer there to greet her. Would she be angry, thinking I had pushed on and forgotten her? Or would she believe something was wrong?

I hated the trail in that moment, but more than anything else, I hated my *own stupidity*. I hated my frugality, which had possibly cost me my life, and I hated the people out there that said I would never make it to Katahdin. Because they had been right.

Torry was a day away, and the only guy I had seen thus far was miles ahead of me. I was alone.

I closed my eyes feeling tired, sleepy, cold, and scared. I wanted to see my mother and father again, and while my instinct had been to cry in that moment, all I could do was sit there. I no longer felt alive, only existing in thoughts as my heartbeat continued slowing. I felt a pit in my stomach all the same, just knowing deep down that I had done so much and had come so far only to die on the side of the trail like a nobody.

I would be the next topic for a few days in the current events and local newspapers as hikers commiserated over how stupid it was for me to be out there unprepared, and others would say, "Better him than me."

I looked at my surroundings briefly as my breathing slowed down to tired jerks. I couldn't even call it breathing anymore because my mind was too foggy to care. I watched a drop of rain dangle on the frozen edge of a dark-green rhododendron leaf for what felt like hours.

"I'm sorry," I thought I remembered whispering, but I was so close to gone I could've imagined it. My last thoughts before drifting off were of Melody and how her midnight-black hair fell across her face the first time we had made love.

Her smile.

And the goosebumps that ran down my back when she had leaned down to whisper into my ear just how much she loved me.

April 13, 2013—tree regrowth within the stump of one long gone

CHAPTER 8

In the "Nick" of Time

I HAD DRIFTED OFF FOR a couple of seconds.

When I awoke, it had only been because I had stopped breathing all together. Terror shot through the roof of my skull, and I felt my heartbeat quickening as adrenaline began pumping through my frozen veins. I tried desperately to stand but continued to fall, as my legs simply wouldn't work right.

I wasn't a religious person, but in that moment I was any- and everything to stay alive. I saw sparks live and die in flashing milliseconds within my eyes. Tiny bright white beads, like fireworks hundreds of miles away against a black backdrop, began to form as my head swam back and forth and the colors of my world had started to gray over.

"Please…" I cried out to anybody that could hear. I had started dragging myself out from beneath the tree.

I had overworked myself and had become so tired, I felt I had just gone fifteen rounds with a heavyweight boxer while doing this though.

I started to forget where I was and remembered in delirium, calling out the name "Jasper."

The moniker had been from a family dog of ours when I was growing up, a treasured animal from the years when my sisters and I still lived at home.

For some reason, I started to call her name from under that tree. I didn't see visions of her, nor were any memories coming to mind. At least none that I could remember.

I sank beneath that whirlpool leading to brain death, and the only thing that had brought me out of it again was the confusion in hearing my own voice call for an old family dog from childhood. When I felt a sliver of ice fall down the back of my shirt and break me out of my moment of absentmindedness, I came back to the dark, cold, wet, and dismal world before me. I had started to actually "feel" again.

I managed to roll onto my stomach, and using the branches as support, I forced myself to stand by getting to my knees.

I shoved out from beneath the frozen rhododendron leaves as water and ice rained upon me. My eyes searched wildly for signs of civilization or other people and found nothing but silence and the hushed whisper of freezing rain falling around me. I tried a light, painful jog down the trail, simply dragging my backpack on the ground behind me, but it was pointless, and I fell to my knees, having overworked myself again after less than a minute. Propping the pack against a tree stump, I slowly lifted it and set it down atop the stump itself. I managed to slip each arm beneath the frozen, ice covered straps and slowly carry on.

I had learned that trick from a hunter back in the Uwharries, who at the time had scoffed at my stupidity and ignorance. Now, in a way, he had maybe saved my life.

It was twenty minutes later when I finally saw Sassafras shelter down a short knoll to the left and stumbled for it in dire desperation.

I turned the corner of the structure to see the guy that had been ahead of me stripping his frozen clothes off and shaking violently in the cold. He too was jerking about rather uncontrollably.

"Wow, you don't look good bro," a third individual, about my height, with a heavy beard, said.

"N...n...nee...need to b...bo...boil wa...water... please," I stuttered. It took forever to get the words out.

"I can see what I got, but I don't have much fuel left," he said, as I was already dropping clothes. The guy who had been hiking ahead of me stood naked, covering himself and pulling out a down under quilt from his backpack.

The bearded hiker saw how dark purple the skin on my stomach and upper torso was after I'd removed my shirt.

"Dude, you're in pretty bad shape," he muttered with a grave tone, as if I didn't have much longer to live.

It was a strange kind of luck that while I was freezing to death mere minutes before that, the wind had miraculously decided *against* picking up again until I'd actually reached the shelter. I say that because gale-force gusts started to pound angrily against the old three-walled structure. I had just managed to escape its icy grip.

Oddly, having removed the wet clothes made me feel a bit warmer as well. My wet, exposed flesh was all that kissed the freezing air.

I tried to unzip the side pocket of my soaked backpack, and after several attempts, the bearded hiker finally helped me. "F...fuel, t...t...take it," I said, pointing to the spare canister I had inside.

"Call me Saint Nick," he said, offering his hand.

I thought it was an odd place to give introductions, but I nodded a hello of sorts all the same, without shaking his hand. He used my canister to boil water for both me and the other hypothermic hiker.

"Do you have a spare set of dry clothes?" he asked, and I nodded my head as I turned my back toward him and dropped my soaked boxers.

I put on my thermals as well as my second set of dry clothes. While doing this I had a moment to look at the color of my skin. My thighs and lower torso around my stomach were maroon red while my arms, legs, hands, feet were pallid white, and the skin rather hardened and numb.

After Saint Nick had filled my Gatorade bottle with the boiling water, he put it inside my sleeping bag, which I had already rolled out within the shelter. I crawled inside it despite the fact that rain and ice had soaked through my backpack in different areas. This had caused my sleeping bag to become wet in several places. I didn't care though because the boiling water bottle was radiating heat pretty well, and the sleeping bag was catching it and keeping it contained inside. I zipped up my bag until nothing but my head poked out.

"If you want, I can boil you guys some hot cocoa. That is, if you don't mind me using your fuel," Saint Nick said.

"P...please," I said, as my teeth chattered and chinked together. I could barely form any words and the other hiker just sat silent as he watched everything unfolding with a shocked look on his face. He had managed to use his own cook kit to boil some more water and had copied exactly as Saint Nick had done for me by putting a second hot bottle in the base of his sleeping bag.

Turns out he went by the name Sinner.

"Y...you...your...M...M...Mohawk," he said, shivering inside his sleeping bag.

I touched the top of it. "F...frozen," I replied.

He smiled painfully and replied, "Y...yes..."

My Mohawk had actually frozen in the freezing rain—straight up. I crunched my hands on the ice that had formed around it and carefully pulled it off and tossed it outside the shelter.

The wind began to pick up as Sinner and I thanked Saint Nick for essentially saving our lives.

"I guess I understand the name now," he said. I looked at Sinner as if he may possibly understand the backstory that Saint Nick was talking about, only he appeared just as dumbfounded as I was.

"I manage to help a lot people on the trail," he said half-laughing once it was obvious we didn't know what he was talking about. "I had to walk a guy who'd had a hernia operation before he'd hiked the trail out to the

NOC. His intestines had literally just dropped and were bulging just below his stomach and above his pubic area," he said.

"W...wow" was all I could reply. The image that came to mind looked painful enough.

"Every step he took, he was crying in pain. I couldn't imagine," Saint Nick said, shaking his head slowly.

I had wrapped my hands around the hot water bottle and the pain as feeling came back into my fingers was absolutely miserable, but welcomed.

The cutting wind picked up, slicing into our shelter relentlessly.

Small gaps between the logs in the structure made the wind almost impossible to stand any longer, even while slightly warming up.

"Who...whose plastic t...tarp," I stuttered, pointing to the folded material in the corner of the shelter's awning.

"Don't know. Why?" Saint Nick asked. The answer seemed pretty practical, but maybe with all of the commotion, he had overlooked it.

"W...we need to pin that sh...sh...sheet up as a fourth wall. C...cut out some of this w...wind."

"Yes, please," Sinner added while tucked into the nest of his down bag. I knew his sleeping bag was at least a hundred times warmer than mine, and I envied him only momentarily before the cold brought me out of it.

Above us, the tin roof had fallen victim to broken branches and huge blocks of falling ice. The pangs rattled off like machine-gun bullets and made our conversations turn much louder.

"G...got any spare p...para cord?" I asked as I began to crawl out of the warmth that was my bag. Already I was second-guessing my decision as I slipped on my camp crocs.

"Yeah, I got some you can use. There's also another tarp underneath this base right here," he said as I stepped out of the shelter and down beneath the awning. Scraps and crumbs of food lined the dirt, along with several mouse droppings. This place looked to be rather infested by the gross amount of tracks and droppings left behind. If I didn't die from hypothermia, I was sure to die from toxoplasmosis[17].

I took out my own soaking, spare rainfly as well, and we spent the next thirty minutes tying up hole-riddled tarps and plastic sheeting as wind blocks.

The patchwork was rather shoddy but to be expected with no nails or tools.

When we were finished, the three of us looked over our work.

---

[17] Toxoplasmosis: A disease stemming from a parasite (gondii) usually obtained by inhaling or accidentally ingesting infected mouse feces. This disease typically causes flu-like symptoms and can become fatal if the infected individual has a weak immune system.

"Well it *feels* a little warmer in here...and hell, I'll take whatever I can get," Saint Nick said.

I nodded, consciously barely there, feeling sleep tugging heavily on me. It was three in the afternoon, and not too long after that, I found my way back into my sleeping bag after pounding down what food I had that didn't need to be cooked.

Saint Nick had been gracious enough to gather Sinner and I more water, truly becoming the hero his legendary trail status was making him out to be.

Suddenly a fourth individual poked his head into the structure.

"Hey guys, just to let you know, we have a hypothermic child coming into the shelter now. We're going to need some room in here," he said. The entire second-floor loft was wide open, and we more than graciously accepted him.

The fourth individual had been a scoutmaster that went by the name Walker. When he saw the shoddy wall work we'd done with what little wind-block materials we had available, he allowed me to use his tent as well as an extra tarp to further block out air flow from the outside. As more people piled in, we scrunched tighter and tighter fitting fifteen, and then sixteen, people within a fourteen-person shelter. The heat rose maybe ten degrees, and with all of that body warmth dispersed throughout the structure, maybe another eight degrees on top of that.

It was freezing, don't get me wrong. But it could've been a lot worse.

Beside me, people I had never met or known before that day slept tight against my body as we all struggled for warmth and rest on rotted floor planks in below-freezing weather. Our only comforts were the broken destitute boards wrapped about us and a flimsy tin roof that was receiving more and more dents and broken planes from falling branches. Sections of ice that fell through the night occasionally awoke us, like bombs going off above our heads.

Throughout the evening, with the fear of death still strong on my mind, I didn't find much comfort or rest. I couldn't stop believing that every time I started to drift off to sleep that I may stop breathing like I had earlier in the day beneath that rhododendron.

It made for an impossibly restless night of fear.

More than that, I began to question being out there. Maybe I'd gone far enough, and my path in life was to take Melody's hand and go back home to reestablish my life.

I knew there would be dangerous days out there when I had first started, but I'd never imagined anything like that. Something so sudden and immediate from completely out of left field had threatened my life.

I would have expected this kind of weather in the Arctic, but not North Carolina in early April. And for somebody who had never been knowingly as close to death as I had been that morning, I was absolutely terrified.

"I don't want to be here anymore," I muttered, half in and out of sleep to myself. When I look back on that sentence now, I'm not sure if I meant the shelter or the actual trail.

"None of us do, sweetie," a female hiker sleeping beside me replied. I opened my eyes and looked at the puffy red ridges surrounding her dark-brown orbs, just barely visible in the night.

"But we're stronger for trying, aren't we?" she asked, with a broken voice as two tears fell down her cheeks.

I closed my eyes.

I didn't know who she was, nor did I know her name, but I could imagine she probably had just as horrible a day as I'd had, to be in tears.

I awoke to a half-emptied shelter and the scoutmaster's tent, and tarp taken down. It had left a large gaping hole in my wind block, and already I could feel the heat bleeding from the structure.

The whole Boy Scout troop that had been with him was gone.

As conditions had been tight and *nobody* had smelled good, it was a rather horrible night.

Sinner, who had slept on my left side, had a wicked case of body odor (not that I was a bouquet of spring roses myself), and as a result, every time he turned in his sleep, a huge, heated waft of onions and garlic blasted me in the face.

Everyone was moving back and forth, snoring, farting, or just plain stinking. I never *like* to stay in shelters if they're going to be crowded, but due to the conditions the day before, I'd had no choice.

Besides, the shared body heat was welcome, even if the smells weren't.

Outside, rain with ice pelting the ground said good morning to me in its whispering hum. My shoulder groaned in pain as I sat up slowly, still tightly bound within my sleeping bag. When I removed my shirt, I looked at the large, dark bruise forming around my collarbone and shoulder from where I had rammed the rhododendron's tree trunk the day before when I'd fallen beneath its protective leaves.

I massaged the sensitive spot as I peered out at the destruction laid before us.

Branches had smashed into the roof of our shelter during the night, and around us were the shattered remains of their assault.

Huge chunks of ice had weighed down the limbs and split a number of trees in two along the sides of the trail. Several of these white or red oaks had crashed around us the day before and were still falling today. The path before us was an absolute massacre.

As I limped off that morning like a geriatric bat out of hell, I had decided on not even stopping to take my medicine or daily vitamins or to even eat breakfast. And despite the fact my boots were iced over inside and out when I put them on, I was only 6.7 miles away from Stecoah Gap, and *nothing* was going to hold me back. I struggled up hills with no views and coasted down the other sides along the ridgeline, trying to shave off as much mileage as quickly as possible.

This wasn't achieved very easily as I slipped and fell again and again. Some of the descents became quite precarious, as the ice hadn't completely melted from the boulders or hard rock surfaces, and I sometimes found myself scooting down hillsides on my butt.

I knew the next few days were going to be spent in a woman's arms, I was going to be warm and clean, and my aching bones were going to have time to recover. It was the *only* reason I pushed as hard as I did that morning.

It was the only saving grace in a mind-set that felt exhausted and disillusioned toward a previous love for the trail.

The fog was miserable and soaking. There was nothing to see further than ten feet in front of me at any given moment. And the wind only gave the impression that it was going to clear the path ahead.

My down jacket that I'd been wearing the day before was drenched through. It hung off of me in wet, feathery clumps as the ice that had formed the day before on the tree branches rained upon me throughout the day without yielding.

Eventually I removed the pointless material and stretched it over the back of my pack.

I scrambled up flat, iced-over slicks and held on to tree roots that were jutting out from the earth.

Pushing past Cheoha Bald, I still found I had no views, and a depressing mist was all I got to be treated to.

It was here that I managed to slip and fall knee first into a slanted slab of granite. I immediately cried out in pain.

"Get up…*get up*!" I shouted angrily at myself. If anyone had seen me or noticed my talking to myself at that very moment, I didn't care because all I had wanted to do was get down that mountain and leave the trail.

When I angrily jerked on the trunk of the tree in front of me to stand, a huge sheet of ice fell from a top-heavy branch and crashed into the same shoulder I had bashed against the tree the day prior. As a result, I fell to my knees into a section of thawing mud, howling in pain.

It was then that I cursed the trail.

I cursed the assholes who made it, maintained it, and had dreamed it up.

Finally, I cursed myself for being so weak.

It took a lot to get back up on my feet, but I did.

As I stumbled through heavy fog and icy rain, I began to second-guess my ability to finish this trip because of my near-death experience the day before and the added frustrations of the following day. Even now, the cold was beginning to set in again as my clothes were now drenched.

My knees were yelping again, and now my Achilles heel was starting to throb. I had put far too much stress on myself over the past couple days looking forward to that small piece of light at the end of the tunnel that was *Melody*.

I sat on a log, shivering, as mist swirled around me in the breeze, trying to catch my breath. I was on a narrow ridgeline, and the fog had begun to swirl like little whirlpools in the air. I tried to take a picture, but my camera battery was dead. Angrily I threw it out on the ground and quickly took out my smartphone to take a picture...only the wind stopped and the whirlpools vanished.

"Of course," I muttered miserably. I jammed my wet phone violently back into my drenched coat pocket and tied it back onto my pack.

After retrieving my camera, I marched on, stomping through mud puddles and falling or slipping on inclines due to the ice chunks on the trail. I shivered endlessly in the cold and swore or cursed more routinely now than I ever had before in my life, screaming a guttural growl at one point in rage when I took a tumble over a slick boulder and landed on my right hip.

Everything felt hopeless in those moments.

"*Fuck you!*" I shouted as I fruitlessly kicked and stomped the boulder I'd slipped on. I went to stand, and the immediate sharp pang against the bone told me I wasn't going anywhere.

"Fine, I'll just sit here and fuckin' die," I said to myself, as if attempting cheap psychology of some sort. In some way, shape, or form, I was looking for an inner strength to break the negative bonds that were on me. Ones that had told me to *leave the trail.*

Told me to *give up.*

My joints felt as if they had been filled with broken shards of glass. I was sore, swollen, bruised, or bleeding from head to foot in some way or another, and in that moment I was sure I was done.

I had given up everything to make this a reality, and it was clear that I was too weak to see it out.

I stood and stumbled carefully down the trail, as I had already started running sentences together in my mind, trying to figure out *how* I was going to tell Torry that I was headed back home with Melody.

That I had given up.

But that's when everything stopped.

Dead silence was in the air and the mist had faded away if only momentarily and suddenly I could see directly in front of me.

I took a deep breath as a warm gust of air came in from the southeast. It was there I saw sunlit rays raining down and tearing holes through the clouds like large spotlights of yellow brilliance.

This was the first time I got to realize how narrow the ridgeline I had been walking on actually was.

Farms and distant mountaintops erected into the valley below me as the breeze pushed away the mist and chilling fog and opened up the view for me, as well as the path ahead.

As if *only* for me.

It was so strange, the feeling of warmth that came over me in that moment. I had hated myself for being out there. I had discounted my ability to go on. My confidence had all but left me.

Yet the ice had still melted and was thawing still around me.

As I sat there upon that overlooking cliff, I had dropped my pack from my back, exhausted. Sunlight spilled through, eventually warming even me. The pains and the mental words shouting self-doubt into my brain had all vanished as the radiance of the sun cleared away the clouds and beamed down directly atop me.

I turned my wet, wearied, muddy face up toward the skies to greet its warmth.

I'm not too proud nor am I ashamed to admit that my eyes welled up with tears in that moment.

It was stunning. Everything I came out here for, everything I had pursued to experience within this life had awakened my frozen senses.

I was still alive.

And while I might have possibly been on the brink of giving everything up only moments before, something was telling me of the brighter future to come. It told me to push on.

And as I wiped the tears from my face, that's exactly what I did.

When I reached Stecoah Gap, a Boy Scout master was waiting for his troop at the bottom of the hill leading to the parking lot.

"Hey there!" he called out to me. At first I wasn't sure if he was talking to me or the guy hiking behind me.

"Was wondering if you two happened across a group of Boy Scouts. I've been waiting here to pick them up for quite some time," he explained as he removed his dark-green cowboy hat.

"There was a group last night that stayed at the Sassafras shelter with us. But they left before I got up this morning," I told him as I thought back to the tent-turned-wind-block that had been taken down.

In fact, I hadn't even seen the group or passed by them that morning, and I was so zoned out in hate and cold that I couldn't seem to remember if there had been other trails for them to have branched off on.

"One of them was possibly suffering from hypothermia, but luckily he made it to the shelter and had warmed up last time I'd heard," I added.

The scoutmaster appeared a bit more worried once I mentioned that but quickly put on a strong face.

"All right, thank you. I think I'm gonna try to call Walker again," he said as he gave himself some distance and took out his cell phone.

I found a nearby picnic table and sat down in the sun. The heat was so radiant that steam started to drift off my pants and wet jacket as I sat there. When I glanced back at my sopping backpack, I began to remove things from it and set them out in the sun to dry.

I looked at the other hiker, who had broken out his Appalachian Trail guide as well as his phone.

I didn't really have an idea of what I was supposed to do next, as the brain fog hadn't completely lifted yet, or so it seemed.

I was tired and sore from head to toe, and the insurmountable weight that had been on my shoulders within that hopeless forest was only now vanishing.

It had been replaced with a comfortable numb.

But these moments of bliss didn't always last forever, and I knew that I would have to start moving again before evening rolled in, hand in hand with the cold.

I texted Melody as I drug my wet items out of my backpack to dry in the sun. "feel like staying in something called the San Ran motel?"

"already booked us a room at Microtel," she replied forty minutes later. "at work, cant talk. bye"

I turned off my phone and stuck it back in my pocket. I had wanted to gush to her about my close call with death but felt it was too massive a story to get into right then and there, when all I wanted to do was find a warm bed and sleep.

I looked out at the highway and began to pack my things. The other hiker that had come down off the mountain behind me had already started sticking his thumb out on the side of the road, and I walked over to him.

"Mind if I hitch with you?" I asked.

"Not at all," he replied, chewing on a toothpick. I wondered if he used to be a smoker. I actually *always* wondered that when I saw people chewing on toothpicks.

After my ordeal, I personally wanted a cigarette more than ever but thought better of it, as nobody wanted to pick up a smoking hitchhiker.

"If hitching doesn't work out, we could always call Ron and catch a ride into town," I offered, thinking out loud as cars blew by us on the highway.

"That's right. He had said that we could call that phone number back in Franklin if we needed a ride from here," the other hiker stated as he thought about what I'd just said.

So we proceeded to call the number that he had provided, only we found that unless we were going to stay at the San Ran motel, nobody would be picking us up.

I hung up and shrugged sadly. "So much for that idea," he said, and went back to sticking his thumb out.

"We could always lie, you know," I offered.

"What do you mean?" he asked.

"Well we could just *say* we're gonna stay at the motel and then just head out once they drop us off. They can't arrest us or send us to jail or hold us prisoner," I said.

The other hiker laughed, with a look on his face like he was actually contemplating the idea.

"I don't think that'll be necessary," the scoutmaster who had been waiting for his troop replied as he closed his flip phone and placed it into his pocket.

The two of us looked back at him, and he walked over toward us.

"I just got a text from the other scout leader, and they're on their way. I've got enough time to drop you both off in town."

"That…that would be awesome!" I said as he nodded his head, firm faced. He was wearing fancy dark-green hiking apparel that looked as if it hadn't seen a day of dirt before in its life, but I didn't care. My judgments weren't based on the history of this man's clothing as much as they were on his promise.

To take us into town.

On the drive down, he looked at us warily before rolling down the windows.

"I'm sorry we smell," I said, ashamed of my own stench.

"You get used to it, hauling around dirty Boy Scouts after a few days of camping," he replied, staring ahead.

He dropped us off at the Microtel, where both the other hiker and I would be staying, and removed my pack for me from the back of his Jeep Cherokee.

"Well, can I give you guys a few bucks or anything? You got food or something?" he offered. I thanked him wholeheartedly with a handshake and assured him that I was fine monetarily.

"My girlfriend's coming, and after two and a half weeks on the trail, I'm ready for a break," I exclaimed.

After I'd said it though, I thought about the words I had chosen.

Was she still my girlfriend? What in all honesty could you call what we had together?

"You OK?" he asked, tapping my shoulder. I came out of my thoughts momentarily and smiled at him, though there was no joy in it.

"Y…yeah. I'm good. Just ready to go to sleep. Thanks again," I said as he waved.

The other hiker took off without so much as a good-bye, and suddenly I realized I was blocking the door to the building. I stepped aside as a few guests passed, with distrusting glances. I looked at my reflection in the glass automatic doors as they closed and saw how absolutely trashed I actually looked. My clothes were drenched and caked in mud in various places and my greasy hair was matted and filled with debris from trees and branches. My beard was wild on one side and smashed against my cheek on the other.

I thought back to Melody and hoped that these next few days would be the ones that won her back.

I took *everything* out to dry and cranked the heat full blast in the room Melody had purchased for us. It didn't take long for it to smell like rotten eggs in there though, as I spent hours scrubbing my gear and washing my equipment in the bathtub.

On my way for a walk across the street, I stopped at an open janitor's closet in the Microtel and took a large black garbage bag that was almost as tall and wide as I was. When I reached the laundromat/diner down the road from my hotel room, I ordered some food and then made my way into the bathroom, where I removed all of my clothes but a pair of boxers. I then punched a hole through the top of the bag for my head to poke through. I did the same for both arms and was now donned in a large garbage-bag T-shirt that went down to my knees.

I garnered quite a few laughs from locals eating in the diner as I took my bag of chips, two Coca-Colas, and two grilled-cheese sandwiches outside that I had ordered from the grill, and ate in the sunshine while my clothes washed. I didn't care. It was warm down in the valley, and the black garbage bag was soaking up heat from the sun like an electric blanket.

It felt good to be warm.

After my lunch, I sat on a stoop in a ditch with snow melt passing beneath as I ate a birthday-cake ice-cream cone I had purchased at the Scoop.

I enjoyed life's little moments like these, where I could watch leaves traveling down ditches filled with water on a sunny day, with no responsibilities or time constraints, and enjoy the simplicity of an ice cream cone.

After the dark days before, I was finally happy as I awaited Melody's arrival.

"I was scared, more so than I'd ever been before in my life," I said as I forked fresh salad greens into my mouth. They tasted so good, if for no other reason than because they weren't chock-full of preservatives like all of my meals had been out on the trail.

Melody glanced up at me solemnly and then shook her head as she looked back down to her plate.

"Quit exaggerating. You asked for this, John. I don't know what you expect me to say. Come home if you don't like it," she replied coldly.

I set my fork down slowly. Something just snapped inside me. It was like a *pop!* in the back of my head as I fumbled over the words she had just spoken to me, trying to process them. Maybe it was the recent stress or the rush of emotions I'd felt in my last few days. Maybe it had something to do with coming to terms with the fact that I felt I was the biggest wimp the world had ever seen, being so close to hypothermic death and still terrified by it a day later.

But maybe...just maybe...it was the condescending tone and the unbelieving pitch in her voice that accompanied the words she had chosen to use.

"I...I'm sorry, did you say," I began, with a small, incredulous laugh, "did you say, *quit exaggerating*? Please tell me you didn't just say that." I felt my eyes begin to sting.

My face flushed with fury.

She looked up at me and saw my hands gripping the edges of the table, slightly shaking. I was infuriated and mortally hurt all at once. But those were just words and did nothing to encapsulate the storm that was rising within me. And while she had been right in that it had been *my idea* to come out on this journey, it was *never* my intention or purpose to *die* in the process.

As childish as it may have seemed, all I had wanted, even if she was only *pretending* to care, was for her to tell me everything would be OK. And that she believed in me and what I was doing.

Melody swallowed the mouthful of pasta she had just forked into her mouth and then set the utensil down slowly.

"Maybe a wrong choice of words," she clarified, holding her hand over her mouth.

I felt my anger begin to withdraw inside me.

"If it was up to me, you'd be back home with me, John. That's all I'm going to say," she said as she took a sip of her wine.

I was no longer hungry and pushed my plate aside as I rested my head in my hands. I was disgusted.

"What's wrong now?" she asked.

I slowly turned my eyes and trained them upon hers.

"Nothing. I'm just tired," I lied, distant in my thoughts.

I was a lot of things, but tired was the least of those at that moment. I was scared and already thinking about the trail, despite the fact that I had the company of my part-time, uncaring girlfriend right there in front of me.

I was mulling over what I had sadly called a relationship as well.

And while I could get over my anger rather quickly and move on at times, I'd always had the problem of letting the memory of them linger on, regardless.

It's not hard to give a complete distortion of facts to friends and family or sometimes even to yourself in lieu of wanting a relationship to work. *Everything is* great *between us. I couldn't be happier!*

How many times had I said that to the people I called friends? I had lost count. How many times had people said, "You guys are perfect for each other!"? How many times had I lied as I wrapped my arms around Melody's waist and agreed?

Melody was never a *bad person*. She was intelligent, stunning, and extremely ambitious. She was strong willed and one of the most successful and hardest workers I had ever met. At the same time, she was cold, calculated, and cunning at times. She was dedicated to success and normally always won at anything she was competitive at, and in turn, she carried a little bit of that cocky ego with her.

It came out in her laugh and her sarcastic smirks whenever I challenged her knowledge.

She was so much more the realist than I could ever comfortably be. It was how she had shaped her life and her education. It was how she became so successful and surgical—and it was also her biggest flaw.

How I longed for the minute details or displays of love more often than I ever received from her. The gentle brushing aside of my hair as it fell into my face. The midnight whispers of love when she thought I was too far in reverie to hear them.

Maybe I was asking for too much. Maybe I felt she owed me more than she truly did. But more and more I was coming to find that what I wanted in a relationship didn't exist between her and me.

And ultimately that was all one needed to move on.

My dream of hiking the trail had seemed paltry and immature to her. It was "pointless," and in the end, *I would have gotten* nothing *from it,* according to her.

"John!" she shouted, breaking me out of my dreaming.

I looked at her, and then the waiter who was standing beside us. "You ready to go?" she asked impatiently. I nodded, apologizing as I handed the waiter my debit card.

"Thank you," I said as I went back to dreaming again. Only this time, I stared at the woman I was *trying* to love.

"Well, what'd you want to do now?"

"You," I replied, without a second's hesitation. It wasn't completely true though. Our lives were scheduled, and this meant our love life too. We would retire to our bedroom in the motel and let our bellies digest the food we had just eaten before we made love. It had already been planned out on her mental schedule.

"You better shave that beard first," she said, laughing.

I smiled momentarily and then placed my hand against her cheek. I cupped her chin and lightly ran my thumb along the bottom of her lip.

"Let's have a good weekend," I said, pleading this one last time for her to become the person I so yearned for her to be.

We spent what little time the weekend truly had to offer holding and kissing each other as if we were distant lovers meeting again after years apart.

We drove to Fontana Dam with our dog, Otis, to explore the piece of trail I'd be walking up ahead once I picked back up where I had left off at Stecoah Gap. I had done some trail magic in the form of Little Debbie cakes, which I placed inside the Fontana Dam shelter with a note stating, "Courtesy of Morris the Cat." I had wanted to put Melody's name as well, but she was dismissive on the subject and bothered by even being there. My spirit had been renewed all the same, if only temporarily between our minor arguments.

The first collision came about because I wanted to introduce her to my friend I'd hiked on and off again beside while on the trail. As it just so happened, we had come across Woodstock in Robbinsville as he was resupplying. When I tried to introduce Melody to him, she smiled from a distance and offered nothing more than a wave and said, "We need to be going, John."

Later down the road, on our way to the Tuskaleechee Caverns, I asked why she had been so rude.

"I didn't come here to meet your hiker buddies. I came here to see *you*. I don't want to waste time meeting or saying hi to people you're never going to meet again," she stated coldly.

"What if he and I become great friends and go hiking all kinds of trails across America together? Don't discount somebody just because you don't think you'll ever meet them again," I said as she mocked me.

"Blah, blah, blah. Who cares? I'll never see him again. I don't give a shit anyway."

I kept silent, with that bitter storm within me rising once again. In that torrid mess was a flurry of sentences and words I'd wanted to string together and let loose, only I kept the lid on my anger and stared out the window.

The second argument came about when I passed another hiker by the name of Prayer Walker.

She was kind enough to say hello, and when I engaged her in conversation, Melody walked off with Otis in anger instead of allowing me to introduce her.

"I didn't come out here to meet these *strangers* and do your stupid…trail…shit for them!" she would shout at me later.

"Trail *magic,*" I clarified.

"I don't care what you call it," Melody shouted, as we drove along the Tail of the Dragon in western North Carolina.

I nodded my head complacently. Patiently, though I meant to argue back with her, once again I kept my mouth shut.

"All right, Melody."

Melody had surprised me by bringing homemade garlic-parmesan wings and pumpkin cream-cheese-iced cupcakes. We retrieved them from the rear of her Audi, in a cooler she had filled with ice.

"Why the hell did we ever go out to eat?" I asked her as she shut the trunk.

"I don't know. You're the one who suggested it," she called back to me as she walked Otis around toward the side of the building.

I made my way inside the Microtel and down the right hallway, past the workout center and the pool. When I had vanished from the front-desk employee's sight, I pushed the door open into the stairwell.

The Microtel charged extra for pets, so we had decided to bypass that fee by sneaking Otis inside. After reaching the fire-door exit, I opened it carefully and let Melody into the stairwell. We then snuck Otis into our room, after he'd snorted heavily while climbing the stairs.

Once we got inside the room, we locked him in the bathroom and collapsed in each other's arms on the bed.

Clothes flew here there and everywhere as we ravenously attacked each other's bodies like starving wolves.

I looked down into her eyes as she lay naked, her lightly tanned, silken flesh illuminated in a ghostly pale by the moon's glow, pouring in through our window.

"I needed these days more than you could ever know," I whispered as she leaned up and kissed my mouth.

"I've missed you," she said softly, with a sad smile. She ran her finger along my jawline.

"I think we can make things work, Melody. I really do," I said with urgency in my eyes. She glanced away momentarily, with a look of uncertainty on her face before smiling up at me again.

"Let's talk about that stuff later. Right now, I want you to kiss me," she said, pulling my mouth to hers.

Getting back on the trail was hard. I had seriously contemplated never going back after my brief brush with death only days before.

I had a lump in my throat and a two-ton boulder sitting in my stomach all day, even up to that very moment, as I thought about the few minutes I had left in Melody's company. Precious minutes before I had to say good-bye and begin my trek with Torry on down the Appalachian Trail again.

As Melody drove toward Stecoah Gap, where she would be dropping me off, I felt my eyes burning.

"You know, I'm glad I decided on going back home to Greensboro with you. Can't wait to start a normal life again," I joked.

If only she could see the truth spoken behind that sarcastic string of words.

She passed me a false smile. "Uh-huh, sure," she replied.

I looked out the passenger's side window, feeling rather displaced.

I watched the passing mountains and distant farm-lands flying by in the reflection of the glass. The sun was starting to set, and I didn't want to believe that the day was ending. I wasn't ready for *our time* to be over just yet.

And as I looked over at her long black hair cascading down her shoulders, all I wanted to do was lie down beside her in bed again as I had that very morning. To feel her fingertips against my cheek and to know her eyes were watching protectively over me as I lay within her arms.

I was surprised at how emotional this journey was truly turning out to be. I was never one to just tear up over anything. In fact, before coming out here, I couldn't even remember the last time that I had. But so much had happened in the days prior to her arrival, I actually began to believe I wasn't strong enough to go on. I didn't feel I mentally had the willpower to continue.

Besides, I had heard the stories from back home. A lot of people from my old job had been following my journal entries. They scoffed, believing I was due to quit any day now. They said things like, "I hope that fat ass dies out there" or "He'll never make it" or "He made the biggest mistake of his life, leaving this job. What a shame."

People I had once called friends didn't even think I could do it. So why even bother *trying* when I hardly believed in *myself*?

"You could always keep driving, you know. I can't physically stop you," I went on, looking out the window at the white line running along the side the road.

"I don't understand why you do this. It doesn't make any sense to me. I could see maybe going out hiking for a week, but this? This is way too much abuse on your body. It's just too much. I'll never understand it," she said, training her view on the road. She hadn't seen my watering eyes.

I quickly wiped my cheek before responding.

"I don't know why I'm out here," I replied honestly. "I wouldn't be lying if I said I had everything I ever wanted and needed to be happy back at home. But some*thing* was telling me to come out here and reset my life," I said distantly. "I don't have an education. I don't have a successful career in my portfolio. I don't have anything. I never *did* anything with my life," I went on, in shame.

"Part of me wants to prove to you I'm strong enough to complete this, and I can't stand the thought of being unsuccessful. Failing at something *again*, like I've failed at *everything else* I've ever tried in my life," I said as my voice cracked. I felt weak and sick to my stomach as I looked away from her eyes, defeated.

"You don't have to prove *anything* to me, John. I would love you the same if you gave up right now. My love for you isn't based on your completion of the trail. My love for you is here, regardless," she replied as we pulled into the Stecoah Gap parking lot. There were a few hikers there I had never met, as well as Torry, with a cigarette hanging from the corner of his mouth.

He waved at us with a cheery smile I didn't feel up to returning at that moment.

As Melody put the vehicle in park, I put my hand over hers. This time, I didn't hold back.

"I'm *scared* to go back out there," I said, with regret in my eyes. I had lowered my defensive walls, and there was no pride left in me. A teardrop ran down along my cheek.

"Then don't go, John. Let's get out of here and go back home together," she replied as she lightly brushed the tear away with her thumb and held my face with her hands. Her eyes had started to fill as well.

I took the moment to glance back out at Torry. He was absorbed in the screen of his phone, like he always was, as he sat atop a picnic table in the afternoon sunlight. Oblivious to what was happening or being said just a few feet away.

"Don't look at him. Look at *me*," she said, turning my face toward her. "Please," she begged. The whites of her brown eyes had begun to turn red, and a single tear fell. "Let's go back home and fix things. Fix *us*. You can find a new job, go back to school. It'll all turn out fine in the end." She let go of my face and grasped my hands tightly. *Needing* me to believe in those very words she spoke.

"I…I was hoping you'd be my strength when I was weak like this," I stuttered, laughing as I wiped my eyes with the back of my hand.

"We can't fix a relationship when you're out *here*. Nothing will ever change," she said finally.

I sighed, confused. Irritated. Sad. Anxious. I didn't know what to do or how to choose my future. It had all come about too quickly, and I had mere minutes to make up my mind. This wasn't the kind of decision you made in moments.

"Everything I gave up…" I began.

"….you can get it all back," she said.

"But the miles I've already done…" I went on, fumbling for strength.

"…don't even matter, when you've got nothing to prove to *anybody*."

"Except my father," I finally grasped. I had been reaching out for anything as I fell away from reasons to go on. Roots, cliffsides, tree branches, *anything* to halt my fall as my love for the trail had all but faded and I fell back toward earth and away from what had once been my dream. "I want to give *him* something to be proud of."

Melody sighed angrily and shook her head from side to side. "You'll *never* understand, John," she said between gritted teeth.

"Melody, I—"

"Just get out!" she said, opening her door and slamming it shut behind her.

I watched her momentarily as she rounded the rear of the vehicle and opened the trunk, struggling with it in frustration until it finally released.

I opened the passenger door and made my way to the rear of the vehicle, just as she had let Otis, our English bulldog, out of his cage to use the restroom.

Torry walked over to us both, joking around and filling me in on his last few days, completely ignorant of the drama unfolding between Melody and me right before his very eyes. While he talked, I watched the woman I loved stare off into the distance with a broken heart.

I couldn't spell it out for her, and part of me didn't even know how to say it, but I knew this would be the last time I ever saw her. I wouldn't see her in a month for another visit...and hypothetical future phone calls between us would be nothing but periodic checkups to make sure I hadn't died.

And even *those* would eventually go away as well.

I knew this was the moment that I either chose our relationship or chose my dream. Melody wouldn't allow me to have both.

Her eyes were puffy as she did her best not only to hide the emotions but the somber look on her face. But her expressions betrayed her.

I removed my pack from the trunk of her Audi.

"You don't have to go," she whispered suddenly, as she began to break apart. She turned her head slowly back toward me, and once again I was looking into the eyes of the woman I had fallen for so many months ago on that beach back in North Carolina. Her lips trembled as I lowered my head.

"And you don't have to *leave me* because I do," I said, looking up at her, pleading for any sign of hope she was willing to give me.

She wiped her eyes and placed her arms around me. Her grip was shaking but calmed to a standstill within moments.

"Take care, John," she said quickly, absorbing all of her emotions instantly.

"Melody—" I began, but she cut me off, suddenly whispering in my ear.

"I loved you. I really did."

When I realized she had said that to me in past tense, I felt my heart drop.

She had perfected the art of turning off the pain whenever she needed to move on. She was surgical with her reactions. It made her robotic. It made her successful. And it was one of her most terrifying traits.

She smiled at me with tears in her eyes, but I was sure that behind that mask of sadness existed nothing but insult.

I watched as she drove off east down 143 toward Highway 28.

I questioned my decision as I glanced over at Torry and then at the white blaze marker on the tree beyond him.

End of Book one. To be continued in…

The World We Left Behind: A Journey from Georgia to Maine - Book Two

About the Author

JOHN MORRIS IS THIRTY-TWO YEARS old and lives in North Carolina, where he grew up. When not writing out the events that took place on his two-thousand-mile adventure, he spends days straying away from civilization, if only to search for what some could call true freedom.

John still keeps in contact with the friends he made and the trail angels he met along the Appalachian Trail.

Upon the completion of his *The World We Left Behind* series, his next plan involves a long-distance journey across America from coast to coast.

Would you like to learn even more about the Author?

HEAD OVER TO WWW.THEWORLDWELEFTBEHIND.COM AND subscribe to Morris the Cat's newsletter for opportunities to win 7 Inch 8GB Kindle Fire Tablets, Autographed physical copies of his books and other prizes!

Be sure to follow the progression of John (a.k.a. Morris the Cat)'s next book as well as future adventures and travel hikes on www.facebook.com/johnmorristhecat

You can also get sneak peeks of upcoming future titles, pictures and videos of his 2013 thru-hike and extra content that had to be removed due to original books length! It's like the "Deleted Scenes" sections of your favorite movie!

And as a final request from me personally:

If you enjoyed this book, feel free to review it on either the Amazon Market Page (click here) or my Goodreads Author Page (click here)

It's always kind to review an Indie Author, such as myself.

For questions or comments, or if you would like to know anything about gear I utilized, places I stayed or how I made my 2013 thru-hike possible, please email me at:

author@theworldweleftbehind.com